Richard Wagner
and the English

Richard Wagner
and the English

Anne Dzamba Sessa

Rutherford • Madison • Teaneck
Fairleigh Dickinson University Press

London: Associated University Presses

©1979 by Associated University Presses, Inc.

Associated University Presses, Inc.
Cranbury, New Jersey 08512

Associated University Presses
Magdalen House
136–148 Tooley Street
London SE1 2TT, England

Library of Congress Cataloging in Publication Data

Sessa, Anne Dzamba.
  Richard Wagner and the English.

  Bibliography: p.
  Includes index.
  1. Wagner, Richard, 1813–1883—Influence.
  2. Music—England—History and criticism. I. Title
ML410.W12E5   782.1'092'4   76—50287
ISBN 0-8386-2055-8

PRINTED IN THE UNITED STATES OF AMERICA

To My Mother

Contents

Acknowledgments 9
Introduction 10

1 The Introduction of Wagner to England:
 Resistance and Acceptance 15
2 Bernard Shaw, Wagnerite 50
3 David Irvine, Schopenhauer, and Wagner 65
4 Wagner among the Literati 87
5 *Parsifal,* Religion, and the English 118
6 Conclusion: 1914 140

Notes 150
Selected Bibliography 172
Index 186

Acknowledgments

I wish to thank the following publishers for having given me permission to quote from published works:

Grove Press, Inc., for permission to quote from Aubrey Beardsley and John Glassco, *Under the Hill*. Copyright © 1959 by John Glassco. Reprinted by permission of Grove Press, Inc.

Hawthorn Books, Inc., for permission to quote from George Moore, *Hail and Farewell*. Copyright © 1925 by Appleton-Century-Crofts. Reprinted by permission of Hawthorn Books, Inc. All rights reserved.

The Society of Authors on behalf of the Bernard Shaw Estate, for permission to quote from Bernard Shaw, *Cashel Byron's Profession*, 1938, and from Bernard Shaw, *How to Become a Music Critic*.

Introduction

G. K. Chesterton once wrote: "A man cannot be wise enough to be a great artist without being wise enough to wish to be a philosopher."[1] Chesterton had George Bernard Shaw in mind, but the maxim could easily be applied to Richard Wagner as well. For Wagner not only composed music dramas but also theorized in his numerous prose essays that opera should be something more than mere vulgar entertainment. He maintained that the ideal art of the past had been Greek tragedy. Its form included music, dance, and poetry, a synthesis of the arts. Its subject matter was myth, which Wagner defined as "a view-in-common of the essence of things," and its performance was a religious occasion in which the entire community took part. By the nineteenth century, Wagner argued, art had retreated from its lofty function in Greek civilization and had reached its nadir in opera. Indeed, attending the opera was an opportunity for social preening and display, and it scarcely mattered what took place on the stage as long as a pleasant aria or two were sung and as long as the girls in the chorus were pretty. Wagner set out to change all that. He insisted that the lights be dimmed during a performance, that latecomers remain outside, that the prelude be heard in silence, and that the applause not interrupt every scene. He demanded an improvement in the standard of acting in opera, and he required careful and appropriate staging, although Wagner's particular taste in staging is no longer popular. Generally speaking, he succeeded in inducing the public to take opera far more seriously than it had before.[2] However, when Wagner's art was

10

advertised not only as an entertainment but also as a religious experience and when his music dramas violated previous musical and moral conventions and appeared to expose or to arouse inner, often repressed, archetypal human emotions, then his art became much more controversial.

In nineteenth-century England, a small group of individuals or, as Shaw explained, "an inner ring of superior persons," made the first effort to understand Wagner's music and concepts. The group consisted largely of men and women in the creative arts and of members of the Anglo-German community. Later, as these individuals attempted to win converts, they helped make Wagnerism a highly partisan issue. The phenomenon of Wagnerism in the nineteenth century has been obscured by events in the twentieth century. The memory of Nazi Wagnerians persists. Their racism, maniacal nationalism, and worship of force and brutality mocked and subverted the traditional ideals of European civilization. English Wagnerites in the nineteenth century did not, on the whole, share these Nazi attitudes.[3] To be sure, they sometimes indulged in racist thinking. In 1900, for instance, Jessie L. Weston wrote a study of the legends of Wagnerian drama in order to prove that they belonged not only to the Germans but also to the Anglo-Saxon nations by a "hereditary right of possession."[4] In fact, such racist attitudes were common in the late nineteenth century in all western countries. It is often easier to find examples than exceptions. However, what is noteworthy is that the English Wagnerians tended to ignore racism. It is sometimes implied in their writings, but it is almost never stated outright. They made almost no original contributions in this area that either augmented or diminished the racism of their times or drove it in any particular direction.

On the contrary, from the documents of the period it appears that many Wagnerians were primarily concerned with the inadequacies of the reigning scientism as a metaphysic. Wagner has been accused of "diverting Romanticist thought from vitalism to materialism,"[5] but among English Wagnerians the case was just the reverse. Instead, they enlisted Wagner as their guide to regions beyond mechanistic materialist philosophy, to the realm of spiritual truth. They believed that Wagner had successfully transformed medieval into modern religious myth, suitable to the modern temperament. They thought that his art was richer in live transcendental inspiration than was the moribund contemporary church. They earnestly argued for the enobling, elevating effect of his music.

The following study examines English Wagnerism as represented by its nineteenth-century adherents, not their twentieth-century successors, in order to isolate the specific elements of Wagner's appeal in that period.

Richard Wagner
and the English

The Introduction of Wagner to England: Resistance and Acceptance

i

The young Richard Wagner and his wife Minna made their first visit to London, unnoticed and unacclaimed, in August 1839. The usual eight-day voyage from Riga to the Thames was made in an abnormally stormy three weeks, a trial that later inspired Wagner's composition of *Der Fliegende Holländer*. They stayed only a week before moving on to Paris. After the first night at the Hoop and Horseshoe, 10 Queen Street, Tower Hill, they moved to the King's Arms, Old Compton Street. Since Wagner knew no English other than a few words from Shakespeare, he could converse with no one. Nevertheless, he took the opportunity to see the sights. He also sought out two Englishmen, Sir George Smart, conductor of the Philharmonic Society, and Sir Edward Bulwer-Lytton, novelist and politician. He had mailed Smart his *Rule Britannia* overture earlier in the summer, but Smart was not in town and the fate of the overture remained unknown for some time.[1] With Bulwer-Lytton, Wagner hoped to discuss the operatic dramatization of his novel *Rienzi*. Bulwer-Lytton was not in town either, but on 15 August Wagner spent an absorbing few hours in Parliament, where he had hoped to waylay the novelist. A courteous stranger escorted Wagner to the visitors' gallery of the House of

15

Lords and later showed him the meeting place of Commons. Wagner could not afford to attend the opera, and after a few days of wandering about town, he and Minna departed on Tuesday 20 August.

The earliest mention of Wagner in the British press seems to have occurred in the *Harmonicum* of May 1833. In a report from Leipzig it was announced that a symphony by Richard Wagner had been performed and applauded.[2] Nine years later, in November 1842, the successful production of *Rienzi* in Dresden was noted by both the *Musical World* and the *Musical Examiner*.[3] In September 1845 the *Musical World* gave notice of the production of *Tannhäuser*, also at Dresden. In 1852 London again heard the name Wagner when Wagner's niece Johanna came to sing.[4] Actual public performances of Wagner's music in London did not occur until 1854, when both the Grand March and the Overture from *Tannhäuser* were played. The Amateur Musical Society, conducted by G. A. Osborne, played the march at the Hanover Square R ooms on 10 April; the original score and parts not being available, a new arrangement was made. The "New" Philharmonic (1852–79) performed the overture on 1 May. The overture was also included several times in the winter programs of Louis Antoine Jullien's orchestra. In 1855 Wagner was asked to serve as guest conductor of the "Old" Philharmonic for a series of concerts.

Throughout the 1840s and early 1850s English critics had greeted the news from the Continent regarding the new prodigy with considerable skepticism. Two of the leading critics were Henry Fothergill Chorley (1808–1872) and James W. Davison (1813–1885). Chorley reviewed for the *Athenaeum* from 1830 to 1866. Davison contributed to the *Musical World,* the *Musical Examiner,* and, from 1846 to 1879, the most-important *Times.* Chorley was the more conservative of the two. Davison, an amateur composer himself, encouraged the production of new British music and also championed the music of selected foreigners, especially that of Felix Mendelssohn. However, "the two camps into which the musical politicians of London became divided, the larger of the *Times* and the smaller of the *Athenaeum,* joined their forces when the 'music of the future' was in question."[5] Rumor had it that Mendelssohn was falling out of favor and that established musical forms were under attack. Critical comments about competing oratorios at the Norwich Festival of 1852 are indicative. A Dr. Bexfield, London organist and native of Norwich, had composed *Israel Restored* in the conventional style, and it had enjoyed a favorable reception at the festival the previous year. Bexfield's composition was now to be played again, together with the *Jerusalem* of Henry Hugh Pierson. Pierson had obtained his musical education in Leipzig, and his name was "associated in the minds of British musicians with the rising schools of Schumann and Wagner."[6] According to Davison, Pierson's oratorio was a composition of "vagueness and incoherency, its subjects made up of a multitude of beginnings without middles or ends—wanting in general plan and musical development of ideas."[7] As far as the new German school was concerned, Chorley wrote: "As regards composition, its aims, limits and means, young Germany is in a fever which should it last, will superinduce an epilepsy fatal to the life of music."[8] Though Bexfield and Pierson[9] are of little interest today, the controversy demonstrates these critics' inclination to misunderstand new musical trends.

The invitation to Wagner to conduct in 1855 was an act of desperation on the part of the Old Philharmonic. Its conductor, Sir Michael Costa, had just resigned. The society was unable to hire Berlioz or Spohr in his place and faced serious competition for audiences from the New Philharmonic. Thus the society could not overlook a suggestion by its first violinist and deputy conductor, Prosper Sainton.[10] Sainton had heard about Wagner but actually knew nothing of his music or writings. Part of what he had heard had come from his close friend, a German named Charles Lüders. According to Wagner, "When Sainton, having proposed me to the directors, had to explain how he knew me, he told a fib—that he had himself seen me conduct—since, as he said the true ground for his conviction would have been incomprehensible to these people."[11] Wagner's acceptance of the assignment was also a mark of desperation: he needed money. As it turned out, the English climate, both physical and musical, was difficult; the money, £220, was eaten up by the cost of living; the scoring of *Die Walküre*, which he had hoped to finish in London, remained incomplete; and the hopes of further invitations to mount full performances of his own operas under his direction went unfulfilled. [12] His letters of the period testify to the bitterness of his complaints.

Wagner arrived at London Bridge on Sunday evening, 4 March 1855. From there he traveled four miles across London to his lodgings for the night, the home of Ferdinand Praeger, which he reached about midnight. [13] He was to conduct eight concerts on the following days: 12 and 26 March, 16 and 30 April, 14 and 28 May, 11 and 25 June. Of his own music, he conducted only the Prelude, Procession to the Minster, and Wedding March and Bridal Chorus from *Lohengrin* on 26 March, and the *Tannhäuser* Overture twice, on 14 May and 11 June. The number of his personal acquaintances in London expanded only slightly from 1839. There was the amiable Ferdinand Praeger, a German music teacher and composer who had settled in London in 1834. [14] Another German acquaintance was the twenty-four-year-old Karl Klindworth, a pupil of Liszt. Klindworth came to London in 1854. He and Wagner commiserated together over the London musical scene. Klindworth later arranged the *Ring* and several of Wagner's other late works for piano; his adopted daughter, Winifred, married Wagner's son, Siegfried. Dr. Hermann Franck, a Dresden friend; the 1848 exile Malwida von Meysenbug; Gottfried Semper, another 1848 revolutionist and the architect who would later be hired to design the Festival Theater that Wagner hoped to build in Munich; Malwida's friend Professor Frederic Althaus; Sainton; Lüders; and Berlioz complete the list of Wagner's non-English acquaintances in London. Among the English, Wagner expressed an interest in John Lodge Ellerton, composer and already a Wagnerian, Cipriani Potter, also a composer, and George Hogarth, secretary of the Old Philharmonic, at whose home Wagner had an awkward meeting with Meyerbeer. In short, Wagner made few English friends, and on 26 June he departed from London with great relief.

An evaluation of Wagner's reception during these four months must take into account that he was judged primarily as a conductor and only secondarily as a composer. For a performance of a complete Wagner opera, Londoners would wait until 1870, when they finally heard *Der Fliegende Holländer* in Italian. Moreover, Wagner's arrival in London in 1855 was preceded by a confusing Continental notoriety. It was believed that in his prose essays the composer did little more than make arrogant claims for himself and nasty remarks about the other musicians. Then, too, he was known as a friend of Franz Liszt, whose personal and musical reputation was still controversial.[15] Conditions of performance must also be considered. There were certain comic aspects to the London musical scene.

> There was the usual mixture of professionalism and dilettantism in the public music-making; there was the usual fatuous confidence that any orchestral concert programme whatever, could be adequately carried out with one rehearsal, or at the most, two. English orchestral players being so super-competent that they did not need as many rehearsals as their weaker brethren on the Continent; there was the usual crowd of professional and amateur-professions practitioners, several of whom were such manifest mediocrities that to us of today it is a mystery why they escaped knighthood. There was *The Times,* already bearing with conscious dignity the heavy burden of responsibility that had been laid upon it by Providence.[16]

Finally, in 1855 Wagner refused to pay any of the customary duty-calls on the critics.

Wagner assumed that most of his critics were in the pay of his enemies, in that of Meyerbeer in particular. Wagner was correct in assuming that English critics of the time customarily accepted flattery and occasional small tokens of appreciation from composers. However, he erred in thinking that these gifts influenced the critics' judgment. Davison, for instance, is generally regarded as having been honest.[17] In fact, the critics developed their hostility independently and became more, rather than less, hostile to Wagner as the concerts progressed. That their humor did not improve was owing largely to Ferdinand Praeger's intemperate articles directed against Davison, not to bribery.

The articles that Davison wrote prior to Wagner's arrival demonstrate a good-humored neutrality. His repetitious banter and badinage do not reveal any serious enmity. In the

Musical World, 27 January, 1855, Davison commented that "we shall see what we shall see" and displayed his secondhand knowledge of Wagner's prose.[18] On 10 February he urged Philharmonic subscribers to make themselves familiar with Wagner's art doctrine: "Remember that Richard is on the way. His shadow is before him on the rail, as far as Cöln. He will be here shortly, and then it may be too late. Send the books—the books—all the books! In them there may be hope."[19] Meanwhile Ferdinand Praeger contributed to the New York *Musical Gazette* of 24 February an article that would later be summarized in the London papers. It held Davison up to scorn: "The engagement of Wagner seems to have affected his brain, and from the most amiable of men and truthful of critics, he has changed to the—well, see his journal."[20] In the same article Praeger mentioned Wagner's until then pseudonymous tract *Judaism in Music* (first published in Germany in 1850) in which Meyerbeer and Mendelssohn were severely criticized. Praeger declared that "the editor of the London *Musical World,* considering himself one of Mendelssohn's heirs, and Mendelssohn having (so it is said) hated Wagner, *ergo,* must the enraged editor also hate him? He certainly seems to do so, *con molto gusto.*"[21] *Judaism in Music* was unknown in England until Praeger did Wagner the dubious service of introducing it. According to Ashton Ellis, "In some odd corner of his marine-store of miscellaneous information the bomb must have lain for four years; he flings it at the very moment when a friend of prudence would have buried it for good."[22] Only after the New York article arrived a fortnight after Wagner himself did Davison raise the Mendelssohn-Judaism issue.

Chorley of the *Athenaeum* opposed Wagner's music from the beginning. In his *Modern German Music,* published in 1854, Chorley had already commented unfavorably on *Rienzi, Der Fliegende Holländer,* and *Tannhäuser.* He protested that he had never been "so blanked, pained, wearied, *insulted* even (the word is not too strong), by a work of pretension as by this same *Tannhäuser*"[23] and he longed for the coherence of Meyerbeer. Thus, in the 27 January issue of the *Athenaeum* Chorley wrote that the appointment of Wagner was nothing short of "a wholesale offence to the native and foreign conductors resident in England" and on 3 February noted that 1855 was likely to be "a year of confusion" and that the Old Philharmonic had shown "a want of reason" in choosing Wagner.[24]

On Saturday 10 March Wagner led the usual single rehearsal two days before the performance with moderate success. Two days later he conducted Hayden, Mozart, Spohr, Weber, Mendelssohn, and Marschner before an audience of approximately eight hundred people. This audience, according to Ellis consisted almost exclusively of the "unemotional middle-aged"—that is, well-to-do patrons, not likely to be swept off their feet.[25] Even Davison admitted to the usual coldness and apathy of the Philharmonic crowd. The first reviews came from the *Morning Post* and the *Daily News* of 13 March. William Howard Glover[26] of the *Post* concluded that the Old Philharmonic had made a wise selection, that the concert was admirable, and that many portions of Hayden, Beethoven, and Mendelssohn's work had "never, in our recollection, been so well played in this country."[27] The *Daily News* article, as well as subsequent articles in the *Illustrated London News,* were all written by George Hogarth.[28] Wagner assumed that Hogarth, who was secretary of the Old Philharmonic, had no choice but to praise the guest conductor. So it was that Hogarth wrote:

> Whatever differences and controversies may exist as to the doctrines and tenets of the musical school to which Wagner is said to belong, and as to his own character as a composer—disputes into which we do not enter, because we are as yet unacquainted with their merits—on one point he has left no room for question—his consummate excellence as an orchestral chief.[29]

Davison in the *Times* of 14 March noted, as did Hogarth, that Wagner was surprisingly well received by the audience, but he declined to offer a final opinion as to the merits of Wagner's conducting. The Old Philharmonic could not accustom itself to Wagner's rubato, as soon became apparent. But Davison did label Wagner as "a man of intelligence and firmness, an original, and perhaps, an intellectual thinker."[30] Davison's article in the *Musical World,* 17 March contained the first direct allusion in an English journal to Wagner's anti-Semitism, but the point was not belabored. The rest of the article contained another discussion of the first concert, which followed the same lines as Davison's *Times* review. Chorley on 17 March questioned whether it was worth sending a deputation to Zurich to secure Wagner's services "for no better result than this?"[31] Lastly, on 18 March, appeared the critique of Henry Smart, nephew of Sir George, in the *Sunday Times:* "It is not probable that a better choice would have been made. Wagner is certainly a remarkable man."[32] All in all, the critics were not unimpressed, and the audience seemed to like the performance, although there was some hint of a difference of opinion as to Wagner's tempi.

The program of Wagner's second concert on 20 March, for which he was granted two rehearsals, included Beethoven's Ninth Symphony and the first English performance of selections from *Lohengrin,* as well as pieces by Weber, Cherubini, and Mendelssohn. Hogarth and Glover remained favorable, though the latter complained that the *Lohengrin* selections exhibited none of the expected epoch-making innovations and that a great deal of the music was "excessive and needlessly luxurious in mere loudness and meretriciousness of sound."[33] Henry Smart complained of the incompatibility of the conductor and the musicians. He did not doubt that Wagner was a man of genius, but he added: "We can in no way satisfy ourselves that music is, in his case, its appropriate form of utterance."[34] He thought that the music lacked beauty. His seems to be the view of an honest critic struggling, but failing, to understand the possibilities in the new music. His future understanding, however, could hardly have been assisted by the insults in Praeger's next American article, reproduced in the *Musical World* of 9 June:

> A new opera by H. Smart is in promise. We shall hear it and see whether H. Smart has any more pretensions to fame than that of being a nephew of Sir George Smart, who again dates his celebrity from one noisy evening at court, where reeling royalty indulged in playing ball with knighthoods, one of which most innocently hit the good old gentleman, and made him what he is—"a Sir!"[35]

Chorley issued a long harsh critique. Davison did not review the second or third concert in the *Times,* but he did discuss it in the *Musical World*. He did not like the *Lohengrin* selections, although he admitted the difficulty of dealing with mere music-snippets. Meanwhile Praeger falsely accused the Old Philharmonic directors of deliberately trying to create a fiasco for Wagner. These samplings of reviews demonstrate that, after Wagner's first two concerts, the critics appeared to be struggling with the genuine difficulties created by the music, while at the same time being goaded by the personal attacks of Praeger and by his offensive remarks about native English talent.

Succeeding concerts therefore produced stronger negative criticism. By the end of June the relatively neutral critics, Glover and Smart, were in opposition. Davison was up in arms, and even Hogarth was uncomfortable, whereas Chorley remained unflaggingly critical. On the subject of Wagner's conducting, loyal Ellis "felt morally constrained to give them reason for once, and admit that Wagner was not a first-class Mendelssohn conductor."[36] Ellis attributed most of the animosity to Praeger, to Wagner's refusal to meet the press while in London, to a lack of good translations of Wagner's prose, to the alienation of the "native-talent school," and finally, to the limitations of the critics. As Ernest Newman appraised them, "They were men of ordinary intelligence brought face to face, for the first time in their professional lives, with a contemporary phenomenon that was extraordinary, and failing to see how much bigger it was than themselves."[37] The verdict after Wagner's departure was indeed harsh. Glover maintained that "it is truly ludicrous to observe how a professedly conservative society can throw itself into the arms of a desperate musical democrat like Herr Wagner, and strive to uphold the present of British art by falling back upon its past."[33] Henry Smart called the final Wagner concert the least creditable in twenty-five years. While he could not fault the Old Philharmonic for giving the pretentious man a hearing—"It was but fitting, then that in England, where all the greatest music is more thoroughly known than in any equal number of square miles on the surface of the globe, this apostle of a new creed in art should have a hearing"—nevertheless, he was glad that the experiment was over.[39] Davison concluded that Wagner was unfit as a conductor, that the *Tannhäuser* and *Lohengrin* selections were dull and commonplace, that "the admirers of Mendelssohn, however, may console themselves with the reflection that nothing such a mushroom musician as Herr Wagner can possibly say against his compositions will rob them of their value."[40] Hogarth in his memoirs acknowledged that the season had been neither pleasant nor successful.[41]

What Wagner lacked in critical acclaim or wide popularity, however, was largely made up for by the approbation of Queen Victoria. The seventh concert, on 11 June was a command performance. The queen's brother-in-law, Ernest II of Saxe-Coburg-Gotha, was both a Wagnerian and a composer of opera himself. Possibly, he was one of the sources of the royal couple's curiosity.[42] In any case, the queen, Prince Albert, the Prince of Wales, Prince Alfred, the Princess Hohenlohe-Langenburg, Princess Adelaide of Hohenlohe, and the Princess Feodore of Hohenlohe were present, attended by the duchess of Sutherland, the duchess of Wellington, the Lord Chamberlain, the Master of the Horse, and the Lord Steward. Wagner retained happy memories of the episode. In a letter to Wilhelm Fischer on 15 June, he quoted the queen as saying: "I am delighted to make your acquaintance, your composition has enraptured me!"[43] In a letter to Liszt, 5 July, he remarked:

> In truth they were the first in England to venture to speak up for me without disguise: if one reflects that they were dealing with a political outcast, under warrant of arrest for high treason, one will surely think me right to thank the pair of them right heartily.[44]

The critics concentrated on the fact that the queen had heard on the same program George Macfarren's Chevy Chase Overture, an example of native talent. Ellis pointed out that five years later, in a letter to Mathilde Wesendonk, Wagner mentioned that Queen Victoria had wanted to hear *Lohengrin* in English in 1860. Wagner was not able to leave Paris, and Ellis speculated that, had it not been for the death of Prince Albert the following year, perhaps the entire *Lohengrin* would have been performed in England fifteen years earlier than it actually was.

In conclusion, Wagner was almost wholly unknown in England in 1839, notorious by 1855, and more notorious after having given the eight concerts. Several explanations may be given for this. First, Wagner's conducting—his primary obligation at the concerts—was poor; even Wagnerians admitted that. Second, Wagner exhibited what seems to have been regarded by the critics as a character disorder; that is, he had "pretensions," a ubiquitous word in many of their articles. Pretensions they were, although they were not well understood. Third, the selections for *Tannhäuser* and *Lohengrin* were regarded as cacophonous.[45] Fourth, the leading critic was Mendelssohn's partisan. And finally, as Ellis speculated, the alliance of the "Old," more conservative Philharmonic with Wagner was unnatural, and the society's patrons, in the midst of the Crimean War, had more serious things to worry about than a musical radical. Such a diagnosis has merit, although it should be stated that Wagner's previous *political* radicalism was not made much of during the controversy. On the other hand, it is remarkable that the *Musical World* continued to publish Wagner's *Opera and Drama* in issues from 19 May 1855 to 26 April 1856,[46] and that interest in Wagner's music was kept very much alive in private circles throughout London.

ii

There were no public performances in England of Wagner's music drama in the late 1850s and 1860s, with the exception of portions of *Tannhäuser* and the "Entry of the Mastersingers," played by August Manns in his orchestral programs at the Crystal Palace in 1868, and the *Rienzi* Overture and Battle Hymn, which appeared on his military band programs.[47] According to Manns, the excerpt from *Die Meistersinger von Nürnberg* disappointed everybody. But the friends of Wagner in London persisted.

In 1867 a private group calling itself the Working Men's Society undertook to play the later works of Beethoven and

Schumann and arrangements of Liszt, Berlioz, and Wagner at one another's homes. The group included Karl Klindworth; Fritz Hartvigson, the Danish pianist who was a pupil of Hans van Bülow and music master to the princess of Wales; the painter and singer William Kümpel; Alfred James Hipkins; Walter Bache; and Edward Dannreuther. Hipkins was an authority on old instruments. He "became attached to the cult in 1866, not from admiration—that came later and is now a passion—but from the feeling that Wagner was being condemned in England unheard." [48] Walter Bache was a pupil of Liszt and his foremost champion in England. Edward Dannreuther—born in Strasbourg, brought up in Cincinnati, and musically educated in Leipzig—first came to London in 1863, where he quickly became established as a pianist, music commentator, and professor at the Royal College of Music. He eventually was naturalized as a British subject. These men met almost weekly for two years. Klindworth, the oldest, "fathered" the meetings and "from him in particular came that impetus for Wagner." [49] Hipkins kept a private memorandum of the meetings. For instance, on 6 December 1867 Dannreuther "led off the Wagner campaign" with Liszt's transcription of the "Spinnelied" from *Der Fliegende Holländer.* On 18 January 1868 Klindworth led the study of *Das Rheingold; Die Walküre* was next on the agenda. On 6 March 1868 Bache played Liszt's transcription of the *Tannhüser* March, on 20 June Klindworth gave a portion of *Tristan und Isolde,* and on 4 July Dannreuther played a considerable part of *Die Meistersinger,* while Kümpel sang one of Walther's songs. Also in July, Anna Mehlig played Liszt's E-flat Concerto. [50] Although this group also played the music of composers other than Wagner, the importance of these meetings lies in "the quiet unobtrusive propaganda" it made for him. [51] During the same years another private group, centering around John Payne, poet and translator, was also listening to private performances of Wagner's music. [52]

Reviews of Wagner's publications abroad appeared in a few London periodicals. A noteworthy substantive article, "Lyric Feuds," came out in the *Westminster Review* in July 1867. It reviewed musical quarrels of two centuries, including Handel versus Bononcini and Glück versus Piccini, and then turned to Wagner, "the chief exponent and the recognised leader of that new school of musical thought whose influence is, at the moment, so rapidly spreading through Europe."[53] After a brief biography and a discussion of Wagner's aesthetic principles, the author went on to describe *Tannhäuser:*

> Looking, however, to the profound impression which a (necessarily) somewhat imperfect selection from *Tannhäuser* created at its performances in a series of orchestral concerts, we cannot think that justice will much longer be denied to the self-sacrificing labours of its conscientious, earnest, and original composer.[54]

A golden future for the music was predicted. So passed the sixties.

In 1870 the Old Philharmonic played the Prize Song from *Die Meistersinger,* and at last, the first British stage performance of any Wagner opera took place—*L'Olandese Dannato* was performed in Italian at Drury Lane. The Kaisermarsch was played at the Crystal Palace on 21 April 1871, and in 1873 Walter Bache included the *Huldingungsmarsch* in one of his programs. Meanwhile, the Wagner movement was gaining momentum. In 1869 Franz Hueffer had arrived in England. He was a young Ph.D. in literature who was imbued with a devotion to Schopenhauer and Wagner. A genial character, he soon found his way about London and, in particular, frequented the circle of Ford Madox Brown and the Pre-Raphaelites. He married Brown's youngest daughter and became a British subject in 1882, changing his name to Francis. On 15 March 1871 he published in the *Academy* a long article based on Wagner's 1870 pamphlet about Beethoven. This article is commonly considered the first important public declaration of the English Wagnerites. Hueffer expanded the essay for the *Fortnightly Review* and in 1874 published *Richard Wagner and the Music of the Future.* According to Hueffer:

> There is a certain poetic justice in the fact that, as Wagner in 1855 had been, as I said before, snuffed out by an article, so the way for his triumphant return in 1877 was paved by a literary movement which was started when only a single opera of his had been performed in this country, and when little more than his name was

known to the general public. Of that movement it beseems the present writer to speak with modesty and a certain reluctance for the reason that it was he who began it.[55]

In the *New Quarterly Magazine,* April 1875, Hueffer explained Wagner's *Ring,* particularly Wagner's use of the sagas. Approaching the matter philosophically, he said that the mythical was superior to the historical or domestic as subject matter for opera because "the latter only represents what actually happened; the former leads us back to the fount of unalloyed volition, from which all actions flow—to the *noumenon,* indeed of which the world and its appearance are only the shadow."[56] In the *Examiner,* 19 August 1876, he summarized the story of the *Ring* and commented on the Bayreuth Festival. Fortunately for the Wagner cause, Hueffer would soon succeed Davison as music critic of the *Times.* In 1877 there was a change of editor, and "Davison was informed from headquarters that he had lost his own working powers. It was remarked that much that interested the general public and gained ample notice in contemporary papers passed unnoticed in *The Times.*"[57] Despite the fact that Davison had mellowed toward new musical trends, Hueffer in 1878 was appointed officially to share his duties. Hueffer had already begun to contribute reviews to the paper even before his appointment, and gradually Davison was phased out.[58]

Also of great importance was the formation of the Wagner Society in 1873. The founder was Edward Dannreuther, while the first president was Lord Lindsay, earl of Crawford and Balcarres. Hueffer was secretary. The society sponsored on 19 February and 9 May 1873 the first public concerts in London that consisted primarily of Wagner's music. The *Athenaeum* reported having received the society's prospectus. It announced that the concerts were being held to raise money for the first performance of the *Ring* at Bayreuth. The *Athenaeum* also concluded that another objective was to popularize Wagner's works in London. Despite what the *Athenaeum* regarded as a splendid orchestra and "an instrumental performance rarely surpassed in this country," the journal doubted that the question of how Wagner's operas would be received by the English public had been settled.[59] In fact, parts of this Wagnerian program became "wearisome." Six more concerts were given in the late autumn of 1873 and early spring of 1874. The *Athenaeum* praised the decision to include some non-Wagnerian works in the program, whereas Hueffer deplored the move and thought it responsible for the concerts' declining revenues. After the six performances, the enterprise was allowed to drop. According to the *Athenaeum*, regardless of the fate of Wagner's operas, one fact was certain: Wagner's *orchestral* works were now completely accepted in the repertoire. "Public opinion has given so unequivocal a verdict, that Wagner is enrolled amongst our classics. . . . So far, the Wagner Society has succeeded in its mission."[60]

Both Hueffer and Dannreuther were present at Bayreuth, 22 May 1872, when the foundation stone of the Festspielhaus was laid and Dannreuther published a series of essays on Wagner in the *Monthly Musical Record*. These appeared as a collection in 1873 under the title *Richard Wagner: His Tendencies and Theories*. In them Dannreuther speaks of the "genuine curiosity . . . only of late arisen" concerning Wagner and of the beginning of a favorable reaction to him since the 1870 Drury Lane production.[61] In order to "explain" Wagner to Englishmen, Dannreuther resorts to Walt Whitman and quotes from the preface to *Leaves of Grass:* "The clearest expression is that which finds no sphere worthy of itself and makes one."[62] It was to Wagner more than to any other living poet that Dannreuther would apply Whitman's prophetic words. In the first section Dannreuther defends Wagner's criticism of past aesthetics as necessary to the work of every great art and artist:

> In all directions men go back to scrutinise the actual instinct and forces which rule over life, to get behind them, and to see them as they really are, to connect them with other instincts and forces, and thus to enlarge our whole view and rule of life. Philosophy generally, and philosophy of art particularly, is more than ever needed; and it is, in short, a strong philosophical power, coupled with abnormally pronounced capabilities of receiving and retaining impressions from actual life, that form the indispensable characteristics of every great modern artist.[63]

For Wagner's previous unpopularity, he blames the publication of his theories before his later musical works were known, his social and political heresies, and his attacks on living men of repute. In part 2, Dannreuther discusses "the utter absurdity of the dramatic grimace known as grand opera"—that is, opera as merely a vehicle for a singer.[64] Part 3 deals with drama and poetry. Part 4 treats the subject of Wagner's *Ring* and concludes:

> It is no more a reformed opera than man is a reformed monkey; it can be measured as little with an ordinary yardstick as with the conductor's baton of an absolute musician. It is new from end to end and it carries its own criterion of excellence in the high and intense emotions a correct performance of it may and will arouse in everyman who, in Pistol's phrase, "hears with ears."[65]

Part 5 discusses the national theater of Germany, and part 6 draws Wagner's biography, pointing to the unfortunate public interest in his personality rather than in his works. Finally, Dannreuther advertises the Wagner societies then springing up in various German cities, in Milan, New York, London, and so on, dedicated to raising funds for an adequate *Ring* performance.

In 1875 *Lohengrin* was presented in London both at Covent Garden and at Her Majesty's Theatre. The future Edward VII heard the Covent Garden performance. Interestingly, the *Musical Times* reported that the "London Germans" in the house kept order:

> The Teutonic element in the house had a marvellous effect in teaching the audience that "Lohengrin" was not to be judged by the ordinary standard; so when the usual round of applause was given for the favourite singers on their entrance and the boisterous marks of approbation burst forth after an effective *morceau*, a very decided "hush" convinced the astonished Opera habitués that the vocalists must be considered as secondary to the work they were interpreting, and that any congratulations to individual performers must be reserved for the fall of the curtain.[66]

The *Musical Times* believed that this influence was all to the good.

In 1876 Covent Garden presented an Italian *Tannhäuser*. It was also the year in which the *Ring* was at last performed at Bayreuth. British Wagnerians and critics were there. James

Davison, nearing the end of his career, arrived hot, dusty and suffering from a leg injury. His humor improved, however, as he found himself surrounded by his literary comrades and hospitable local people. In his *Times* articles dispatched from Bayreuth, he pronounced the festival "an incontestable success."[67] When Siegfried presented Brünhilde with the ring in *Die Götterdämmerung*, Davison spoke of "another opportunity for the display of Wagner's marvelous facility in giving expression, after his individual manner, to the emotions of passionate love."[68] In 1855 to Davison Wagner's only marvelous facility had seemed to be for doing the wrong thing. Now Davison mentioned "charming" melody, "fresh, inspiriting, and appropriate phrases," and "delightfully tuneful strains." In an article of 20 August, Davison, in his own individual manner, demonstrates that he had learned about the relationship of poetry in music drama to orchestral music and had developed an awareness of its haunting quality.

Thus in concocting the drama of the future, that poet and musician must be one and inseparable would seem to follow as a Wagnerian deduction. It is hardly too much to say that, apart from the drama to which it is allied, the orchestral music of the *Ring* would signify little more at best than a succession of chords, scales (not infrequently chromatic), figures and snatches of tunes, distributed capriciously among the instruments, "*tremolandoes*" (*ad infinitum*), strange and unheard of combinations, perpetual changes of key, etc.,—a chaos of sound, in short, now more or less agreeable, now more or less the opposite, and, deprived of the weird and singular fascination that attends it when obviously explained by what is being said and done upon the stage, almost unmeaning. Wagner's symphony may be likened to an omni-coloured kaleidoscope, where the same bits of painted glass incessantly appear and disappear, yielding prominence to others that have been seen before, and puzzling the eye of the examiner, as the Wagner orchestra puzzles, while it frequently enchants the ear.[69]

In the same article, Davison points to the many melodies that, "while never ceasing to haunt the memory, cannot be repeated or hummed," and poetically compares Wagner's music to an Aeolian harp under the influence of shifting wind currents. Davison also pays tribute to the orchestra, to the singers, and to Wagner's "magnetic influence" over them. He liked Mme Materna as Brünhilde with her helmet, shield, and spear. What he found fault with were the scenic appliances: the rainbow bridge, the steam apparatus (which martyred the dwellers in the orchestra pit), all the water scenes, and the dragon. But, all in all, Davison thought that the experience was worthwhile, though he doubted that such a spectacle would ever be feasible again.

Davison's great friend Joseph Bennett (1813–1911) also attended the Bayreuth *Ring* cycle. Most of his "letters from Bayreuth" appeared in the *Daily Telegraph.* He also wrote for the *Musical World,* and in 1873 he began a thirty-year association with the *Musical Times.* Bennett preferred "human interest" to fantastical gods and goddesses and liked plain, honest melody and moral plots. Like most people other than the most uncompromising Wagnerians, he found Bayreuth dull and commercialized and the food unpalatable. His fun derived from observing the other tourists. For instance, he asked: "Why, then, is it, that faith in the Art-Work of the Future goes in company with spectacles, long hair, and funny headgear?"[70] On another occasion he noted that when a Berlin critic said something particularly obnoxious about the Nibelungs, the critic received a beer mug in his face and had to retire with a broken nose. The incident stimulated a free-for-all, ending in the arrest of the violent Wagnerian. Bennett paid five marks to dine in the same restaurant where Wagner dined and there he observed

> enthusiastic Yankee ladies, in a chronic state of ecstasy about "darling Liszt," whose shadow they hoped would fall upon them by-and-by; wild-looking Germans of various types . . .; unbelieving Frenchmen, always keeping together as though for mutual assistance, and always meditating epigrams of the most withering character; and English pilgrims not a few, looking at one another askance, as who would say "If you don't agree with me about this business take care when I catch you at home."[71]

Bennett referred to his countrymen as "a swarm of English."

Bennett did not care for "the strange world" of *Das Rheingold*, but he did like Wagner's orchestration: "Whatever may come of the festival in other respects, we now know fully what an orchestra can do, and where in a theatre it should be placed."[72] *Die Walküre* had "strong human interest" and approached "as nearly as possible to that which we commonly know as music."[73] Bennett loved the "Ride of the Valkyries," as did the audience, but the droning dialogues of Wotan, Fricka, and Brünhilde bored him, and the incest of Siegmund and Sieglinde disgusted him. He considered *Siegfried* a stupendous work and regarded Siegfried's singing in scene 1 of the second act as "a grand addition to the world's store of beauty."[74] *Götterdämmerung* he found a disappointment since it was inconsistent with Wagner's own theories and did not make the most of the magnificent opportunities supplied by its situations. "Oh, for a Verdi," he wrote.[75] In general, Bennett argued that the old pagan myths were "dead as a dodo" with regard to their power to move modern audiences and that Wagner had ignored what there was of human interest in the chronicles. Concerned also with the moral purpose of the *Ring,* he complained that the message was lost in the machinery that worked it out:

> The presentation of crime on the stage is only justifiable by strong reasons; what are the reasons in Wagner's case? Are they summed up in a desire to show that the rule of love is stronger than that of force, or that the pursuit of power leads through devious and dirty ways? If so the lesson is almost lost in the complexity of the fable. Surely it was not needful to take up four evenings, and parade thirty-four gods, giants, imps, and mortals for such an elementary purpose.[76]

Thirteen years later, in 1890, Bernard Shaw discovered Bennett still writing articles on Wagner's life and works for the *Musical Times.* However, Bennett's views had mellowed: "Mr. Bennett is one of those few unhappy ones who, having shied all the bricks they could pick up at Wagner, whilst he lived, have now reluctantly to build their missiles into a monument for him."[77] Shaw could not refrain from being amused at the change in Bennett's attitude.

From an anonymous private account comes another English view of Bayreuth in 1876:

I came away more than ever filled with admiration for the wonderful genius which not only wrote the words and music—music which in itself seems sometimes more than earthly—but which also conceived, and has carried into execution, every little detail that goes to make their performances the grandest, the most thoroughly perfect, that this age has witnessed, or will perhaps ever witness again. [78]

The young enthusiast also enjoyed the "jolly evenings" spent with other Wagnerian friends and the glimpses of royalty that furnished additional excitement at the performances. His visit to Wahnfried provided "a glorious ending to a month of such happiness as can come only once in a life—a never-to-be-forgotten real day dream." [79]

Wagner made his third and final visit to London in 1877 to conduct at Albert Hall. This time Wagner's music only was played, and Hans Richter assisted him in the matter of conducting. There were six concerts in fourteen days, in addition to two others at popular prices. [80] Unhappily for Wagner, who was deeply in debt at Bayreuth, the concerts once again were not a financial success, the entire business having been mismanaged by Wagner's agents, Hodge and Essex. However, the public considered the concerts a success. In fact, "from this year, then we may say that in views of the British musical public, Wagner had at last 'arrived'." [81] The *Athenaeum* remarked on "the long-continued cheering and the demands for repetition" that must have pleased Wagner, although the *Athenaeum* steadfastly maintained that the audience's admiration was limited to the instrumental pieces, and did not extend to the vocal settings. [82] Likewise, the *Musical Examiner* reported how pleasing the music was and how "this effect was produced on a vast miscellaneous audience, totally indifferent to Wagner's theories and unacquainted with the mythological significance of Loge and Wotan." [83] Even the commentator in *Punch,* who had burlesqued the concerts as a carnival of "Wagnerian waggeries," admitted that "many who went to scoff remained to praise." [84]

Wagner lodged with the Dannreuthers at 12 Orme Square. The Dannreuther home has been described as "old and full of quaint rooms and halls, and the composer had added a concert room. The walls were covered with Morris papers—the design lemons and pomegranates—and hung with pictures of Burne-Jones and his school."[85] Those were gala evenings at the Dannreuthers. Several accounts remain. Hueffer remembered an evening when Wagner was

> the life and soul of a large and distinguished gathering, including amongst others, George Eliot and Mr. G. H. Lewes. Madame Wagner, who speaks English perfectly, served as an interpreter, and her conversation with the great English novelist—who took a deep interest in music, although her appreciation of Wagner's music was of a very Platonic kind—was both friendly and animated. "Your husband," remarked George Eliot, with that straightforwardness which was so conspicuous and so lovable in her character, "does not like Jews, my husband is a Jew."[86]

Hueffer did not record any reply by Cosima Wagner. He did explain to his English readers his opinion that Wagner's anti-Semitism was theoretical and "did not extend to individuals."

Moncure Conway, an American clergyman and author then living in London, remembered either the same or a similar occasion:

> Before the concerts began, Wagner was entertained by the Dannreuthers, the guests being not only musical artists, but painters and writers. G. H. Lewes and his wife were present, and I remember a display of enthusiasm by George Eliot. Wagner performed on the piano a piece just composed, unknown I believe to his nearest friends. It was a song, and in it were one or two passages that one might suppose beyond the compass of any voice; but Materna mastered them one after the other, the composer's face reddening with excitement until the last note sounded, when he leaped up and seized the hands of the singer. Then George Eliot moved quickly forward to shake hands with her, though whether Materna was aware of the distinction of the woman who congratulated her was doubtful. For George Eliot, who could probably not have been drawn to so large a company by any less attraction than Wagner, had sat in her usual reserve until this brilliant performance by Materna.[87]

Novelist Eliot and G. H. Lewes were Germanophiles, translators and expositors of German poetry and philosophy. Eliot apparently had heard *Tannhäuser, Lohengrin,* and *Der*

Fliegende Holländer in the summer and autumn of 1854 at Weimar. At that time she wrote that she was delighted with *Der Fliegende Holländer*: "The poem and the music are alike charming. The *Tannhäuser*, too, created in me a great desire to hear it again. Many of the situations, and much of the music, struck me as remarkably fine."[88] On the other hand, she disliked the declamation in *Lohengrin*. In 1877 she attended the concerts with Cosima.

Hubert Parry (1848–1918) on 2 May wrote in his diary: "In the evening I went to Dannreuther's to meet Wagner."[89] On 5 May he recorded that "there was a goodly company of artist folk to see Wagner, who was in great fettle, and talked to an open-mouthed group in brilliant fashion."[90] He too mentioned Eliot. She and Cosima had attended a performance together. Cosima reported, according to Parry, that Eliot "wept plentifully over the heavenly scene between Siegmund and Brünhilde."[91] Parry's diary is of special interest because he later became a composer well known in England, a music historian, and director of the Royal College of Music. A pupil of Dannreuther's, Parry attended Bayreuth in 1876 and "never was so perfectly satisfied in my life."[92] Subsequently, his own compositions, especially *Scenes from Shelley's "Prometheus Unbound,"* showed the technical influence of Wagner in Parry's revolt against the confining traditions of his social, artistic, and religious upbringing.

Among the others who met Wagner were Robert Browning; Rudolf Lehmann; Sir Herbert von Herkomer, portraitist of Wagner; his old friends Sainton and Lüders; and the photographers Elliott and Fry. Cosima visited the home and studio of Georgiana and Edward Burne-Jones.[93] Although he did not meet Wagner, Herbert Spencer attended the 1877 performances. In his autobiography he came to the conclusion that Wagner was a great artist, but not a great musician, in that he understood better than other composers how to marshall his effects:

To make a fine work of art it is requisite that its components shall be arranged in such a way as to yield adequate contrasts of all orders: large for the great divisions and small for the sub-divisions and sub-sub-divisions; and that there shall be contrast not of one kind only but of many kinds. Wagner, I think, saw this more clearly than his predecessors. . . . Wagner specialized the uses of his instruments better than most. . . . I hope his example will be followed and bettered.[94]

In short, Spencer found Wagner's musical phrases to be uninspired, but he liked his orchestration. Dannreuther finally brought Wagner and James Davison together for a brief conversation in French. Davison acknowledged that he had seen the *Ring* and now desired to hear *Parsifal,* and Wagner kissed him good-bye, continental style. To conclude the list, the queen received Wagner at Windsor on 17 May.

Thus the seventies brought general acceptance of Wagner's orchestral music by much of the public. The newspaper reviews suggest that acceptance was underway by the time of the Wagner Society's concerts in 1873 and completed during Wagner's visit in 1877. Furthermore, it appeared that pilgrimages to Bayreuth would become socially fashionable. Much of the preparation for Wagner's reception had been conducted by English artists and a coterie of Anglo-Germans. There remained skepticism as to the larger significance of Wagner's operas and theories. The debate on the latter rose to its most passionate heights in the 1880s and early 1890s.

iii

In 1882 the English for the first time saw the stage performance of the *Ring, Die Meistersinger,* and *Tristan und Isolde* in the original language.[95] Of these performances Hueffer commented: "English people like serious music and like the stage but they do not care for serious music on the stage."[96] The 1877 Albert Hall orchestral concerts led to the Richter concerts. The public liked these much better; "musical and fashionable London flocked to them."[97] In 1883 when Wagner died, the *Times* pronounced him "the greatest musician of our time."[98]

The *Saturday Review* labeled him "a man of extraordinary poetical, dramatic, and musical feeling" and reminded its readers of the "wild admiration and equally wild dislike" that he had engendered.[99] The *Athenaeum* admitted that Wagner's reforms in opera "have already been accepted to a very large degree" and that the world had lost "probably the greatest musical genius since Beethoven," but it entered the caveat that Wagner at times carried his system of leitmotiv to an excess and that in some of his work dramatic truth was sought at the expense of musical beauty.[100]

The death of Wagner gave his movement a renewed drive. In 1884 the Wagner Society was refounded as the London Branch of the Universal Wagner Society.[101] It was organized as a rallying point for the composer's admirers, as a way of selling tickets and raising funds for Bayreuth, and as a means of furthering the study of Wagner's music dramas—"of his aesthetic and philosophical works, as well as the dissemination of the art principles which he held and taught."[102] Beginning with 54 members, by 1890 it boasted 309. Again, it appeared that Wagner's support came from persons of German origin living in England, together with the English artistic community. Among the members mentioned by name in the society's journal, the *Meister*, are Louis N. Parker, playwright; Alma Murray, the actress; Alfred Forman, Murray's husband and literary scholar; Ferdinand Praeger; George Bernard Shaw; Edward Dannreuther; Charles Dowdeswell, art dealer; Edgar F. Jacques, editor of the *Musical Times* from 1892 to 1897 and music critic of the *Observer* and *Sunday Times;* William Shakespeare, singer; Julius Cyriax, German-born pharmaceuticals merchant; Carl Armbruster, itinerant Wagner lecturer; H. F. Frost, organist and critic; C. A. Barry, composer and writer; A. L. Birnstingl; J. B. Moseley[103] and W. H. Edwards. The *Daily Telegraph* maintained in 1893 that one-sixth of the membership was of German origin and praised this phenomenon as a way of keeping "a natural and laudable Teutonic patriotism viable."[104] The new society's president was William John Manners, ninth earl of Dysart (1859–1935). Almost totally blind for the greater part of his life, Manners found much solace in music—Wagner's and early church music.

Politically he was inconspicuous.[105] In 1895 he resigned, and Edward Dannreuther replaced him.

From 1888 to 1895 the society published a quarterly journal, the *Meister,* inspired by the Parisian *Revue Wagnérienne.* The journal reflected the society's aims and provided a description of its activities. Its editor was William Ashton Ellis, one of Wagner's most faithful English adherents. Ellis was a physician by profession, but he spent much of his time writing a biography of Wagner, translating Wagner's entire prose works into what has become the standard edition in English. He also translated many of Wagner's letters. He wrote *Richard Wagner as Poet, Musician, and Mystic* in 1887, and *Wagner-Sketches: 1849, A Vindication* in 1892. He joined the Wagner Society, having already championed Wagner for ten years previously.[106] He seemed to have spent so much of his life and substance on Wagner's behalf that Bernard Shaw, in a letter to Lord Haldane on 16 November 1907, urged that when Haldane became prime minister, one of his first acts should be "to give me that pension for Ashton Ellis (who is pawning his spare scarf-pins) and to abolish the censorship of plays."[107]

The aim of the journal was to demonstrate to the English-speaking world Wagner's many-sided genius. His genius, the *Meister* emphasized, was not only musical but philosophical.

> Had he never composed one bar of music and never conceived one scene of drama, his prose works alone would have ranked him amongst the foremost thinkers of his day.... Through art he fought his way to social problems of the deepest interest, and to the vital questions of religion and a higher world.[108]

According to Ellis, even though more and more English were thronging to Bayreuth,[109] few who drank in the music ever stayed to question "what deep thought lies underneath the vesture of the poems."[110] Elsewhere, Ellis had placed Wagner in the reaction against scientific materialism.

The *Meister*'s cover design illustrated its preoccupations.[111] The theme was the pre-Socratic division of the universe into the four elements—water, earth, air, and fire—in the same order as they occurred in the *Ring.* A female figure resembling a mermaid and carrying a shield typified the dual nature of man—animal and material in the lower part of the body, human and spiritual in the upper. Her shield presented on its left the sword of power, *Nothung,* and the Nibelung's ring, the symbol of "self-devouring Time"; on the right of the shield was the swan of *Lohengrin,* representing the soul, and the chalice, or vessel of divine reason. Other aspects of the picture included a laurel wreath of victory, a lance—Parsifal's spear—denoting the power of spiritual truth, and the masks of comedy and tragedy. Crossing the entire composition and uniting it was a flamboyant scroll bearing the name of the journal; the flames of the scroll symbolized the purifying fire of love.

When in 1888 Bernard Shaw saw the first copy he recoiled at the cover design and complained about the editorial tone. The former was too exuberant: the latter not exuberant enough. "There is an evident indisposition to provoke hostility," he wrote. [112] What the periodical needed, he went on, was a fighting editor. Thus complimented, Ellis proceeded to reproduce translations of Wagner's writings, discussions of his dramas, reviews of books and concerts, poems, a few advertisements, discussions of related issues (such as Schopenhauer's philosophy), and notes on the meetings of the Wagner Society.

Volume I (1888) opened with a panegyric by "Evelyn Pyne" on the anniversary of Wagner's death:

> Sing of strong Love the Redeemer,
>   Self-less who comes but to save:—
> Deathless he lives in thy music—
>   Tearless we stand by thy grave. [Etc., etc.!]

It also included excerpts from Wagner's *Art and Revolution,* a series on Schopenhauer's *The World as Will and Idea,* and a translation of *Tristan und Isolde* by Forman. Illustrating Ellis's religious bent was his explication of *Parsifal,* introduced by the remark: "We feel that Wagner has gone behind the mere forms of worship, and shown us its essence in a light such as none of the custom-dulled rites of Churches can now hold aloft." [113] In its notes, the *Meister* reported the activities of Carl Armbruster, the Wagner circuit lecturer. George Bernard Shaw later remarked that Armbruster's lectures "unmistakably aroused considerable interest and curiosity," and that "he does for Bayreuth what our University Extension lecturers do for Oxford and Cambridge."[114]

In 1889 the *Meister* carried Wagner's *Religion and Art,* notes on Wagner's childhood, and notes on the Vienna Wagner Museum. *The Meister* also editorialized on what had become known as "the Bayreuth hush." Technically, "the hush" was the quiet Wagner demanded of his audiences. In particular, they were not supposed to stop the performance by applauding their favorite signers, as they might with Bellini or Donizetti. According to the *Meister,* "One enters with the hush of expectation, one passes hours spellbound in the hush of realization, and one leaves amid the hush of meditation."[115] Of particular interest in this volume is William C. Ward's lengthy interpretation of the *Ring,* challenged here and there in a footnote by Ellis but by and large meeting with his approval. The true subject of the opera, the article argues, is "the gradual progress of the human Soul, its contests, its victories and defeats, and its ultimate redemption by the power of Divine Love."[116] Ward explains, as did others subsequently, that Wagner had taken the teutonic myths and brought them home to the heart and made them intelligible to the intellect of the nineteenth century.

A summary of the progress of Wagnerism in the eighties opened volume 3 (1890). The parent Wagner Society now numbered eight thousand members in three hundred branches. In England, the society mustered over three hundred members. At the Bayreuth festival, "the English and Americans form[ed] an almost preponderating portion of the audience."[117] Finally, the *Meister* pointed out that the English critics, with one or two exceptions, were now favorable to Wagner. The third volume also included a study of *Die Meistersinger,* in which, according to the author of the analysis, Wagner seems "to teach us . . . the lesson that heroism and devotion, manliness and pure love, are not to be found alone in regions far removed from our daily life, but can be brought down even into the lowly shoemaker's workshop."[118]

In the fourth volume (1891) Ellis announced that his translations of Wagner's prose works could not be completed in the four yearly issues of the magazine; therefore, they would be published separately and made available to members at a reduced rate. This volume concentrated on *Tannhäuser* and its message. "The one dominant idea around which the whole drama revolves, is that which perhaps no other poet has dwelt on so lovingly or so nobly, the saving efficacy of woman's love, a love which reaches far beyond the creature, and expands its wings to brood over the universe."[119] This Wagnerian theme was heightened in *Parsifal,* where love, robbed of sex, reveals its inner essence as suffering with one's fellow man, the basic quality of the lives of Jesus and Siddhartha.

A eulogy in memory of Julius Cyriax in volume 5 provides an interesting glimpse of the Wagnerians.[120] Cyriax was one of the founders of the London branch of the Wagner Society; he financed it during its infancy and "by his contagious enthusiasm brought the largest number of members."[121] Ellis called him "my sheet-anchor in the Wagner cause" and recalled having first met him in 1882. "I looked upon him as one of those who had fought the good fight when it was *indeed* a battle."[122] Cyriax introduced Ellis to Cyrill Kistler, a minor composer of Wagner-like operas, and, with the encouragement of Cyriax and Ellis, Kistler had some success in England.

Volume 6 (1893) included a study of *Tristan and Isolde* and Louis N. Parker's paper on "Wagner as Playwright." Ellis also mentioned a Spanish painter, R. De. Equsquiza, whose etchings of Wagner, Schopenhauer, and characters from Wagner's operas were apparently selling quite well in London. The seventh volume (1894) discussed *Lohengrin,* serialized Liszt's letters to Wagner, and presented "Wagner as Melodist," by Edgar F. Jacques. The last volume (1895) recommended H. S. Chamberlain's biography on Wagner. The *Meister* previously had published installments of C. F. Glasenapp's adulaatory biography. Indeed, in every issue Ellis made an effort to explain Wagner's character to the English in the most favorable way. Ellis also lectured publicly on Wagner. For instance, the *Meister* quoted a review in the *Musical World* of an Ellis talk, given 15 March 1889 at Trinity College, Mandeville Place:

The lecturer showed by various extracts from the letters how completely Wagner was absorbed in the task of artistic creation, how lovable and genial (with all his little temporary outbursts of trouble-bred petulence) was his character and how entirely his nature vibrated to the great chord of Mother Nature herself.[123]

Ellis also analyzed the infamous "money-letters," proving that of 314 letters of Wagner to Liszt, only 12 were direct appeals to Liszt's own purse. He put it to his audience whether or not any one of them, lacking bread and fuel, would not have appealed similarly to a trusted friend. Thus, in the *Meister* Ellis emphasized three points that many Wagnerites regarded as crucial: the goodness of Wagner's personal character; the importance of his pronouncements on society and art in his prose essays; and the moral and religious interpretation of his music dramas.

With volume 8 the *Meister* ceased publication without any warning and without editorial farewell. The reasons for termination are not entirely clear. Most probably it was because of a quarrel within the society—a quarrel that revolved around Ferdinand Praeger and his memoir *Wagner as I Knew Him,* published in 1892. Ellis argued in the *Meister* that Praeger's book was a fraud, that the man had much overrated his role in bringing Wagner to London in 1855,[124] that his memory of the incidents of Wagner's visit and of other biographical details was very inaccurate, and that he had inexcusably altered much of his correspondence with Wagner. Ellis was so thorough in his attack that most biographers today regard Praeger as unreliable. Ellis was aware that "uncritical friends in the London Wagner Society took a little offence" at his exposure of the shortcomings of their old acquaintance, but he believed that it was his duty as editor of the *Meister* to scrutinize Praeger's work.[125] He pointed out that he had scarcely known Praeger, who died in November 1891, and had even written a laudatory epitaph for the *Meister* based on reports that he had heard from other members of the society. But, having read the memoir in February 1892, Ellis felt obliged to act. What seemed to trouble Wagner's acolyte most was Praeger's description of Wagner's role in the revolution in Saxony, 1848–49,[126] and his handling of Wagner's character. Praeger, he argued, seemed to expand his own importance at the expense of Wagner's. In Ellis's words, "One is astonished to find that 'original thinker' as Wagner was, it was always Mr. Praeger who got the best of the argument, and one cannot smother the impression of an encounter between a schoolboy and his tutor."[127] Likewise, although Praeger called himself a friend of Wagner, he always seemed to place the composer in an odious or absurd light.[128] Because Praeger's was the first English biography of Wagner, Ellis was anxious to correct any wrong impressions. In the last issue of the *Meister,* Ellis published a communication of Houston Stewart Chamberlain's that informed the public that the German edition of Praeger's book had been removed from the market by its publishers, Breitkopf and Hartel, because of its many inaccuracies. Subsequently, Ellis and Chamberlain were attacked in the newspapers by Praeger's champions and "threatened with all sorts of dreadful things soon after."[129] In Chamberlain's case, an attempted legal action failed for lack of evidence. The earl of Dysart, to whom Praeger had dedicated his book and who had supported Praeger presumably in good faith, then resigned as president of the society.[130] Breithkopf and Hartel had removed the book from circulation without fanfare but the publication of the Chamberlain letter, together with Ellis's critique, brought the matter into the open and apparently made it impossible for Dysart to continue. Dannreuther finished out Dysart's term. Possibly as a result of this dispute, both the journal and the society disbanded in 1895. Actually, their task had been fulfilled. Wagner's ideas had been brought before the public.

During the eighties and nineties, Wagnerian criticism and explication also moved to a more neutral ground: they found voice in the Royal Musical Association, established in 1874 as a scholarly rather than as a performing group. Papers read before the association were published in its proceedings, together with the discussions that took place after the lectures. In introducing *Die Meistersinger* to the association in March 1881, C. A. Barry asserted that he need no longer apologize for his choice of the opera as a subject, something he might have had to do several years earlier. After concisely and interestingly describing the literary origins of Wagner's plots, he proceeded to give a sketch of the action. He concluded that the opera represented "the victory of genius, aided by good sense, over pedantry and conventionalism."[131] The moral that the work sought to convey is that art is progressive and that rules are useful, to be broken only by those who have learned to observe them. The discussion revolved around the importance of the libretto in Wagner's work, the question of whether Wagner's music was "noisy," and the expense and difficulty of staging the opera.[132]

H. F. Frost's paper on *Tristan und Isolde,* delivered in May 1882, was more controversial. There was, he said, a danger that the libretto of the work might be termed "a hideously immoral book," and therefore he had to spend much of his lecture describing the plot. He specifically pointed out that there is nothing to prove that "the marriage between King Marke and Isolde has been consummated, while there is circumstantial evidence to the contrary."[133] The total effect of the music drama, which Frost said was inimitable and should not become a model for young musicians, was "a mental exhaustion that may have been partly caused by intense emotional pleasure but which in itself is more akin to pain."[134] One of the discussants agreed:

It did produce on me a feeling of extreme weariness, though I fancy it was not exactly the kind of weariness to which our friend Mr. Frost alluded. . . . I missed the full closes—I wanted the cadences of which he has spoken as being absent; and the music, I think I may say, instead of giving one a definite impression of a completed subject, went on in what one can only call a rambling way—the various motives were so jumbled up in the laborious orchestration that I could not longer detect them . . . my only feeling was, that the sooner it was over the sooner my torture would end.[135]

No one mentioned the alleged immorality of the plot in the discussion.

J. S. Shedlock reviewed the Wagner-Liszt correspondence in April 1888. He noted the charms that private letters of famous men held for biographers and also the danger that they might be used unscrupulously for party purposes. Shedlock found that the Wagner-Liszt letters contained seeds of both good and evil:

So far as I have understood the book, I make out that Wagner was a man thoroughly in earnest. He felt he had a mission in life, and that mission he sought to fulfill. But the fates were against him: his mind was strong but his body weak; he meant well but often acted ill. He must not be judged by an ordinary standard, his faults were to a great extent the result of his genius. He had a sharp pen, a sharp tongue, but it needed strong weapons to fight a way from Dresden to Bayreuth. [136]

Of special interest was a letter from Wagner to Liszt in 1851 referring to Wagner's pamphlet *Judaism in Music*. Shedlock said that for years Wagner had seen Mendelssohn and Meyerbeer making their mark in the world, whereas he was unsuccessful. Wagner wished in particular to prove that he had nothing in common with Meyerbeer, but it would have been better, according to Shedlock, "had he left his friends and the world to make this easy discovery for themselves." [137] The discussion was monopolized by the chairman of the day, Ferdinand Praeger. He claimed that he understood these letters "better than anyone." [138] The meeting closed with a vote of thanks to Shedlock for the balance struck in his lecture.

When the Reverend Henry Cart found himself lecturing before the association in February 1890, he stated that he was only following the spirit of the age. It seemed, he said, that everyone was talking about Wagner. Cart simply summarized what was then known of Wagner's life. He thought that the liking for Wagner was mostly a fad: "I am morally certain that the English do not appreciate and cannot understand Wagner or his works." [139] Several of the discussants challenged Cart on this point. The most interesting comment, however, was that of a Mr. Herbert, who stated the classic English case against Wagner—that he was a danger to public morality:

First, he [Cart] thought all great musicians had bad tempers; but as against that I would think of Hayden, Mozart, or Mendelssohn. Then came a statement that the acts of great geniuses were to be judged by a different standard from the rest of the world, *apropos* to Wagner seducing his friend's wife. There I differ from him entirely. And in speaking of great musicians, he said Beethoven was the first; but I think Mr. Cart forgot Sebastian Bach. I am a most uncompromising enemy of Wagner in every possible way, but at the same time I admit that I came to the task twelve years ago (1878) prejudiced; for all I had heard abroad from professional musicians, and all I had read in his works certainly prejudiced me against him. To mention one or two instances, he said that the music of "Don Giovanni" would one day not be worth the paper on which it was written. After that he could not, by any possibility, find any sympathy from me. Then there was the matter of the pamphlet containing the attack on Mendelssohn and Meyerbeer and the rest. In fact, on the moral side, Wagner's character was such as to prejudice me very much against his compositions. Pougin says . . . how difficult it is—almost impossible to separate a man from his compositions, and there I entirely agree with him. [140]

But it was Wagner's music, not his morals, that was at stake, remonstrated the next speaker.

Two years later, in 1892, William Ashton Ellis presented a paper on Wagner's prose, which he found to be "a fund of general knowledge, of deep thoughts on almost every branch of art and life, that in itself is a liberal education." [141] However, to give morality its due, Ellis claimed that *Judaism in Music* was one of Wagner's less important writings and said that of all his writings, the only one that he "should honestly like to see suppressed" was the *Capitulation,* Wagner's diatribe against the French after their defeat in 1870. [142] Ellis catalogued the translation, or mistranslation, of Wagner's prose works into English as they appeared and traced Wagner's ideas in relation to Feuerbach, Schopenhauer, and others. Actually, Ellis found the prose quite moral: "The one great principle to which Wagner comes ever back, as the foundation and the governor of all art, is that of Communism against Egoism." [143] And, as for Wagner's personal character, Ellis preferred Wagner to the Uriah Heaps of life.

Finally, the *Proceedings* contained E. Algernon Baughn's essay on the development of opera and E. W. Naylor's comparison of Verdi and Wagner. [144] It was clear that the main issues regarding Wagner had by then been exposed to the English public in a rational and well-informed fashion, although some biographical details were still to come, and that most of his operas had been performed at least adequately in London or Bayreuth. The public was in a much better position to evaluate Wagner in 1895 than they were in 1855 or 1877. Of course, unanimity was unattainable.

In *Wagnerism: A Protest* (1882) Major H. W. L. Hime declined to accept the composer as either a preacher or a prophet. According to him, the *Ring* was a ridiculous bunch of old legends, some of them scandalous, "in a jingling, alliterative verse, accompanied by declamatory music almost entirely without melody, and spun out to insufferable length."[145] He compared the leitmotiv to the use of the trumpet in battle: "This is a most convenient system of conventional signs but it can hardly be called very high art."[146] Edmund Gurney in 1883 railed against "the displacement of coherent form by incoherent colour" and complained that color had become the bane of music.[147] He found in Wagner's melody even at its finest "a faint flower of disease, something overripe in its lusciousness and febrile in its passion."[148] J. F. Rowbotham in 1888 assured his readers that the "Wagner bubble" had burst and proceeded to attack Wagner and Wagnerism in the angriest article yet to appear. He attributed Wagner's ideas to pique and spleen alone and charged Wagner with every possible license and irregularity in music.[149] The article was so vitriolic, and in many places so obviously inaccurate, that it prompted a rejoinder from C. Villiers Stanford, composer and professor of music, who, though not a professed Wagnerian at the time, felt moved enough to descend "for the first time into the sanguinary arena of Wagnerian controversy," in the interest of fair play.[150] The Wagner bubble had not burst.

Ten years later, in 1898, J. Cuthbert Hadden pleaded: "Let us by all means give Wagner the honour that is his due, but let us not forget his limitations."[151] Above all, he urged that "the Wagner mania" should not act as a check on the originality of new young composers. Wagner had progressed from underdog to tyrant. Though Wagner's theories, music, and personality would always remain repugnant to some, on the whole, the public in the nineties heard Wagner's music frequently and with pleasure. Wagner had been introduced by the few and now belonged to the many. Ironically, his operas were heard less often than selections or "numbers" from them, just what he had hoped to avoid. While many called for Wagner simply because it had become the fashionable thing to do, others became blindly devoted. Still others, more creative men and women, enlisted Wagner in their attack on bourgeois philistinism and in their search for new styles of life and art in an age that was to become increasingly uncertain and dissatisfied with itself. To these individuals the following chapters are devoted.

2

Bernard Shaw, Wagnerite

i

I saw him, day after day, poring over Karl Marx's *Das Kapital* and an orchestral score of Wagner's *Tristan und Isolde.*

> William Archer, having first met Shaw at the British Museum[1]

Bernard Shaw was seventeen in 1873 when the London Branch of the Universal Wagner Society was founded. He had had little to do with the initial efforts of Francis Hueffer and Edward Dannreuther to mold a favorable public opinion for Wagner's music. Nevertheless, he proved to be one of the best music critics in England, incorruptible though freely admitting his subjectivity, generous-minded in searching for the worthwhile in both the old and the new, severe in the name of excellence, and a joy to read.[2] As Jacques Barzun has said, with some truth, "Who now reads Chorley or Dr. Franz Hueffer?"[3] Among Shaw's particular contributions to Wagnerism were the interpretation of the *Ring* as a socialist allegory, the proposal of an English Bayreuth in keeping with his and Wagner's ideas on the role of national theater, and the balancing of the more extreme views of other Wagnerites.

Shaw's first opportunity in the field of music criticism came in 1876 when he ghosted some articles in the *Hornet* for voice teacher G. J. Vandaleur Lee, a friend of Shaw's family. Shaw made his second attempt in 1883. He offered his services to the *Times* and the *Musical Review* as "a modern musician very fond of *Der Ring*" but "not fiercely contemptuous of *Il Trovatore*."[4] He submitted an article entitled "Music for the People" that met with Hueffer's abrupt disapproval. Shaw later claimed that he had written that the English public did not know good music from bad, but Hueffer had replied that Shaw knew nothing about the public, that nobody had ever seen him in really decent society, and that he moved among cranks, Bohemians, unbelievers, and agitators.[5] Nevertheless, Hueffer published the article.[6]

Shaw's third sally took place five years later. In May 1888 he became music critic for T. P. O'Connor's *Star*. He chose the pseudonym Corno di Bassetto because he then "had no name worth signing, and G. B. S. meant nothing to the public."[7] Shaw once explained how this journalistic assignment came about. Originally he had been hired to write about politics, but his articles were too passionately Socialist for the editor's taste. Therefore he and O'Connor compromised. Pitying Shaw's poverty, O'Connor arranged that Shaw might keep his job, on the condition that he abandon politics for music criticism. Although it is true that the two men differed politically, Shaw's music career began more casually than the sentimental tone of his memoirs would suggest. Actually, the *Star* already had a music critic, Ernest Belfort Bax. Whenever Bax was out of town or had to review simultaneous musical events, Shaw covered for him. Eventually, Bax resigned, and Shaw replaced him.[8]

Shaw was convinced that the London public assumed that Corno di Bassetto's unconventional criticism was an elaborate put on by a man who had absolutely no knowledge of music.[9] But as he had said, "Among the pious I am a scoffer, among the musical I am religious."[10] There was nothing frivolous in his love of music, nor was his musical knowledge slight. He had been interested in music from his youth. His mother was a mezzo-soprano of local fame in Dublin; her teacher, the aforementioned Vandaleur Lee. Since neither of them took pains to give Shaw a formal music education, he apparently taught himself. When Mrs. Shaw moved to London in the hope of bettering the family fortunes, the young Shaw remained in Ireland working in an office. He detested offices; his real life was in music and literature. Through studying the score of *Lohengrin,* he made "the revolutionary discovery of Wagner."[11] He migrated to England and joined his mother, whom he used to drive "nearly crazy" with his renditions of the *Ring.*[12] To the end of his life he was capable of sitting down at the piano and singing excerpts from Mozart, Handel, and, especially, Wagner.

Shaw wrote about one hundred articles for the *Star,* twenty of which deal at some length with Wagner. Only six, however, were entirely devoted to him. Of these, the most interesting are Shaw's descriptions of his first visit to Bayreuth between 25 July and 4 August 1889. The occasion was a performance of *Parsifal,* and Shaw's comments reveal both his iconoclasm and his appreciation. His travel on the Continent made him wish for a Channel Tunnel. He found Bayreuth "a desperately stupid little town" and the drab interior of the Wagner theater unpromising.[13] The staging was "marred by obsolete contrivances," such as the obvious electrical connections in the glowing ruby bowl of the Holy Grail.[14] Shaw did not hesitate to attack the Bayreuth shrine when he believed that it was necessary. He refused to let the theater become "a temple of dead traditions."[15] On the other hand, he pointed out that the *Parsifal* performance was an emotional and artistic success for its audience:

> Hardly anybody has the slightest idea of what it all means; many people are severely fatigued by it. . . . Yet *Parsifal* is the magnet that draws people to Bayreuth and disturbs their journey thence with sudden fits of desperate desire to go back again.[16]

Once the prelude began, the listener discovered that he was in the "most perfect theatre in the world for comfort, effect, and concentration of attention."[17] No one laughed at the clumsy stage machinery. "It is a point of honor not to laugh in the Wagner theatre."[18] By the conclusion of the performance the listener was "converted to the Church and Stage Guild's view that the theatre is as holy a place as the church and the function of the actor no less sacred than that of the priest."[19]

In 1890 Shaw joined the *World,* a weekly newspaper, where his criticism appeared until 1894. Here amid hundreds of references to Wagner, there appeared perhaps twenty articles predominantly concerning Wagner or Wagnerism. Typically, Shaw commented on the productions and did not raise the matter of philosophical interpretation. In fact, in reviewing the first performance of *Siegfried* at Covent Garden, he deliberately said "nothing of the great drama of world-forces which the Nibelung story symbolizes, because I must not pretend that the Covent Garden performance was judged on that ground."[20] On the other hand, he criticized the London Wagner Society for not trying to establish a Wagner Theater in England:

> Why in the name of common sense does not the London Branch of the Wagner Society declare itself an autonomous English Wagner Society, and save up the fifty pounds a year which it now spends in sending coals to Newcastle to form a fund for placing a Wagner Theatre on Richmond Hill.[21]

He also accused the members of Wagner-idolatry and of preferring imitation Wagner to genuine Mozart:

> For in art, as in more personal matters, there is a love which means hating everybody else, and which ought to be capitally punished; as well as a love which spreads to everyone else, and which increases your regard for every man or woman, or piece of music, for the sake of one man or woman or piece of music.[22]

More often than not, Shaw steered between both Wagner's idolaters and his enemies.[23]

Perhaps a more profound defense of Wagner's creativity than Shaw's newspaper articles came in his *Sanity of Art,* first published in 1895. Two years earlier Max Nordau had written *Degeneration,* an attack on modern art as a symptom of the decline of the race of Western man, and had branded Wagner as "the last mushroom on the dunghill of Romanticism."[24] The American anarchist and Wagnerite Ben Tucker had then approached Shaw and asked him to write a rebuttal. To Nordau's charge that Wagner's work, by violating the fixed rules of the theory of composition, was undisciplined and therefore uncivilized, Shaw replied that there are no fixed rules and that "the severity of artistic discipline is produced by the fact that in creative art no ready-made rules can help you," and finally that Wagner's composition did indeed exhibit a strong regard for design, order, and symmetry.[25] So great was the logic of his works that once his melody and harmony had become familiar to the public, it would seem even as mechanical as that of Handel to those who did not appreciate its dramatic inspiration. Shaw's rebuttal was effective. Even Nordau admitted its validity.[26]

Shaw's interpretations of Wagner's symbolism appeared in *The Perfect Wagnerite,* published in 1889.[27] He considered the *Ring* a socialist allegory. In this work also are intimations of the vitalism that would be developed more extensively elsewhere in his works. Shaw declared that the *Ring* was not a folk-myth put to music but a drama of contemporary society, supremely relevant to the nineteenth century. Readers of the original sagas would recognize some names and episodes, but the meaning was hardly the same, for Wagner's *Ring* was a parable of modern capitalism. Shaw said that the *Ring* was very attractive dramatically and orchestrally apart from its political philosophy, particularly since there was not a bar of "classical music" in it; however, it should be understood that the whole work had "a most urgent and searching philosophical and social significance" recognized by "an inner ring of superior persons" to which Shaw professed to belong.[28]

Das Rheingold opens with the theft of gold by an ugly dwarf who renounces love for the gold and its power. "Such dwarfs are quite common in London," writes Shaw; they have enslaved millions of working men and women.[29] "All this part of the story is frightfully real, frightfully present, frightfully modern."[30] Opposed to the plutocrats, however, are higher powers, sometimes called the Godhead, which Shaw describes in vitalist terms:

> The mysterious thing we call life organizes itself into all living shapes, bird, beast, beetle, and fish, rising to the human marvel in cunning dwarfs and in laborious muscular giants, capable, these last, of enduring toil, willing to buy love and life, not with

suicidal curses and renunciations, but with patient manual drudgery in the service of higher powers. And these higher powers are called into existence by the same self-organization of life still more wonderfully into rare persons who may by comparison be called gods, creatures capable of thought, whose aims extend far beyond the satisfactions of their bodily appetites and personal affections, since they perceive that it is only by the establishment of a social order founded on common bonds or moral faith that the world can rise from mere savagery.[31]

But because of the stupidity of the world, the gods are not able to rule by purest wisdom. They resort to law, punishments, and rewards, and are obliged to uphold the law even when it ceases to represent their thought, ceaselessly broadening and evolving with life into new directions. They are compelled to acquire the external trappings of authority. Into this situation comes Alberich. The gods illegally capture his power and are thus further compromised. They become, in Shaw's terminology, the Establishment, and they long secretly for a hero, an anarchist, who will destroy this mechanical empire of law and establish a "true republic of free thought."

Essentially for Shaw, this is the story of the tetralogy. Alberich could be an industrialist and his subterranean home might just as well be "a match-factory, with yellow phosphorous, phossy jaw, a large dividend and plenty of clergymen shareholders."[32] The giants Fafner and Fasolt are unthinking, conscientious toilers, who, like Alberich, worship money. Wotan represents any monarch or pontiff who violates his own statutes; Siegfried, "the ideal of Bakoonin, an anticipation of the 'overman' of Nietzsche."[33] Foreseeing public doubt and outrage, Shaw refers the public to Wagner's participation in the revolutions of 1848 and to his treatise *Art and Revolution.* For Shaw, the culmination of the tetralogy is Siegfried's defiant splintering of Wotan's world-governing spear. Everything else—another opera and a half—is anticlimax.

Götterdämmerung is nothing but old-fashioned grand opera in style and content. It offers the panacea of love, "a romantic nostrum for all human ills," and a most sexual version of love at that.[34] Shaw was disappointed. He said that "the only faith which any reasonable disciple can gain from *The Ring* is not in love, but in life itself as a tireless power which is continually driving onward and upward . . . into higher and higher forms of organization."[35]

In the third edition of *The Perfect Wagnerite*, Shaw offers a new explanation for *Götterdämmerung* in keeping with his historicopolitical point of view. Originally, he explained Wagner's change of style by the twenty-five years that had lapsed between the beginning and the completion of the cycle. In this work he suggests that "the Siegfrieds of 1848 were hopeless political failures, whereas the Wotans and Alberics and Lokis were conspicuous political successes."[36] Shaw's interpretation resembles Lenin's later appraisal of the hardihood of capitalism. Wagner, Shaw asserts, had an excellent sense of political reality and had changed his mind about the ending by the time that he scored it. Shaw is also aware that consistency did not often trouble Wagner: "Wagner was not a Schopenhauerite every day in the week, nor even a Wagnerite."[37]

Perhaps a simpler Shavian solution to the problem of the ending of *Götterdämmerung* exists, although unexploited, in *The Perfect Wagnerite*.

> In the old-fashioned orders of creation, the supernatural personages are invariably conceived as greater than man, for good or evil. In the modern humanitarian order, as adopted by Wagner, Man is the highest. In *The Rhinegold* it is pretended that there are as yet no men on earth. There are dwarfs, giants, and gods. The danger is that you will jump to the conclusion that the gods, at least, are a higher order than the human order. On the contrary, the world is waiting for Man to redeem it from the lame and cramped government of the gods. Once grasp that; and the allegory becomes simple enough.[38]

Siegfried, of course, still qualifies as one of the gods, being descended from Wotan (as was Brünhilde). Hence when the stage is cleared at the conclusion of *Götterdämmerung*, all the gods have failed and the task of world-building is left to an audience of mortal men. Shaw does not see it that way, however, because he also considers the dwarfs, giants, and gods to be dramatizations of different kinds of men. Siegfried therefore is not the last of the gods (and so good riddance!) but an advanced kind of man, in whom Shaw is grossly disappointed.[39] Actually, for Wagner socialism was a pose. Shaw's socialism is real.

In the fourth and last edition of the book, Shaw sees no reason to revise his interpretations. He does note, however, that his description of Bayreuth as the ultimate in modern stage production is out-of-date, but he remains convinced that World War I had not invalidated Wagner's allegory. The main difference is that "Alberic is richer."[40]

The reception of *The Perfect Wagnerite* was mixed. Many English Wagnerites refused to believe Wagner's active role in the revolutions of 1848 and wrote letters of protest to the newspapers. On the other hand, the thesis of the book produced scarcely a ripple of interest among the Fabian Socialists. According to Shaw: "The Fabians were inveterate Philistines. My efforts to induce them to publish Richard Wagner's *Art and Revolution* . . . fell so flat that I doubt whether my colleagues were even conscious of them."[41] Though frequently sold and presumably read, *The Perfect Wagnerite* did not stimulate other socialist interpretations or uses of Wagner.[42] The public at large was interested in Wagner as musician, passionate Romantic, or religious prophet, not as critic of capitalism.

ii

If Shaw did not do as much for the Wagnerian cause as is sometimes assumed, Wagner did much for Shaw, as an examination of Shaw's novels and plays will reveal. In his first and appropriately titled novel, *Immaturity* (1879), Shaw makes mention of both music criticism and Wagner. An iconoclastic dinner guest, Mr. Musgrove, takes issue with an established critic, Mr. Weeks. He accuses music critics of trying to overwhelm the public with technical jargon and of relying too much on tradition and reputation. "Except when they prophesy after the event, musical critics are invariably wrong."[43] Musgrove points out that after thirty years of disapproving of Wagner, all of the critics have rushed to champion him in order to catch up with public opinion. Whereupon the hostess, Lady Geraldine Scott, threatens to leave the table unless they stop talking about music.

In *Cashel Byron's Profession* (1882), an episode more crucial to the plot than is the table conversation in *Immaturity* utilizes the theme of Wagner once again. In this novel Lydia Carew, a well-educated, rational woman who never stops intellectualizing, meets Cashel Byron, a champion boxer and a man of action and impulse, who scarcely ever reasons. Shaw seems to have believed that such intellect and such vigor would make a good combination (perhaps a minor contribution to human evolution, although Shaw is not explicit on this point). At an evening party, Cashel holds forth and puts down a rival named Lucian Webber. Lydia does not yet know the nature of Cashel's profession. Cashel indirectly defends his profession by discussing the importance of fighting a good and stylish fight in order to preserve one's interests in life, society, and politics. Here he draws on Wagner to illustrate how one "artist" can shed light on another:

> I made out from the gentleman's remarks that there is a man in the musical line named Wagner, who is what you might call a game sort of composer; and that the musical fancy, though they can't deny that his tunes are first-rate, and that, so to speak, he wins his fights, yet they try to make out that he wins them in an outlandish way, and that he has no real science. Now I tell the gentlemen not to mind such talk. As I have just shown you, his game wouldn't be any use to him without science. He might have beaten a few second-raters with a rush while he was young; but he wouldn't have lasted out as he has done unless he was clever as well. It's the newness of his style that puzzles people. . . . You will find that those who run Professor Wagner down are either jealous, or they are old stagers that are not used to his style, and think that anything new must be bad. [44]

And then Cashel makes a prediction: "Just you wait a bit, and, take my word for it, they'll turn right around and swear that his style isn't new at all, and that he stole it from some one they saw when they were ten years old." [45] He went on to prove his point about "game" and "science" by catching Lucien Webber off-balance and knocking him into a chair with just a touch of his hand. Apparently, Shaw could not resist mentioning his music hero even in a drawing room boxing demonstration.

Unsuccessful at the novel, Shaw turned to drama. *Widowers' Houses,* his first play, published in 1892, was begun rather accidentally in 1885 as a collaboration with William Archer, a fellow journalist and literary critic. In 1883 Archer wrote a lengthy but unpublished work on Wagner and his theories.[46] Discovering that Shaw had written novels, Archer confessed an ambition to write plays. He proposed to devise a plot if Shaw would do the dialogue. The play was to open on the banks of the Rhine. There was to be "a capitalistic villain, tainted gold, and finally a grand gesture of throwing the tainted gold back into the Rhine."[47] The collaboration failed. Much to Archer's annoyance, Shaw ignored nine-tenths of his plot. Shaw noted in his diary that a long argument ensued, and his letters indicate that when the play was read to him, Archer first laughed and then snored.[48] Shaw claimed that the central idea was good, but that it was surrounded by romantic hallucinations and unreal plot mechanisms. Hence *Rhinegold* was set aside for seven years, until 1892, when it became *Widowers' Houses.* Its subject matter is slum landlordism. The first act takes place in a small Rhineland hotel. There is no palpable gold nor Scribe-like turn of plot, but the attack on moneyed power remains. The play was not well received, except by some socialists.

Reverberations from the *Ring* are again to be found in *Man and Superman,* published in 1903. The published version of the play contains an appended section, supposedly written by the main character, John Tanner. It is called *The Revolutionist's Handbook and Pocket Companion.* The *Handbook* and the chapter "Siegfried as Protestant" in *The Perfect Wagnerite* contain similar arguments. In each Shaw asserts that man as he now exists is not capable of further progress, but that he must be replaced by a superior animal through some form of selective breeding or purposive willing. Tanner himself is not a Siegfried; rather, he is an intellectual mated unwillingly, but inevitably, to a woman whose charm and guile are placed at the service of her desire to reproduce. Perhaps they will create the Superman together. In the famous third-act dream sequence known as

Don Juan in Hell, Don Juan/Tanner is an apostle of the Life Force. The devil comments that "Wagner once drifted into Life Force worship, and invented a Superman. But he came to his senses afterwards."[49] The devil then quarrels with Nietzsche, and Nietzsche leaves for heaven in a huff. Don Juan too migrates to paradise, even though he suspects that it is boring, whereas Wagner, having betrayed his Superman, according to Shaw, remains in hell.

Shaw paid his greatest tribute to Wagner's tetralogy by writing his *Back to Methuselah* (1918–20), "a metabiological pentateuch," which he thought to be his own *Ring*.[50] *Back to Methusaleh* is a legend of Creative Evolution, a sort of moral and religious science fiction. The first play is an adaptation of the Garden of Eden story; the last play takes place thirty-one thousand years after the birth of Christ, when human evolution is fully completed. Shaw was an iconoclast, a gadfly, the ultimate anticlerical. He was a fighter for the new styles both in politics and in music. Nevertheless, he also hoped to be remembered as "redistilling the eternal spirit of religion and thus extricating it from the sludgy residue of temporalities and legends that are making belief impossible."[51] In the preface to *Back to Methusaleh,* Shaw presents an excellent survey of the devastating impact of Darwinism on nineteenth-century religion. He offers an alternative, based on Lamarckian principles, reasserting the role of purpose, consciousness, and progress in human development. *Back to Methusaleh* is to be "a contribution to the modern Bible."[52] The pentalogy provides "an iconography for a live religion."[53] Creative Evolution is to be the basis of "a new Reformation."[54] According to Shaw, "We must either embrace Creative Evolution or fall into the bottomless pit of an utterly discouraging pessimism."[55] Deliberately, he refashions the legends out of old traditions, and, in a sense, performs an act of conservation. He regards Mozart's *Magic Flute,* Beethoven's *Ninth Symphony,* and Wagner's *Ring,* as "reachings forward to the new Vitalist art," and he hopes that *Back to Methusaleh* belongs to that group.[56] Actually, by the conclusion of the last play, Shaw abandons both socialism and biology. Social science has destroyed the world, and future beings are about to divest themselves of their flesh and enter a vortex of pure thought.

Much ink has been spilled on the question of the influence of Schopenhauer, Nietzsche, and Bergson on Shaw. He himself denied any such influence and claimed that whatever he knew came from English writers such as Samuel Butler (certainly, a neo-Lamarckian), Ernest Belfort Bax, and even the seventeenth-century John Bunyan. Very likely, Shaw should be taken at his word. What he knew of Schopenhauer may have come through Bax; however, his use of the concept of the will and his notions of the role of the sexes differ greatly from Schopenhauer. Shaw could not have known much of Nietzsche before writing *The Perfect Wagnerite* beyond the term *Übermensch,* which Shaw acknowledges as Nietzschean and translates as "overman."[57] Bergson published *Creative Evolution* in 1907, nine years after *The Perfect Wagnerite,* in which Shaw expresses the vitalism that he reiterates in *Back to Methusaleh.* In the latter, of course, he borrows Bergson's phraseology. Apart from his appropriation of these terms, the influence seems to be indirect. Shaw's work reflects the kinship and the shared concerns of men of the 1890s. Certainly, Wagner appeared on Shaw's intellectual horizon before either Nietzsche or Bergson.

References in succeeding plays pointed either to Wagner's personal character or to his tribulations. In *The Doctor's Dilemma* (1906), Shaw discusses, in the climactic scene, the importance of kind treatment for animals. The conversation is a paraphrase of Wagner's *An End in Paris* (1841, a story concerning the death of his Newfoundland dog.[58] In his preface to *Androcles and the Lion* (1912), where he discusses the role of marriage, the family, and revolution, he writes: "It took a revolution to rescue Wagner from his Court appointment in Dresden; and his wife never forgave him for being glad and feeling free when he lost it and threw her back into poverty."[59] In the preface to *Saint Joan* (1923), where Shaw comments on modern and medieval cruelty, he mentions that as recently as the period of Wagner's youth, the composer had observed and avoided a crowd of persons hastening to see a soldier broken on the wheel. Since Shaw has discussed at one time or another almost everything under the sun, such references to Wagner need not have a special importance. However, they do add to the portrait of the playwright as fully informed of nearly every anecdote and biographical detail concerning the composer.

Besides reference to Wagner in Shaw's novels and prefaces and plays, and his use of myth in the "metabiological penta-teuch," Shaw's writing style very much reflects his interest in opera. According to Martin Meisel, Shaw's use of operatic conceptions is fourfold.[60] First, he made direct allusions to opera. Second, he cast his characters with a concern for vocal balance. Third, he consciously conceived his scenes musically as recitatives, arias, duets, trios, and the like. Fourth, he used musical terms to describe his art; they abound in his rehearsal notes and acting directions.[61] None of this is exclusively Wag-nerian, necessarily. However, like Wagner, Bernard Shaw had a lofty concept of the role of drama as a vehicle for religious knowledge. Said Shaw: "The theatre is really the week-day church; and a good play is essentially identical with a church service as a combination of artistic ritual, profession of faith, and sermon."[62] Shaw distinquished between most nineteenth-century opera as the drama of passions and the Wagnerian music drama, such as the *Ring,* in which ideas are made flesh. Thus, according to Meisel, "In Wagner's music-drama Shaw believed he had found the possibility of conveying impassioned thought to an audience, thought interpenetrated with intense feeling."[63] Shaw believed that in order to create his own "drama of impassioned thought," of heroic ideas, he would have to bring the world of music into his playwriting. Wagner had found opera in the nineteenth century a spectacle for the tired business man and had tried to make it into an occasion more like that of the community experience of the Greek tragic festivals. In so doing, he had abandoned plots that served merely as framework for arias and substituted a music drama in which both words and music existed together to convey serious meaning and to provide an intellectual and emotional experience. Shaw in creating a drama of ideas could not be satisfied merely with the bon mot or didactic aphorism.

He gave his ideas life and intensity through their orchestrations. Though Shaw's characters neither reveal their psychic depths nor provoke as vehement an audience reaction as do Wagner's, Shaw created through his artistry "a music of ideas—or rather, perhaps, it is a music of moralities."[64]

The strong artistic and emotional influence of Wagner's works on Shaw, coupled with his continued defense of Wagner during the years of the First and Second World Wars, added fuel to the fires of debate on Shaw's political affiliation with Germany. Shaw's appreciation of German music, his interest in German philosophers, his admiration for German socialists, together with his frequent criticism, even scolding, of the English nation do not make him a supporter either of the Kaiser or of Hitler. In World War I, his public statements called for the defeat of Germany. Yet his delight in contrasting German virtues with British sins made it seem as though Shaw were pro-German.

> The result was that although he was never universally condemned in England, the British except for a few socialists who agreed with him, considered him at worst a traitor and at best a poor sport; while Germany celebrated him as a paragon of straight-thinking and converted some of his published remarks into propaganda favoring the Central Powers.[65]

Between the two world wars Shaw's contempt for British "sham democracy" and his agreement with Mussolini on that point led to an exchange of passionate letters between the Italian historian and liberal patriot Gaetano Salvemini and Shaw. Likewise, Shaw's disapproval of Oswald Mosley's wartime imprisonment without trial raised for the British public the question of Shaw's sympathy with fascism and nazism. According to both his detractors and his defenders, Shaw's attitudes on these points seem in any case to have been determined by his political ideas and not by any cultural affinity for Germany or liking for German—or Italian—music.

To conclude, Bernard Shaw was a wise music critic in general and a hearty satirist of the Wagner cult in particular. The following statement from an article in the *Hawk,* 13 August 1889, is both illustrative and irresistible:

The first time I ever heard a note of Wagner's music was in my small boy days, when I stumbled upon a military band playing the Tannhäuser march. I will not pretend that I quite rose to the occasion; in fact, I said just what Hector Berlioz said—that it was a plagiarism from the famous theme in *Der Freischutz*. But a little after this bad beginning I picked up a score of *Lohengrin;* and before I had taken in ten bars of the prelude I was a confirmed Wagnerite in the sense the term then bore, which committed me to nothing further than greatly relishing Wagner's music. What it commits a man to now, Omniscience only knows. Vegetarianism, the higher Buddhism, Christianity divested of its allegorical trappings (I suspect this is a heterodox variety), belief in a Fall of Man brought about by some cataclysm which starved him into eating flesh, negation of the Will-to-Live and consequent redemption through compassion excited by suffering (this is the Wagner-Schopenhauer article of faith); all these are but samples of what Wagnerism involves nowadays. The average enthusiast accepts them all unhesitatingly—bar vegetarianism. Buddhism he can stand; he is not particular as to what variety of Christianity he owns up to: Schopenhauer is his favorite philosopher; but get through *Parsifal* without a beefsteak between the second and third acts he will not. Now as it happens, I am a vegetarian; and I can presume enormously upon that habit of mine, even among the elect. But for an unlucky sense of humor which is continually exposing me to charges of ribaldry, I should have been elected a vice-president of the Wagner Society long ago. [66]

But to say only that Shaw laughed at the Wagnerites is to miss the point. Shaw himself succumbed to Wagner emotionally as well as artistically. The iconoclast at Bayreuth fell in love with the *Ring:* "Most of us are at present so helplessly under the spell of *The Ring's* greatness that we can do nothing but go raving about the theatre between acts in ecstacies of deluded admiration." [67] It is just possible, as G. K. Chesterton said, that music, and especially Wagner's music, might "itself be considered in the first case as the imaginative safety valve of the rationalistic Irishman." [68] Finally, it is important to say that Shaw succumbed not only as a man but also as a writer. In his novels and plays he showed a love of music, particularly opera, and in what he regarded as the most explicit statement of his own philosophy in *Back to Methusaleh,* he had adapted Wagner's conception of the mission of art to the prose theater.

David Irvine, Schopenhauer,
and Wagner

Schopenhauer's *Die Welt als Wille und Vorstellung*, though published in 1819, was neglected thoroughly until the second half of the century, when it began to enjoy a remarkable vogue. Schopenhauer's philosophy was first introduced in England by John Oxenford in his article "Iconoclasm in German Philosophy" in 1853.[1] Several articles and a biography appeared in the 1870s.[2] Schopenhauer's major treatise was translated by R. B. Haldane and J. Kemp in the years 1883–86; the rest of his works found translators in the nineties. According to Thomas Mann, Schopenhauer's thought permeated the intellectual atmosphere of the second half of the nineteenth century, "the air of youth and home for those of us past sixty."[3] Indeed, in England many young people in the 1880s read and effected to worship Schopenhauer.[4]

For Schopenhauer, the world is the blind, tragic, striving of the will. If the world is will, then it is full of pain and suffering, for it is not possible to satisfy the demands of desire. Wisdom in man consists of transcending the absurd appetites of will and finding rest in contemplation. Often man's wisdom is only the rationalization of what the will has done; however, sometimes the intellect disobeys the will. It may therefore be possible to develop the power of the intellect or consciousness so that it can rise above the strivings of the will. The deliverance of knowledge from servitude to the will can best be accomplished through philosophy and through art. Thus contemplation of the tragedy of the world through art, particularly through music, which Schopenhauer valued above all, can elevate us and give us moments of peace. Schopenhauer's combination of ethical pessimism, emphasis on the erotic aspect of the will, and the hope of redemption through art appealed enormously to artistic souls who experienced cultural or religious despair and who did not, like Max Nordau, blame their despair on degeneracy.

Admiration for Wagner in England was nearly inseparable from admiration for Schopenhauer. Francis Hueffer and William Ashton Ellis proclaimed the worth of Schopenhauer and Wagner in several articles.[5] Charles Dowdeswell's translation of Schopenhauer's *Die Welt* occupied many pages of the Wagner Society's *Meister*. John Payne, the Pre-Raphaelite poet, dedicated poems to both Wagner and Schopenhauer. Alfred Forman, who was the best English translator of Wagner's dramas in the nineteenth century, was also devoted to Schopenhauer. Forman's work *Sonnets,* privately printed in 1886, illustrates the mood of these Germanophiles.[6] In the poem "Medusa" he names Schopenhauer the "Great Prophet of the World's Despair," who shows reality as it truly is and "strips back the veil and strikes us into stone."[7] In "The Will-to-Live" he speaks of man "drunk with the fury of the Will-to-be," taking up his burden and playing out his dismal part.[8] It appears that only Wagner can offer him solace:

> . . . Great Spirit! Thou by whom alone,
> Of all the Wonder-doers sent to be
> My signs and sureties Time-ward, unto me
> My inmost self has ceased to be unknown! . . .
> Thou only so hast dealt with me, that I
> Can be no more as if thou hadst not been.[9]

Forman had not seen *Parsifal* and wrote longingly of his desire to hear the grail king's music.[10] He found that Wagner's music achieved what Schopenhauer found to be the purpose of music, "a painless sympathy with pain."

Of all the English admirers of Wagner and Schopenhauer,

David Henderson Irvine was the most systematic and persevering in connecting the two.[11] Unlike George Bernard Shaw, Irvine was not a many-sided public figure and was not known apart from his Wagnerism. Born in Scotland in 1856, he seems to have lived from independent means primarily in London, where he published eight books on or relating to Wagner.[12] Shaw mentioned in a letter to his wife in 1897 that he was going to dine at the home of H. W. Massingham (editor of the *Daily Chronicle*) in order to meet "David Irvine, the Wagnerite."[13] Very likely Irvine belonged to the London Wagner Society. William Ashton Ellis described Irvine as his friend.[14] It is certain that he was a lifetime member of the *Schopenhauer Gesellschaft*. Membership lists of the society show that Irvine moved from London to Australia sometime between February 1913 and February 1914, probably early in 1914. In Melbourne he lived for a time with Herman Theodor Schräder, formerly professor of music at the Melbourne University Conservatorium. The 23 April 1914 issue of the *Argus,* a Melbourne newspaper, published a letter by Irvine in defense of Wagner and Cosima in their dealings with Cosima's first husband, Hans van Bülow. In 1919 Irvine moved to Sydney, where he died on 17 January 1930. He was buried in a Presbyterian cemetery.[15] He was not married. He did not publish anything during his old age in Australia, nor is it known why he left England in 1914. Although the fact that he was devoted both to German and to British culture might seem a plausible explanation for his departure in early 1914, when war between Great Britain and Germany loomed, he probably left England months before that war became certain.

Irvine was a severe critic of all theistic religion, including that espoused by the Church of England, and political conservatism, anything that he considered to be the Establishment. He was a proponent of liberalism, by which he meant "a compound of radical politics, Protestantism, and Rationalism."[16] He hoped to modify liberalism and make it more profound by freeing it of excessive individualism and giving it metaphysical roots in Schopenhauer's philosophy.[17] He believed that Schopenhauer's pessimism was exactly equivalent to *real* Christianity divested of its hypocrisy and ecclesiasticism.[18] He was also convinced that philosophy was "the theoretic counterpart of Art," and that these two met "in the employment of analogy and of symbolism."[19] Since art was instinctive, pure, and "objective" in the Schopenhaurian sense, it was the higher of the two. Thus Wagner, who admired Schopenhauer and whose works developed a Schopenhaurian aura, could serve as a guide to expose both the church and conservatism and to strengthen liberalism. Hence, Irvine championed Wagner's ideas against his critics and gave support to those who found a message in his music.

Irvine's first book, *Wagner's "Ring of the Nibelung" and the Conditions of Ideal Manhood,* published in 1897, stresses the contemporaneity of the drama. Like Bernard Shaw, Irvine recognized Wagner's dramatis personae to be modern. They spring "from the character of the age and life in which Wagner lived and not from the *mythos* at all."[20] The Nibelungs, however, are not Shaw's proletarians, but slaves of egoism and, "more likely," members of the upper classes; the giants and Hunding rise above egoism to conventional law; the gods strive both to stand above nature and to be closer to it.[21] All these characters whether designated as dwarfs, dragons, or gods, are representations of "man and not any power outside man except what we find in nature."[22] According to Irvine, the conventional or artificial appear in Wagner's works as evils opposed to what is natural, loving, and free from the restrictions of corrupt social institutions. The Christian church is one of the worst evils. In his book, Irvine divides the chapters into sections dealing with the earlier prose works of Wagner, the characters of the *Ring,* the drama, and the music, all interlaced with his own social comment.

Characteristic examples of Irvine's view of the nineteenth-century church may be found in his discussion of Mime, the Nibelung who raises the orphaned Siegfried to manhood. Mime insistently reminds Siegfried how much the child owes him and how much he has sacrificed on his behalf. Mime claims to be both father and mother to him. At the same time Mime intends to use Siegfried in his plan to seize the ring. Irvine comments:

Mime is thus that spirit which superficially appears as the educator of mankind, and when intelligence begins to perceive that nature is its true educator and the other a mere charlatan, with which it has nothing in common, then craft and subterfuge are called into requisition in order to turn this step, leading to a truer knowledge of things, into the further service of self-interest. Mime is thus the craft which finds its best soil in the Church impressing every one in early youth, before judgment is ripe, with the belief that it is a spiritual father and mother. [23]

Irvine observes that "the birth and growth of religion in man is in spite of the Church and not in virtue of it." [24] In the second act, after the forest bird has informed Siegfried not to trust Mime, the dwarf approaches Siegfried with a drink, as he says, to refresh the young man. At the same time he tells Siegfried of his intention to poison him with it. "What then is meant by this fatuous declaration of Mime, telling to Siegfried's face what Siegfried knows already?" [25] Evidently, Irvine does not realize that Siegfried, having tasted the dragon's blood, can read the thoughts behind Mime's words and that Wagner had to use the words that Siegfried understands, not those he actually hears, for the audience's benefit. Instead, Irvine provides an explanation of his own. Mime has tried to use the natural intelligence of mankind to his own corrupt end. Therefore he is like a sect or church that binds differing individuals only by virtue of its opposition to all rivals, although claiming to have exclusive truth. Here Irvine quotes Laurence Oliphant, the author of *Scientific Religion* and a critic of orthodoxy—hence a favorite of Irvine: "The only monopoly a Church has a right to claim is a monopoly of the errors which are peculiar to it—what truth it has is generally common to all. [26] Mime is thus single-minded in opposition to Siegfried, but two-faced when it comes to the truth.

Mime now represents one body with conflicting views. Thus in the same breath he refutes himself without in any way knowing he does so, just as the contradictions of the Church members refute unity without apparent knowledge of what is therewith implied. [27]

Irvine recommends, "as happened to Mime," that "the

Church with an eye on its own welfare at the expense of the individual, has to be slain by the intellect."[28] This characterization of Mime is not the only opportunity that Irvine found for criticism of the church. For instance, of the incident in which Loge urges Wotan to steal the ring from Alberich, Irvine remarks:

> Robbing now is of no consequence. One church helps itself to another's wealth. *That* is right, God smiles on that deed. But if a democratic state wishes to take possession of that wealth for obvious reasons of good to the community, that is shameless robbery.[29]

In general, Irvine speaks of Christianity "degraded through hypocrisy and half-heartedness," allowing itself "to countenance the oppression of the people."[30]

In Wagner's *Ring,* according to Irvine, "the essence of Christianity is more nearly approached than by any sect or church."[31] In his explanation, Irvine relies heavily on the philosophical concepts of optimism and pessimism, the framework within which he makes his entire evaluation of Wagner's works. Optimism is the "belief in the goodness of nature as known to our senses."[32] Nature's worthiest manifestation is human energy. Human kind may tap this energy for social ends, but it usually fails. In order to avoid confronting this problem,

> we grasp at some supernatural power, indulge in abstract speculation and conventional reverence. . . . Possessing no means of demonstrating the existence of this supernatural power, we invest it with our own egoism, firstly to justify individual acts in ourselves, and secondly to condemn individual acts in others. The power of making valid the justification of these acts is vested in the state. This forms our pitiable ideas of morality.[33]

There are two kinds of optimism, the egoistic and the altruistic. The egoistic is represented by the church unified with the state and is really Judaic, not Christian, in origin; the altruistic is represented by the destruction of conventional religion, as in Wagner's *Ring.* The destruction of conventional religion and political authority is necessary to return to the goodness of nature.

> Law, imposed by the few on the many, first made sin possible. Man to work his way out of the possibility of sinning, had to cast off the restraints of the law. . . . The *Ring* is thus solely occupied with a conflict between the assumed right of traditional authority and the natural instinct in man to satisfy his desires.[34]

All other laws being abrogated, the law of nature prevails. The law of nature is love, never positively defined in the opera but strongly suggested by Brünhilde and the inward struggles of Wotan. Wotan is the conventional godhead who renounces power for the sake of purely human love. Hence Wagner's optimism in the *Ring* is "not egoistic but altruistic and closer to the Christianity of Christ than the theology of the Church."[35] Love, freedom, and ideal manhood are one and the same.

Both in his explication of the *Ring* and in *A Wagnerian's Midsummer Madness,* Irvine traces the development of altruistic optimism through Wagner's early essays. Wagner's *Art and Revolution* is "little more than a prose poem . . . directed against the hypocrisy of the age."[36] *Opera and Drama* celebrates "the victory of the human over the artificial" and proposes a complete artwork containing the poetical idea that "appropriates virtue to the heart, dramatically opposed to legal or official virtue."[37] In *Communication to My Friends,* once more Wagner finds "the divine, the moral feeling of the heart, in this world instead of a problematic heaven."[38] In *Art-Work of the Future* the bondage of man to conventional authority is compared with the parallel bondage of art. In the operas, the hero of *Der Fliegende Holländer* seeks an earthly love affair; Tannhäuser wearies of "sensuality in a mystic sphere"; Lohengrin finds the love of a human being. However, Lohengrin turns away from his Elsa, and Irvine considers the opera a failure. Finally, when Irvine returns to the *Ring,* he reiterates his view that Wagner's artistic goal was to separate the human from the conventional and to make the concept *divine* synonymous with *human.* Then, concluding his study of the *Ring,* Irvine dramatically contrasts the views of Wagner and Cardinal Newman. He places excerpts from their works side by side and comments:

> And thus one may say that the poetry of Wagner, the delineation of the purely-human in the dramatic setting has led up to a watershed from which every individual can intellectually judge that a given action serves either to develop or retard the growth of the moral spirit of the age which seeks to rationally justify its drift toward liberty. The official or the artistic: The Pope or Wagner? The issue has long been before the intellect. Never has it obtained such clearness or significance as now; never has a genius thrown such influence into one scale as has been done by Wagner. Into which scale none but a dolt need ask and none but an egoist dispute.[39]

In his next treatise, *"Parsifal" and Wagner's Christianity*, Irvine attempts to prove that Wagner's final music drama moves beyond altruistic optimism to the higher realm of Schopenhaurian pessimism and that Schopenhauer truly understood the meaning of Christianity. Irvine knows perfectly well that Schopenhauer did not believe in God. Schopenhauer's business was "to steer a middle course between Theism and complete Agnosticism."[40] Irvine quotes from *Neue Paralipomena* (nos. 377, 392, 395) to the effect that Schopenhauer believed that he possessed a "better consciousness," that part of the intellect that could subdue the will and lead him into a world where there was no longer personality or causality, subject or object. Schopenhauer did not believe that the better consciousness was God, but he was willing to allow the word *God* to be used symbolically. Irvine suggests that Wagner did not believe in God either but that, like Schopenhauer, he believed that if the public had to hold on to traditional terminology, it was welcome to it. Wagner would interpret metaphysical truth, often using the old symbols, through his art.

Whereas in the *Ring* the problem is social contention and strife, in *Parsifal* the struggle is narrowed to the conflict of two principles within the heart of one man. Or, as Irvine explains it, "There is nothing more striking than the complete, or next to complete, unconsciousness with which the struggle in the *Ring* is carried on, and the complete consciousness in *Parsifal*."[41] For Irvine, the opera's characters reflect philosophical ideas. Titurel represents that which must die out before a restoration may take place: egoistic Jewish Christianity. Klingsor embodies the intellect employed in the services of the will. He is the father of lies. Kundry is a divided character. Sometimes her individual will is captive to Klingsor; sometimes she demonstrates a higher will to serve the good. In discussing Kundry, Irvine raises the subject of sexuality in the idea of God. "In the idea of 'god,' the male and female exist bisexually and her [Kundry's] redemption means nothing more or less than the reversion to that original state where the separation of the sexes was unknown."[42] The divine being both male and female, woman is thus eventually to be freed from the lie that makes her only "the degraded object of man's desire" or "the medium to incite the sexual in man." In this view Irvine seems to have borrowed heavily from Laurence Oliphant, via T. L. Harris and Emanuel Swedenborg. Titurel, Klingsor, and Kundry all represent the mortal part of the will. The wounded Amfortas exemplifies the individual man in his highest capacity. He is supremely conscious of the fact that the misery of the world is identical with its sensuality. Gurnemanz is a simple, good man of faith, a man of the folk, uncontaminated by civilization. Parsifal is "the exceptional man who not only sees what ordinary men do not see, but what he sees equally with them gets inverted in the perspective of his moral vision."[43] The Grail community represents the ideal church. But, Irvine asserts, Parsifal is not Christ, nor are the Grail precincts heaven.[44] The music drama is symbolic and mystical but not intended to bolster any exclusive, and therefore false, sectarian interpretation. Rather, Wagner, and Schopenhauer and Oliphant as well, penetrate in their own ways to the esoteric and universal meaning of Christianity.[45] Furthermore, it is no matter when or even whether Wagner actually read Schopenhauer: "It is a matter here of concomitancy, not of cause and effect."[46]

There is a carry-over from the action of the *Ring* to that of *Parsifal.* Irvine is more interested in Wotan than in Siegfried and in Amfortas more than Parsifal. Accordingly, he compares Wotan to Amfortas. Wotan recognizes his inability to deal with two conflicting desires, the attainment of power and its external demands and the inclination of his own inner nature toward love. To him as an embodiment of authority the triumph of his inner moral side would mean the end of his world. The attainment of the ring typifies one desire; the success of his progeny the Volsungs the other. In the *Ring* only Wotan and Brünhilde reach any sort of consciousness and self-reproach. Apart from these two, the *Ring* portrays an unconscious struggle between the partisans of power for power's sake and the partisans of life and love. In *Parsifal,* on the other hand, the struggle for consciousness is the central feature. Titurel and Kundry can be viewed as relics of Wotan's double character—that is, "Titurel in his will-to-live for the sake of Power, Kundry in her conscious sense of the degradation of sexual intercourse."[47] In the *Ring* Wotan's sin, according to Irvine, is not entirely his own; his virtue, which is his own, is in conflict with the demands of his office. Amfortas's sin is entirely his own and his office is not diminished on that account. "Wotan condemns his conditions and his environment. His abnegation destroys these conditions. . . . Amfortas can only blame himself."[48] As far as Siegfried is concerned, he is a noble savage, has no temptations, and "personates" nature. But Amfortas lives in the center of consciousness and responsibility as does Parsifal, although Parsifal does not share Amfortas's sin. The hope of Parsifal is to achieve consciousness; as Irvine says, no philosophy can offer any insight into the taming of the blind will

> that does not place self-conciousness in the van of all moral reformation. . . . Freedom from the tyranny of individuality is the beginning and end of the divine principle. In the individual the reflecting individual has recognised the universal sin.[49]

Of course, the basis of the blind will is the urge to live and to reproduce. In this respect, Irvine comments that the *Ring* cuts down the laws of human action to love; *Parsifal* reduces love to compassion—that is, love freed from sensuality. Concluding his discussion, Irvine pleads the following case for "pessimism": "To combat the egoistic sensual Will, there is needed the compassionate and spiritual Will. All of this battleground is on this earth. Man is both God and Devil."[50] Such is the essence of true Christian teaching in Irvine's opinion.

Of particular interest in analyzing Irvine's Wagnerism is his attitude toward Wagner's later prose works. These writings and their relationship to the art of *Parsifal* are especially controversial. A recent scholarly biographer, Robert Gutman, believes that *Parsifal* is an allegorical presentation of Wagner's hopes for the regeneration of the racially debased Aryans. Gutman derives this "painful interpretation" of the opera largely from Wagner's own words, expressed in these essays. Although he admits that Wagner's opera may also and "more comfortably be regarded as his final treatment of the themes of empathy, growing awareness, and the love-death," nevertheless, he cannot overlook the fact that *Parsifal* developed from the aging Wagner's racial hatred, impotence, and sexual ambivalence.[51]

At the outset, Irvine admits to meeting with many difficulties. There is the question of Wagner's problematic character, which Wagnerians believed that they were obliged to defend. Wagner, accustomed during his last years to writing for a circle of intimate friends, sometimes expressed in his writing a superior, exclusive attitude. Not surprisingly, however, this confidential style was welcome to a circle acknowledging a master. Irvine agrees that moral exhortations directed to the public from lofty pinnacles can be very nauseating indeed, but he believes that the confidence of Wagner's disciples is both proof and justification that Wagner was no hypocrite. He suggests that Wagner never denied to others the comforts that he enjoyed himself, that criticism of Wagner's character was mostly villification, and that "the revelations of Nietzsche are ludicrously devoid of the recognition of humour in Wagner's necessary, indeed almost playful, adoption in private life of the superior air."[52] On the contrary, what troubles Irvine most are the occasions when Wagner took himself so seriously as to be tempted by asceticism. He agrees with Nietzsche, and contradicts Schopenhauer, in stating that asceticism may be "a perfectly honest hallucination," but in reality it is the most degrading form of egoism.[53] Therefore, having done his best to explain and defend Wagner's character, as he would do over

and over again, he concludes that, while a trace of false supe-
riority does color Wagner's writings, "it seems to be the debt
which the theoretical writer and human being Wagner paid
to the inspired genius Wagner."[54]

Next, Irvine qualifies his approach to the content of Wagner's writings. First, he notes that the philosophical questions
raised by Wagner were weighty and complex. Second, he
acknowledges that Wagner's style was not always clear. Third,
he urges that Wagner's mainstream of thought be kept firmly
in mind so that the subsidiary themes will not appear as
inappropriate fads.[55] For instance, Wagner's vegetarianism
and his antivivisectionist pleadings, if impractical, did have a
legitimate place in turning mankind away from brutality and
egoism. Irvine begins with a discussion of Wagner's *On State and
Religion*, published in 1864. Gutman states that "its infran-
gible syntax does not yield much sense" but that it was probably intended to flatter Ludwig II as "a kind of superman, the
representative of the 'purely-human',", and to assure Ludwig
that Wagner had never really been a revolutionary in 1848.[56]
Irvine, on the other hand, makes no mention of Ludwig or of
the circumstances under which the essay had been written.
Rather, he interprets the essay as best he can in a Schopenhaurian vein. Typically, he reiterates his indictment of orthodoxy, while scolding and admonishing his readers: "If people
cannot understand this; if history, past and present, does not
substantiate it, then it is hard to know what they intellectually
are fit to be entrusted with."[57] More gently, he urges his readers, still enmeshed in orthodoxy's wiles, to suspend their judgment and listen. *On State and Religion* is an exposition of the
ideal duties of a king, who represents the highest consciousness and therefore the highest responsibility. What guides the
ordinary citizen within the community is patriotism. Patriotism demands from the individual an act of renunciation
in the interests of the state. However, as a virtue, patriotism
stops at the boundaries of the nation. For states blindly and
violently strive against one another. On the other hand, what
guides the king who stands above the many in the state is
religion. Patriotism may be the height attainable to the
burgher. The king, however, through religion may aspire to a

greater dignity and justice. To Irvine, this is just another way of asserting the importance of the divine in man.[58] Actually, the subject of kings is uncongenial to Irvine and happily he turns to discussion of the *volk* in Wagner's *German Art and German Policy,* published in 1867.

Of this Irvine says categorically: "Nothing finer, more conclusive, profounder and yet simpler has appeared from any pen the whole century throughout."[59] In this essay Wagner hailed German music as the art that would give birth to a drama surpassing the Greeks. Also, as Gutman and others have pointed out, Wagner eulogized the murderer of Kotzebue in 1819, espoused theories based upon those of Vater John, and gave free rein to his anti-French feelings. The Bavarian government was so embarrassed that it ordered publication of the essay discontinued. But Irvine admires the essay because he appreciates the blows struck at "the conventionality and the artificiality of the Pharisaical upper class."[60] Wagner, of course identifies the artificial, princely authority with French civilization: "French civilization arose without the people, German art without the princes."[61] Irvine concludes with the following comment:

> We must leave this notable essay with a recommendation to the English reader to master it, and then ask himself, with his mixture of Norman and Saxon blood, which of the two lies really at the root of English greatness; which shall he cultivate, the spirit of conventionalism, of artificiality, of ritualism, of pseudo-politeness, or of that blunt honesty which dominates the Saxon spirit. If the popularity of Wagner's music affords any test, then there is no doubt about the issue.[62]

What is surprising is that, immediately following this statement honoring the Saxon spirit at the expense of the Norman, Irvine is moved to quote rather abruptly a single paragraph from Wagner's *What is German?*1865) in order "to keep in touch with Wagner's ideal Christian religion":

> The Christian religion belongs to no specific national stock; the Christian dogma addresses purely-human nature. Only in so far as it has seized in all its purity this content common to all men, can a people call itself Christian in truth.[63]

Possibly Irvine is suggesting that Wagner's ethnic pronouncements not be taken too literally.

If so, what does Irvine have to say concerning Wagner's *Religion and Art,* written in 1880, and its supplements, *What Boots This Knowledge, Know Thyself,* and *Herodom and Christianity?* It is *Religion and Art* that Gutman views as revealing that Wagner's idiosyncrasies were turning to serious aberrations.[64] Indeed Wagner suggested that Jesus was probably not of Jewish stock. Furthermore Gutman chooses to interpret Wagner's statement in *Herodom* that "pride is such a delicate virtue, suffering no compromise such as the mixing of the blood" as outright advocacy of genocide.[65] In 1899 Irvine's darkest imagination did not extend that far, and thus he was probably closer to interpreting Wagner's meaning than Gutman, who had experienced the Third Reich. In discussing *Religion and Art* Irvine stresses Wagner's theme that the spirit of religion is revealed through art. He describes Wagner's view of the vengeful Jewish Jehovah, but he does not mention the composer's view of Christ as an Aryan. What Irvine says is that in order to give Christ his true divine nature, all idea of an earthly father, Joseph, has to be eliminated. This is in keeping with Schopenhauer's doctrine that the will that is derived from the father would otherwise have had its sensuality appearing in Christ. Commenting on Wagner's *Know Thyself,* Irvine informs the reader that Wagner was intent on freeing Christian civilization from Judaism and that Wagner believed that the Jew should assimilate "his method and disposition" with the Christian's.[66] Wagner advocated assimilation, not genocide. Wagner's *Herodom and Christianity,* strongly influenced by Gobineau, deals with a racial theory of civilization's degeneration. Irvine inevitably interprets this theory in the light of Schopenhauer's thought:

> It must now be evident that all conventional ordering of man into higher and lower gives place to another. The lower races are those which allow the Will to lay down the law for their intellect; the higher discriminate. . . . This theory and view of life is solely demonstrable on the basis of Schopenhauer's philosophy.[67]

The best of Schopenhauer has here been used to coat the most vile of Wagner's ideas. Though there is nothing in the text of *Parsifal* that necessitates a biological interpretation, Gutman has used the later prose works in order to judge Wagner's alleged intent in writing the opera. Irvine believes that in the later prose works Wagner actually avoided the deeper problem of the origin of sex itself, and therefore of egoism. He is satisfied only that the prose works did not contradict what the artist had actually accomplished in his music drama.[68]

Having thus interpreted Wagner's major operatic and prose works, Irvine proceeded to criticize the critics of Wagner in three short books: *A Wagnerian's Midsummer Madness, Wagner's Bad Luck,* and *The Badness of Wagner's Bad Luck.* These titles may connote a certain impatience, even mild hysteria. The first contains two chapters on anti-Wagnerism, one chapter on the poetry in Wagner's prose, two translations of German articles on Wagner, and a satirical philosophical essay. Irvine writes of his determination "to carry on the Wagner mission among the slums and backways of the East-end of intelligence."[69] He makes a distinction between the anti-Wagnerism of the past and that of his own time. The former despised Wagner's music and was on the wane. The latter accepted Wagner's music but, unfortunately, ignored his ideas. For instance, one newspaper reported that happily for mankind Wagner had had a few lucid intervals in which he composed music. To this Irvine replies: "This is just your present-day anti-Wagnerism in a nut-shell."[70] He also attacks the *Fortnightly Review* for republishing Nietzsche's *Case of Wagner.*

The publication in 1911 of an English translation of Wagner's *Mein Leben* prompted the next two polemics. In *Wagner's Bad Luck,* the first section lists, with examples, the types of error that marred this translation. These include specific errors in translation, contradictions growing out of loose translation, defamation of Wagner's character—especially in the description of his love affairs—improper usage of English idioms applied to German university life, and omissions—particularly of dates. The second section itemizes single and multiple errors on 430 of the 886 pages of the book. Irvine attacked both the Bayreuth editors and the English translators. He objected to the selling off of Wagner's literary effects to the highest bidders and warned that the commercial spirit would soon ruin Bayreuth. Like Shaw, he objected to the high price of tickets to Bayreuth performances. "Wagner was for the people, not for the salon; and every step away from the people is contrary to the spirit and aim of Wagner."[71] Lastly he heaped his scorn on the "university men" who were the translators:

> The translation, from one end to the other, is so offensively redolent of that English spirit that chiefly prevails at what the "men" call the "varsity" (pronounced "vahsity") that we cannot be blamed for reminding the reader every now and then of the fact. Bless us! the Wagnerian wants simplicity and unaffectedness, not jargon of a mock superior kind.[72]

Irvine's scorn for the translators of *Mein Leben* was a measure of the intensity of his need to place Wagner's character in the best possible light. *Mein Leben* was and remains a controversial memoir.[73] For many years it was asked just what proportion was attributable to Wagner and what to Cosima's redaction. Also, if Wagner were responsible for most of it, as is now believed, how truthful was he, and how should his character and personality best be interpreted?

Irvine returns to the autobiography in his last essay, *The Badness of Wagner's Bad Luck*. This reveals Irvine's ambitions, frustrations as a Wagnerite, and occasional indulgence in fantasy, despite his dogged attempts to keep within the framework of rational discussion. The first ten sections concern the background of Wagnerian criticism. Irvine repeats his estimate of the desperate condition of England philosophically and reiterates the premise that anti-Wagnerism was but a symptom of a radical evil—"The lack of religion to suit the intellectual requirements of the age."[74] Pointing to a deeply rooted conspiracy to demean Wagner, he blames the shallow nature of English thought and the irresponsibility of English journalism. Irvine's general plan of reply is to attempt to instil a new philosophy in the public mind. Thus he mentions the then just published *Metaphysical Rudiments of Liberalism;* another volume on Schopenhauer to come—perhaps his own translation of *Transcendent Speculations on Apparent Design in the Fate of the Individual;* and a third projected work on the specific problem of anti-Wagnerism, to be called *Wagner's "Ring" and Another Ring.* The other ring presumably was to be the anti-Wagner journalistic combine. This last work apparently was never written. Irvine also challenged critics of Wagner to debate. When the leading critic of the *Daily News* admitted that he could not make sense out of the *Ring,* calling it "a hopeless metaphysical muddle," Irvine replied that he had offered to pay fifty pounds to this critic's favorite musical charity "if I could not satisfactorily explain before a judge and jury accustomed to sifting out and weighing contrary evidence the symbolism of Wagner's *Ring.* "[75] The challenge was published in the *Musical Standard,* but the *Daily News* failed to take notice.

Next Irvine turned his attention to various reviews of *Mein Leben.* As usual, the three main themes of his discussion were Wagner's character, Wagner's ideas, and Wagner's music. Those reviewers who liked Wagner's music, but considered his prose unimportant, felt no obligation to defend his character. Irvine, however, felt the need to defend both Wagner's ideas and his character. One typical issue that separated the most avid Wagner cultists from more moderate admirers of the composer was Wagner's relationship with Minna Planer, his mistress and first wife. For instance, the *Spectator,* in an article published in 1911, acknowledged Wagner's mastery as an artist, his "indomitable perserverance in the face of endless difficulties," and his generosity, broadmindedness, and catholicity in honoring his debts to teachers and contemporary musicians. However, half of the *Spectator* article concerned Minna, the "true heroine" of the piece.[76] Wagner's tale, dictated to his second wife, of his conduct toward his first wife, provided a spectacle that was "one of the most repulsive and unholy in all annals of complacent egotism."[77] Irvine's reply makes it appear that the *Spectator* was finding fault with Minna as well as with Wagner in a most hypocritical fashion:

The Spectator is one of those remarkable papers that could hush up the whole business were it a case of some eminent nobleman who, at the same time as he was legally married, kept women, provided he were a social magnate and a wealthy member of the Church of England. But let it be the great genius Wagner . . . then the most trivial fact of these wandering people cohabiting previous to marriage is sufficient for the *Spectator* to enlarge on Wagner's immorality, and to speak slightingly of the two in a relation that does not hold good either to the spirit or to the letter.[78]

Furthermore, Irvine wrote, he would like just once to see the entire staff of the *Spectator* from office boy to editor, "compelled by some irresistible force to devote an entire issue of the journal to as fair-minded and enlightening an exposition of Schopenhauer's philosophy as ever flowed from Wagner's pen or mouth. . . . I would want a kinematographic exposition of the whole transaction."[79] Similar articles in the *Academy* he easily dispensed with, since they reflected "the same Anglican of phariseeism and moral cant" as the *Spectator*.[80] Interesting by way of comparison is the opinion of another Wagnerian, John Runciman of the *Saturday Review.* He said that there was no need to go into the sordid matter since "these things can never be explained and are best left alone."[81] However, he did believe that it was just as well to hear the story related from Wagner's viewpoint, for the truth had too often been distorted in the past by anti-Wagnerian critics. Unlike Irvine, however, he found the translation skillfully done.

By this time a new, young, and formidable English critic had appeared on the scene. He was Ernest Newman, author of *A Study of Wagner,* published in 1899. Actually, he was born William Roberts, but he changed his name in 1905 "in earnest" of his new approach. Inspired by the views of J. M. Robertson, a liberal politician and leading secularist, Newman believed in applying "scientific" procedures to the study of the arts. Accordingly, he aimed to be objective, skeptical, and factual in his music criticism. His four-volume biography of Wagner, published late in his life, has become the standard. However, Newman admitted a great reluctance even to attempt to describe Wagner's metaphysics. Irvine found in Newman a rigorous opponent. Although he recognized Newman's sincerity and skill at musical analysis, he maintained that "where Mr. Newman fails is where the great public begins to recognize in Wagner and Art what it now takes to lie in its priests and churches."[82] Newman, of course, had not failed since he was not at all interested in saving Christianity through art and philosophy.

Irvine attacks Newman's review of Wagner's *Mein Leben* in the last half of *The Badness of Wagner's Bad Luck*. In his article, printed in the *Fortnightly Review*, Newman raises the issues both of Wagner's relation with Minna and of Wagner's financial dealings. To describe Wagner's behavior he uses such phrases as "the depths of moral shabbiness," the "climax of meanness," "amazing vulgarity of soul," and "incredible egoism."[83] On the other hand, he points out that Wagner was not consciously cruel, merely completely self-centered, and that "his case is too abnormal to have any moral or immoral connotations whatever; we might as reasonably censure a blind man for being blind, or flog a hunchback for his hump."[84] But for his willful character, Wagner might never have persevered as an artist. In return, Irvine argues that Newman strove for objectivity, but often betrayed prejudice. According to Newman in the *Fortnightly Review* article, an admirer of Wagner was nearly always "rabid" or an "out-and-out" Wagnerian. Irvine deplores Newman's constant use of such adjectival "tags." He also points to Newman's use of several mistranslations and one abbreviated translation used to put Wagner's character in bad light. For example, Newman writes:

> When, after the fiasco of the Paris concerts, Madame Kalergis offers him 10,000 francs to cover his losses, he [Wagner] tells us: "I felt as though something were being fulfilled which I had always been entitled to expect."[85]

Irvine replies that Wagner looked upon Madame Kalergis's money as given for his art: it was therefore not an egoistic personal claim. Also, Newman makes the sentence stop short at the word "expect" when in fact the sentence continues. Completely translated, it reads:

> It appeared to me as if something was only fulfilled which I always deemed myself justified in expecting, and immediately I conceived in response but the one need likewise to reply to his rare woman by at least being able to do something for her.[86]

Irvine freely admits that Wagner was extravagant and hopelessly incapable of managing money. But at the same time he strongly resents Newman's moralistic attitude. Irvine lists many more such examples in Newman's *Study of Wagner*. "The thing is written for a society of Tartuffes, Scapins, Blifils, Holy Willies, Pecksniffs, Joseph Surfaces, Charles Honeymans, Stigginses, Beckmessers, and Mimes, never for artists."[87]

In the epilogue to *The Badness of Wagner's Bad Luck,* Irvine utters his last word on *Mein Leben.* He agrees with Wagner's critics that the early part of the memoir seems better than the second volume. On balance, he said, volume 2 "does not impress us with a growing sublimity or maturity," largely because Wagner spoke less of his art than of his grievances.[88] Predictably, Irvine is ready with the usual explanation: "Exhibitions of peevish temper and childish actions along with a maturing mind whose free results are hampered, denote something of the sickness that arrives on the constant deferring of one's hopes."[89] Thus, at times, Irvine could recognize Wagner's childishness or his extravagances, but was willing to put them down to the temperament and tribulations of the artist as opposed to the temperament of ordinary persons, and to minimize these defects as thoroughly as possible.

Concluding the epilogue, Irvine totals the score. He reports that he has read some fifty or sixty press notices of *Mein Leben* from throughout England and the British Empire. Forty he grades as fair; eleven definitely favorable; and the rest very bad indeed. Such a rather favorable tabulation would seem to belie Irvine's preoccupation with anti-Wagnerism but for the fact that his ultimate aim was not only to defend a composer but to rejuvenate a religion. This aim compelled him to insist on Wagner's goodness of character with all the rhetorical flourishes and scholarly ammunition he could muster.

David Irvine's integrity and his ambition are impressive. He knew his Wagner and his Schopenhauer very well; he felt obliged to deal systematically with their entire output; and, like the medieval scholastics, he admitted finding inconsistencies, while at the same time trying to reconcile them. His ambition was a new Reformation. It does seem at times that Irvine took a very long way around to come to the conclusion that true Christianity is humanism. However, considering the paradoxical import of that view, perhaps it is proper that he leads his readers gently and lengthily up and down the by-ways of philosophy, stopping often to point out the wicked-ness of contemporary Christianity, so at last when the human-istic conclusion is reached, it is inescapable.

Irvine, like Bernard Shaw, was a radical. Like Shaw, he began as an outsider. He opposed the Establishment, be it identified with the professors; the Anglican, Roman, or Non-Conformist divines; the conservative politicians; or the officials of the state. Like Shaw also, he questioned aspects of Dar-winism. He believed that "moral advancement cannot be explained in terms of physical evolution."[90]

In *"Parsifal" and Wagner's Christianity* he states that "only a recognized socialistic government could evade the conse-quences of our present civilization" and that "only the further-ance of democracy can provide the bed whereon to sow the seed."[91] Unlike the Fabian Socialist, however, Irvine makes no suggestion elaborating an economic basis of reform. The most definitive statement of his ideas appears in *Metaphysical Rudiments of Liberalism.*[92] In that he translates three early essays of Kant, explicates Kant's antitheological inclinations, and, of course, treats the ideas of Schopenhauer. He accuses contem-porary liberals of holding to the creed of optimism, which he deplores becausedt relieves mankind of moral responsibilities.[93] Liberalism and Protestantism should be considered as the true negation of conservatism and theism. It is unlikely that Irvine sees liberalism as a political party.

> Liberalism will never convert officialism to Liberalism. In the nature of things, every Liberal who becomes an official, to some extent, parts with his Liberalism. The philosopher, the artist, and the saint are the only complete Liberals.[94]

Rather liberalism carries above all the responsibility for moral and intellectual leadership. True to his philosophic idealism, Irvine concludes that if philosophy had one sensible word to say about the causes of revolution, schism, dissent and strife, it would be that these "arise from obstructing the intellect in its natural growth."[95] Because Irvine views the artist as the "compleat liberal," it is possible for him to say:

> If I personally were offered the choice of either taking as gospel truth everything Wagner uttered, or repudiating as false everything he uttered, then I would certainly choose the former, not because I agree with everything, but because I am, in my own individual right, convinced that, of all men who have the courage to repudiate the pseudo-protection of a morally worthless conception of God almighty, I get nearest, with him, to my latent ideal of what this life of relationship ought to be. So I decline, with thanks, any past or present substitute.[96]

That statement best describes Irvine's moral and religious Wagnerism.

4

Wagner among the Literati

Wagner's influence on English literature is manifest in poems, novels, and dramas and in the biographies of English authors. First, Wagner was drafted for the task of overthrowing Victorianism. In Somerset Maugham's *Of Human Bondage,* which is set at the turn of the century, a group of English art students in Paris drew up a list of the works of "Great Victorians" to be thrown onto a vast imaginary bonfire. Included among others are works by Tennyson, Dickens, Ruskin, Gladstone, Arnold, and Emerson. Only Walter Pater was exempted.[1] For the English decadents, in particular, Wagnerism helped light the torch. Second, Wagner's music drama was appealing because of its eroticism. It is possible that as sex became liberated from the Christian matrix of society it became a subject of even greater urgency to be reveled in and feared at the same time. Hence, English authors seemed fascinated most by the subjects of *Tannhäuser* and of *Tristan und Isolde* and by the passion of the music itself. Wagner's treatment of these medieval legends were not the only ones of the period. For instance, Matthew Arnold had written a *Tristan and Iseult* in 1852, and later maintained that he had "managed the story better than Wagner."[2] By the end of the century, however, Wagner's versions were the most popular. Indeed, to establish the commencement of an important love scene, the

English writer needed only to seat his hero and heroine at the parlor piano and have them run through passages of a Wagnerian score. The rest, the reader knew, was a foregone conclusion.

The earliest example of Wagner's influence on English letters seems to be *Tannhäuser; or, The Ballad of the Bards,* by Neville Temple and Edward Trevor, published in 1861. Temple and Trevor were the pseudonyms of Julian Fane (1827–1870) and Edward Robert Bulwer Lytton (1831–1891), two young diplomats and men of letters.[3] Both had received some of their education in Germany. Fane was a translator of Heine's poetry and also had an interest in composing music. Both men were personally acquainted with Wagner. Fane has left a record of a meeting with the composer:

> I had lately a delightful evening at Lady B's with Wagner. He read us the libretto of his new (seriocomic) opera, "The Singers of Nuremberg." The work may almost be called a satire on the art-critics of the day. It is full of humour and wit; sparkles with lively versification; and is really rich in thought. He declaimed it admirably, with much histrionic power. I was greatly struck with the man as well as his work.[4]

The young diplomats conceived their *Tannhäuser* ballad as a literary exercise. It developed out of Fane's "enthusiasm for the genius he recognized and his grateful sense of the emotional satisfaction he enjoyed in Wagner's great opera of *Tannhäuser,*" and it was the object of the poem to translate into words the authors' impressions "rendered vivid by an intense enjoyment of the music."[5] The poem pleased the public but not the critics. Its defect was lack of originality. The style and tone were Tennysonian; the plot, Wagnerian. "Between the plot of the opera and of this poem there is a resemblance too close to be accidental."[6] Fane's and Bulwer Lytton's ballad demonstrated their emotional susceptibility to Wagner's music and their desire to re-create the Wagnerian experience in another art form. Their choice of the Tannhäuser theme was repeated in the work of Morris, Swinburne, Payne, Beardsley, Davidson and others. Swinburne indeed drew some of the details of his *Laus Veneris* from the Fane and Bulwer Lytton ballad.

Algernon Charles Swinburne (1837–1909) was early in

his career one of the Pre-Raphaelites. The Pre-Raphaelite Brotherhood was formed in London in 1848 and consisted originally of seven members: Holman Hunt, John Millais, Dante Gabriel Rossetti, William Michael Rossetti, Thomas Woolner, James Collinson, and Frederic George Stephens. Later associates included Oxonians William Morris, Edward Burne-Jones, and Swinburne, together with Theodore Watts-Dunton, William Bell Scott, John Payne, and various others. Frequently, they gathered at the home of Ford Madox Brown the painter. Here they met the Wagnerian Franz Hueffer, who, as already mentioned, was music critic of the *Times*. He was married to Brown's younger daughter. Through Hueffer Wagner's name became known to this circle, and he soon became a subject for discussion.[7]

Wagner's intentions often seem to parallel those of the Pre-Raphaelites. The Pre-Raphaelites were poets and painters who despised materialism and the worship of technology so characteristic of their age. Wagner also railed against cultural decline, particularly the commercialization of the arts. The Pre-Raphaelites reconstructed the Middle Ages to contrast with the modern world; Wagner returned to the Middle Ages for the source of myth and symbol. Many of the Pre-Raphaelites were of "an imprecise religious intention";[8] to Wagner art was a religion. One of the later Pre-Raphaelites, William Morris, sought to change the times through art and medievally inspired socialism. For a time Wagner sought the same goal, although his socialism was short-lived. Dante Gabriel Rossetti believed in art as personal mysticism, as did Wagner, and both men utilized in their art the contrast between the material and the spiritual, the erotic and the redemptive. Finally, the Pre-Raphaelites were outsiders resisting the tyranny of the Royal Academy; Wagner was resisting the domination of the German theater by Parisian and Italian opera Wagner seems to have had no influence on the original brotherhood. However, his impact upon the larger circle of Pre-Raphaelites of the 1860s and 1870s was more than tangential. Morris reacted to Wagner unfavorably. Swinburne proved much more enthusiastic, while John Payne regarded Wagner's music as one of the formative influences of his life.

William Morris was both a poet and a craftsman. As craftsman he battled the alleged ill effects of factory production
and enriched the art of interior decoration. As poet he strove
to revivify the English language through the reintroduction
of Teutonic usages. He visited Iceland and translated the
sagas. Two of his works deal with subject matter that Wagner
used also. In his *Earthly Paradise* (1869), a retelling of the Greek
and Norse myths, he includes a section entitled *The Hill of
Venus*, in which he presents his version of the Tannhäuser
legend. It is a bleak and despairing poem, possibly referring to
Morris's own unhappy marital situation.[9] In the story *Sigurd
the Volsung and the Fall of the Niblungs,* Morris wrote an original
English epic based primarily on the *Volsunga Saga.* Published
the year of Wagner's Bayreuth triumph (1876), Morris's poem
received indifferent notices. Unlike Wagner, Morris adhered
closely to the legends. He did not bring together separate
elements into a new, if somewhat inconsistent, whole. His
technique was to embroider lyrically descriptive passages from
suggestions in the original text. Wagner embellished through
his music, not through his words. Morris also softened the
fierce nature of his characters. Faithful to the sagas, he did not
connect Sigurd's death with the fall of the gods. Furthermore Morris's concept of the new age after the gods' fall
suggests his socialism, whereas the final version of Wagner's
Götterdämmerung expresses his shift in interest from social
revolution to Schopenhaurian resignation.

Morris was acquainted with Wagner's works through
Hueffer and Swinburne, and May Morris noted that he had
seen several of Wagner's operas. But he did not like them. In
1873, H. Buxton Forman sent Morris a translation by his
brother Alfred of the text of *Die Walküre.* Replying in a letter
of 13 November 1873, Morris said that he had not had time
to read it:

> Nor to say the truth am I much interested in anything Wagner
> does, as his theories on musical matters seem to me as an artist and
> non-musical man perfectly abominable: besides I look upon it as
> nothing short of desecration to bring such a tremendous and world-
> wide subject under the gaslights of an opera: the most rococo and
> degraded of all forms of art—the idea of a sandy-haired German

tenor tweedledeeing over the unspeakable woes of Sigurd, which even the simplest words are not typical enough to express! Excuse my heat; but I wish to see Wagner uprooted. [10]

Morris disliked Wagner's stage literalism. Wagner's attempt to condense the sagas seemed arrogant and nearly sacrilegious to him. Ultimately, Morris preferred pure poetry to opera. Although Morris described himself as nonmusical, his friend and biographer, J. W. Mackail, has said that Morris was much moved by the music of the sixteenth and seventeenth centuries: "It was from no want of sensitiveness—rather perhaps the reverse—that he would not admit it into his life." [11] Also, in Mackail's opinion Wagner's art, with its "lack of reticence, its idealized appeals to the senses, its highly coloured and heavily charged rhetoric," was quite alien to Morris's personality. [12] Or perhaps Morris was one of those moved by Wagner's music, while not approving of it. Certainly their concepts of art differed. "For Wagner life was to gain a meaning through a great, i.e., Wagnerian art," while "for Morris great art was to mirror a good life." [13] In 1877 Morris had occasion to meet Cosima Wagner at the Dannreuthers. He was unimpressed. [14] Wagner himself was detained by rehearsals at the Albert Hall. He and Morris never met. Thus the two men, so temperamentally opposed, composed their versions of Norse mythology independently of one another.

Somewhat different was the case of Algernon Charles Swinburne. Swinburne enjoyed the Pre-Raphaelite circle, and he dedicated his *Poems and Ballards* (first series) to Burne-Jones. Yet he did not share the Pre-Raphaelite admiration for the Middle Ages and its religiosity as much as he revered classical antiquity and paganism. This preference for paganism, as it was interpreted in the nineteenth century, influenced his poetry and may also have affected his life. Swinburne's Dionysiac temperament led to excessive drinking, orgiastic revels, and unconventional sexual experiences. In 1879 his friend Watts-Dunton took charge of Swinburne and succeeded in reforming his habits. They moved to Putney, on the outskirts of London, and rarely received any of Swinburne's former companions. Swinburne regained his health, although he may have lost some of his poetic inspiration, and, thus cloistered, he survived until 1909. The evidence of Swinburne's Wagnerism lies in his letters to friends and in the poems *Laus Veneris,* *Tristram of Lyonesse,* and the three roundels composed on the occasion of Wagner's death. Though Swinburne was out of vogue long before he died, the erotic tone of his poetry presaged the era of English decadence, a period that coincided with Wagner's greatest popularity.

Although it is not known when Swinburne first heard Wagner's music, it is probable that he became acquainted with it through George Powell (1842–1882). Powell was a well-to-do Welsh landowner. Like Swinburne, he attended both Eton and Oxford, although the two did not meet, apparently, until Powell wrote to Swinburne praising his *Atalanta in Calydon,* published in 1865. Like William Morris, Powell was an ardent admirer and translator of Icelandic literature. Powell and Swinburne were close companions in the days before Putney, and Powell often used his own money to pay Swinburne's bills. Three poems in *A Century of Roundels* (1883) memorialize Powell.[15] "Autumn and Winter" links Powell and Wagner, reflecting the fact that they died within four months of each other. Swinburne also wrote to his sister Isabel that he wondered if Powell had gone before in order to announce Wagner's coming.[16] Powell was known in London as a Wagnerian, and he was a friend of A. J. Hipkins and William Kümpel, members of Walter Bache's Wagner circle, the so-called Working Men's Society.[17] In various letters to Powell and others, Swinburne mentioned Wagner. For example, on 26 December, 1866 he urged Powell to visit him and "Schumanize and Wagnerize among us to some purpose."[18] On 30 April, 1869 he wrote to Powell praising an article on Wagner that he had read in the *Revue des Deux Mondes;* on 21 October, 1869 he recommended a monograph on Wagner and Schopenhauer by Auguste de Gasperini.[19] In a letter to Powell of 2 August, 1872 he asserted that he was writing a poem on the effect of Wagner's *Tristan* prelude for the magazine *La Renaissance.*[20] Swinburne published nothing in *La Renaissance,* but later he did write two Tristan poems. On 14 February, 1873 he spoke of Powell's being in the thick of the Wagner movement and of an announcement in the *Guardian* of Dannreuther's conducting an all-Wagner concert on 19 February.[21] To John Nicol, probably in 1876, he mentioned:

> some thoughts of going to Munich (of all places) with an old schoolfellow and friend, to see the opening of Wagner's theatre and the performance of his as yet unknown opera which is to take four nights to represent and embody the whole of the Nibelungen. Conceive—if you know *Lohengrin*—what a divine delight it will be. But I presume the destinies will intervene and make it impossible.[22]

These references at least indicate Swinburne's sympathetic awareness of Wagnerian opera.

Laus Veneris, published in 1864, was written before Swinburne met Powell and prior to any mention of Wagner in Swinburne's letters. Nevertheless, Swinburne's biographers have remarked about the "strangely Wagnerian atmosphere" of the poem,[23] and there is considerable speculation concerning the sources of Swinburne's inspiration. It is tempting to link Swinburne and Baudelaire. In 1862 Swinburne enthusiastically reviewed Baudelaire's *Les Fleurs du mal* for the *Spectator.* Baudelaire, already a Wagnerian,[24] responded with a letter on 10 October, 1863 and a copy of his pamphlet *Wagner and Tannhäuser in Paris* (1861). In the letter he wrote that Wagner had exclaimed to him that he would not have believed that his work could be so well understood by a Frenchman, so he, Baudelaire, would not have believed his poetry could be so wisely understood by an Englishman. Unfortunately, Swinburne never received the letter,[25] and he stated in his *Notes on Poems and Reviews* (1866) that he had not received the pamphlet until after he had written the poem.[26] *Laus Veneris* apparently was begun in the summer of 1862 on a weekend visit with George Meredith and Dante Gabriel Rossetti. One version of the episode relates that Swinburne had just made the intoxicating discovery of Edward FitzGerald's *Rubáiyát of Omar Khayyám.* Meredith, Rossetti, and Swinburne spent the day reciting FitzGerald's quatrains to each other, and "then Swinburne snatched paper, a quill pen, and a bottle of red ink, and within an hour wrote the first thirteen stanzas of *Laus Veneris,* in the same pattern as the FitzGerald poem."[27] In December Swinburne declaimed the rest of the poem to Rossetti and

W. B. Scott. Other critics have argued that Swinburne implied in his *Notes* that he was acquainted with Wagner's *Tannhäuser* even before he read Baudelaire's pamphlet.[28] He could at least have heard the overture to *Tannhäuser* in London and probably had read other French accounts of the opera.[29] Furthermore, it is likely at least that Swinburne knew of and was inspired by Fane and Bulwer Lytton's paraphrase of *Tannhäuser*.[30] There are some textual parallels.[31] However, while Fane and Bulwer Lytton concentrated on the episode of the singing contest, with its long descriptions of Elizabeth and Wolfram, in dignified language like that of Tennyson's *Idylls of the King*, Swinburne's shorter version dwelt on the intimate feelings of the lustful Tannhäuser in language more direct and with an impact more immediate. Venus "weaves and multiplies Exceeding pleasure out of extreme pain."[32] Tannhäuser in both the Bulwer Lytton and Wagner versions repents in the end, and the fact that the staff of the Pope does miraculously bloom adds the hope of redemption. In Swinburne's poem, however, Tannhäuser resigns himself to the pleasures of his sufferings:

> For till the thunder in the trumpet be,
> Soul may divide from body, but not we
>   One from another; I hold thee with
>   my hand,
> I let mine eyes have all their will of thee,
> I seal myself upon thee with my might,
> Abiding always out of all men's sight
>   Until God loosen over sea and land
> The thunder of the trumpets of the night
> EXPLICIT LAUS VENERIS

The note of redemption is absent. One might also infer that Swinburne believed that in Wagner's operas the erotic quality of the music triumphed over the message. Though the evidence for Wagnerian influence on *Laus Veneris* will probably remain inconclusive, it is hardly possible to doubt that Wagner's opera at least contributed to the making of Swinburne's poem.

Wagner's *Tristan und Isolde* was completed in 1859, first performed in 1865, and first produced in London in 1882, a month before the appearance of Swinburne's poem *Tristram of Lyonesse*. Again, critics have remarked on the affinities, particularly stylistic, between the two. Samuel Chew thought the parallels too close to be merely coincidental: "I think Swinburne must have known Wagner's libretto."[33] Cecil Y. Lang, editor of Swinburne's letters, has said that Wagner's music "stimulated" the composition of the poem.[34] John R. Reed observed that there was no doubt that Swinburne "did employ, in *Tristram of Lyonesse,* the technique of a conscious and disciplined motif suggestive of musical composition," and thus Swinburne might have noted and sympathized with Wagner's device of the leitmotiv.[35] Also, Swinburne's organized rhapsodies have been called "melodious verbiage," and their effect on listeners may be compared perhaps with Wagner's "endless melody." For example, Ferdinand Wagner once wrote to George Powell:

> I always feel happier and better when I have dived into the turbulent waves of Swinburne's gigantic mind. The masterly hand with which he holds the threads that seem to float unconnectedly—as if driven by the wind—and which he always succeeds in tying together when least expected seems to me exactly like Richard Wagner.[36]

Swinburne once was deprecated as a poet of sound obscuring sense, just as Wagner was criticized by Max Nordau and others for lack of coherence and form.

Later criticism has challenged these views, however. It has been suggested that it is in the philosophic import of *Tristram* that Swinburne differs markedly from Wagner.[37] Wagner's music drama has been described as "a gloomy vision" in which Wagner "takes the inner, nocturnal world of passion as real, and the common outer world as illusory."[38] The words and music united in such a way as to be passion itself enacted on a stage. In *Tristan und Isolde* the insatiability and inevitability of the passion leads the lovers to a voluptuous embracing of death, to drown, as Isolde sings:

> In des Welt-Atems
> wehendem All—
> ertrinken,
> versinken,—
> unbewusst—
> höchste Lust![39]

On the other hand, the tone of Swinburne's poem is radiant, not gloomy or nocturnal. Its major image is "the sungod which is love," and Tristram, Iseult, and the forces of nature all are described in sun-imagery. All unite; as Tristram says, "Love, as sun and sea are thou and I." However different in tone, nevertheless, both Wagner's and Swinburne's works treat love as the force behind all action. Wagner's Isolde sings that love rules all earthly destiny and that life and death are subject to her.[40] Swinburne in his prelude declares that love is "first and last of all things made, the light that has the living world for shade." In both cases the destiny of the lovers is an eternity beyond death. The quality of this eternity is difficult to assess. The concept of Nirvana has always seemed to defy language. In Wagner's opera it appears to be a release, a thoughtless oblivion. In Swinburne's poem love seems to lead men beyond life to an "existence" of peace:

> And so their four lips became one silent mouth,
> So came their hour on them that were in life
> Tristram and Iseult so from love and strife
> The stroke of love's own hand felt last and best
> Give them deliverance to perpetual rest.[41]

This rest is:

> the timeless space wherein the brief world move
> Clothed with light life and fruitful with light
>   love,
> with hopes that threaten and with fears that
>   cease,
> Past fear and hope, hath in it only peace.[42]

Such a conclusion is not totally unlike Wagner's. Furthermore, the special role of music both in Swinburne's *Tristram* poem and in "Music: An Ode" (1882) may possibly indicate more Wagnerian and also Schopenhaurian sympathies.

Several shorter poems by Swinburne are also of Wagnerian interest. Of the two preludes, "Lohengrin" was dedicated to love and "Tristan" to fate. A poem entitled "The Twilight of the Lords" was an attack on the House of Lords cast in the mold of the sagas. Lastly, Swinburne wrote "The Death of Richard Wagner," in which he mourned the passing of a soul wherein the "earth's songs of death and birth, darkness and light, were wont to sound and blend."[43] Wagner was a magician who had changed the forces of earth, seas, fire, and tempest into music.

A third poet whose youth was spent among the Pre-Raphaelites was John Payne (1842–1916). He became known primarily as a translator of the *Arabian Nights,* Omar Khayyam, Hafiz, Boccacio, Heine, and Villon. Founder of the Villon Society, he also admired the modern French poets—Mallarmé, whom he knew personally, Gautier, and Baudelaire. Payne aspired to write great poetry but succeeded only in producing minor works reminiscent of Dante Gabriel Rossetti and William Morris. However, through his Pre-Raphaelite connection and his dedication to Wagner and Schopenhauer he reflected major trends of his time. In philosophy he was moved first by Emerson's essays, then by Schopenhauer, who in turn led him to studies of the Vedantic philosophy of ancient India.[44] "Ideologically he stood in the floodtide of European Pessimism. . . . Payne knew and loved Schopenhauer. He never tired of singing the ennui of life and longing for Nirvana."[45] It was the search for redemption that appealed to him in Wagner's music. Payne was acquainted with Wagner, having met him in Germany. In his autobiography he wrote:

> Wagner's music has always been as much and as essential a part of my life as literature. Although all but untaught . . . I have a species of innate gift for music which enables me to judge and appreciate the strongest and most unconventional compositions and to reproduce upon the piano (without a previous hearing) the most complicated orchestral and other works. . . . I cannot but feel that my love and practice of music are to be traced everywhere in my verses.[46]

According to Payne's friend and biographer, Thomas Wright, sometime in the period from 1867 to 1870, when Wagner was still little known in England, Payne arranged some music from Wagner's operas to be played for his club.[47] Payne also praised Wagner in his own poetry. "Sir Floris" was a grail poem, dedicated to Wagner as the author of *Lohengrin.*[48] "The Building of a Dream" was a rather inconclusive study on the Tannhäuser theme. In it a squire of Poitou is led magically to the abode of Venus. There he languishes uncomfortably, appearing not to derive the slightest twinge of pleasure from his lust. Abruptly he leaves Venus and returns home to die.[49] Next there was a sonnet: "Bride-Night: Wagner's *Tristan and Isolde*—Act II, scene 2."[50] Most important, *Songs of Life and Death* (1872) began with twenty-four stanzas of praise for Wagner. A few lines may serve to show that Payne's idolatrous enthusiasm at the time exceeded his poetic capacities.

> I greet thee with a promise and cheering—
>   I, that have loved thee many weary years,
> I, that with eyes strained for the dawn's appearing,
>   Have clung to thee for hope and healing tears.
>
> . . . .
>
> Be not disheartened, O our Zoraster,
>   O mage of our new music-world of fire!
> Thou art not all unfriended, O my master!
>   Let not the great heart fail thee for desire.
>
> . . . .
>
> For the days hasten when shall all adore thee,
>   All at thy spring shall drink, and know it sweet;
> All the false temples shall fall down before thee,
>   Ay—and the false gods crumble at thy feet.
> Then shall men set thee in their holy places,
>   Hymn thee with anthems of remembering;
> Faiths shall spring up and blossom in thy traces,
>   Thick as the violets cluster round the spring.[51]

Anything further would be anticlimactic; nevertheless, included in *Vigil and Vision* (1903) is one Schopenhauer poem, together with "Wagneriana," a series of five sonnets. Each sonnet is devoted to a Wagnerian character: Sieglinde, Wotan, Brünhilde, Hagen, and Isolde. Though Payne deplored some tendencies of the late Victorian age, such as increasing democratization, he must have been pleased when Wagnerian opera came into its own.

ii

England gave only mild attention to Wagner during the heyday of Victorianism, when it was still a reasonably confident society. But in the late eighties and nineties, when "the nation was out of health," as R. C. K. Ensor and others have suggested,[52] there developed a feeling of need for new cultural patterns and experiments and a willingness to cross the channel for inspiration. Then Wagner's influence became more widespread. This is not to say that he was the prime mover of any one new literary style; rather, he appealed to widely differing personalities of talent—for example, Bernard Shaw and Oscar Wilde—and he served to stimulate and liberate many minds.

One of the newer literary movements that adopted Wagner was that of decadence. Various definitions suggest that decadence was marked by "a special interest in the moral decline of the ancient world and a smacking of the lips over the vices of supercivilization" or by "an avowal of a refined epicureanism and an enjoyment of art free from the chains of moral and religious respect."[53] To a contemporary, Ernest Belfort Bax, socialist, barrister, composer, and Germanophile, decadence in art showed "a morbid craving for, and striving after, bizarrerie. It mattered not whether a thing were beautiful or ugly, provided it were significantly bizarre."[54] Arthur Symons, a decadent himself, viewed decadence as "an intense self-consciousness, a restless curiosity in research, an oversubtilizing refinement upon refinement, a spiritual and moral perversity. . . . Health we cannot call it, and healthy it does not wish to be considered.[55] It was rumored, of course, that Decadence came from France, from the French symbolist poets, and from the pages of Huysman's *A rebours*. But it also had English precursors in Swinburne's "Fleshly School" of poetry, as it was labeled, and in Walter Pater's aestheticism. Among the major English decadents were Aubrey Beardsley, Oscar Wilde, and Arthur Symons. Each was a Wagnerian.

Beardsley (1872–1898) was an illustrator of genius, a writer, and an editor. He preferred candlelight to daylight, the artificial to the natural, and spent his time in museums, theaters, and bookshops, A victim of tuberculosis, he did not live a long or normal life. Like Shaw, he not only loved music but was trained in it. His mother had taught him to play Chopin before he was of school age. Soon he was able to read and understand a full musical score. He frequently attended performances of Wagnerian operas with Frederick Evans, a London bookseller. Arthur Symons reported having seen him at concerts in Dieppe, "always carrying his large gilt-leather portfolio with the magnificent folio-paper which he would often open to write some lines in pencil."[56] In the depths of his illness he wrote to his publisher, Leonard Smithers: "Wagner alone consoles me somewhat"; and when he needed to sell his book collection he retained only John Gray's *Spiritual Poems, The Lives of the Saints,* the works of Saint Theresa, and Richard Wagner's *Prose Works.*[57]

It was at the home of clergyman Alfred Gurney, a friend of the Beardsley family and author of a study of *Parsifal,* that Beardsley and his sister hit upon the idea of taking his drawings to Burne-Jones, by then prosperous and famous, for an opinion. With Burne-Jones's encouragement, Beardsley began a career that brought him considerable fame. Among his illustrations are thirteen of Wagnerian subjects.[58] The three earliest include *Die Götterdämmerung, Tannhäuser,* and *Siegfried* slaying the dragon. The first two seem Pre-Raphaelite in inspiration; the last begins to exhibit Beardsley's obsession with elegant decorative line. A rather slim and frail Siegfried appears, together with his slain dragon, amidst wonderfully exotic vines, trees, and flowers. The later drawings include *The Wagnerites, The Return of Tannhäuser to Venusberg,* a floral design from the cover of Beardsley's own copy of *Tristan und Isolde, Isolde, The Third Tableau of "Das Rheingold," The Fourth Tableau of "Das Rheingold," Tristan und Isolde, A Repetition of "Tristan und Isolde," Frontispiece to the Comedy of "Das Rheingold," Flosshilde, Erda,* and *Alberich. The Wagnerites* shows the public at a performance of *Tristan;* they appear to be wealthy, jaded women, their sinister faces and decolletage highlighted. *The Return of Tannhäuser"* is a second drawing of the earliest subject in Beardsley's mature style. It is listed among the drawings as Tannhäuser's return *to* the Venusberg, but it looks as if Tannhäuser is actually emerging *from* the Venusberg into the sunlit ordinary world. The drawing was given by Beardsley to the publisher J. M. Dent. Dent wrote to Beardsley, thanking him for "The Return of Tannhäuser *from* the Venusberg":

God bless you once more, this little picture speaks wonders to me—
that bit of clear white sky of hope out of all the Blackness and Di-
spair [sic]—and the eyes of Tannhäuser are opening to it—yes,
Humanity will come back from Hades one day—it is coming already. [59]

It is possible that the picture, reproduced by permission of
J. M. Dent, was mistitled in the first and succeeding editions.
The Rheingold drawings were intended for an illustrated edition of what Beardsley called a comedy, "an elaborate piece
of nonsense." [60] The edition never appeared, but the drawings
came out in Beardsley's *Under the Hill,* a pornographic treatment of the much-used Tannhäuser theme.

Under the Hill was left incomplete at Beardsley's death in
1898. Two expurgated installments had appeared in the *Savoy*—
chapters 1–3 in January 1896 and chapter 7, including much of
chapter 5 in a long footnote, in April 1897. An unexpurgated
edition was privately printed in London in 1907 by Leonard
Smithers, to whom the work had originally been sent. *Under
the Hill* is surprisingly lighthearted and rococo. Edmund Wilson has described it well:

He does succeed in investing a sort of pagan world with the artificial graces of the nineties without allowing it to become darkened
and tragic with the fumes of a burning orthodoxy; his Venus, unlike the Venus of Swinburne or the Harlot of Wilde, is not destruc-
tive or terrible, but girlish and agreeable. The grotesqueries and
orgies of her court are to her all quite natural and harmless; she
really approaches much nearer to the naive naughtiness of the
eighteenth-century than anything to be found in Wilde. [61]

There are two direct references expressing Beardsley's Wagnerism. First, the conductor of the Venusberg orchestra is
named Titurel de Schentefleur. He seems to play every in-
strument rather than to lead them; his amatory tastes are unknown; he is called the Virgin. Some biographers theorize
that this is a reference to Beardsley himself. On the significance of the name Titurel, which may come from *Parsifal,*
one can only speculate. Second, on Tannhäuser's first morning after his first Venusberg orgy, he takes to bed with him
the score of *Das Rheingold.*

Making a pulpit out of his knees he propped up the opera before him and turned over the pages with a loving hand, and found it delicious to attack Wagner's brilliant comedy with the cold hand of morning.* Once more he was ravished with the beauty and wit of the opening scene, the mystery of its prelude that seems to come up from the very mud of the Rhine, and to be as ancient, the abominable primitive wantonness of the music that follows the talk and the movements of the Rhine-maidens, the black, hateful sound in Alberich's love-making, and the flowing melody of the river legends.

But it was the third tableau that he applauded most that morning, the scene where Loge, like some flamboyant primeval Scapin, practices his cunning upon Alberich. The feverish insistent ringing of the hammers at the forge, the dry staccato restlessness of Mime, the ceaseless coming and going of the troop of Nibelungs, drawn hither and thither like a flock of terror-stricken and infernal sheep, Alberich's savage activity and metamorphoses, and Loge's rapid, flaming, tonguelike movements, making the tableau the least reposeful, most troubled and confusing thing in the whole range of opera. How the Chevalier rejoiced in the extravagant monstrous poetry, the heated melodrama, and splendid agitation of it all.

No particular literary or pornographic necessity seems to require the inclusion of these passages. Is Beardsley speaking here for himself? Is this the remains of the never completed *Rheingold* comedy? If it is Beardsley speaking as himself, what then is his attitude? Is it the "splendid agitation of it all" that he appreciated in Wagner or was he speaking tongue-in-cheek? The least that can be said is that he gives expression to the operas' very disturbing psychic effect, which some deplored but which others, like Beardsley, apparently relished. Whereas Shaw linked Wagner with socialism, Beardsley linked Wagner with the erotic, the emotional, and the sensual, and thoroughly approved. [63] Also noteworthy is Beardsley's interest in the seriousness of listening to music and his placing of music in the category presumably of the sacred as opposed to that of "the secular influences" of the day.

*It is a thousand pities that concerts should only be given either in the afternoon, when you are torpid, or in the evening, when you are nervous. Surely you should assist at fine music as you assist at the Mass—before noon—when your brain and heart are not too troubled and tired with the secular influences of the growing day. [62]

In 1894 Beardsley became art editor of the *Yellow Book,* conceived as an illustrated periodical of booklike workmanship to represent new and excellent literature. Though many of its contributors were quite orthodox, the magazine became notorious from the first issue because of Beardsley's drawings. It became doubly so when Oscar Wilde was arrested in 1894, a yellow book under his arm, on a charge of homosexuality. As it happened, Wilde's yellow book was not Beardsley's *Yellow Book,* but, although Wilde never contributed to the *Yellow Book* and although he and Beardsley were not friends, Beardsley was forced to resign his editorship. [64] The magazine soon folded, but Beardsley reappeared on the staff of another short-lived publication, Arthur Symons's *Savoy.*

Wilde's novel *The Picture of Dorian Gray* published in 1890, reflects the dual influence of French literature and Wagner. [65] In the novel, an artist named Basil Hallward undertakes to paint Dorian, an unusually handsome individual. Meanwhile, Dorian is taken in hand and "educated" by Hallward's friend Lord Henry Wotton. Wotton gives Dorian a "yellow book" to read, which from Wilde's description has to be Huysmans's *À rebours:* "One hardly knew at times whether one was reading the spiritual ecstacies of some medieval saint or the morbid confessions of a modern sinner. It was a poisonous book." [66] Dorian began to indulge himself in all the passions, vices, and perversions, including committing murder, and in so doing his portrait and his own visage become hideous. He ends as a suicide. According to the author, Dorian would sit in his box at the opera, "listening in rapt pleasure to *Tannhäuser,* and seeing in the prelude to that great work of art a presentation of the tragedy of his own soul." [67] *Tannhäuser* almost becomes a code word for experimentation with forbidden pleasures.

In 1896 the *Yellow Book* was revived as the *Savoy,* edited by Arthur Symons. Symons shared the decadent life-style and was a poet and critic as well. It was he who made the term *symbolism* fashionable in English literary circles when in 1889 he published *The Symbolist Movement in Literature.* Wagnerian subjects appear in Symons's poem "Parsifal" in *Images of Good and Evil,* published in 1889, "Tristan's Song" of 1913, *Tristan and Iseult,* a play of 1917, and "Merlin and Mark," a poem published in 1922.[68] The Parsifal poem recalls the scene of Kundry's magical garden:

> Parsifal has outblushed the roses: dead
> Is all the garden of the world's delight,
> And every rose of joy has dropped its head,
> And for sweet shame is dead;
> Sweet joy being shameful in the pure fool's
> sight.

The Tristan song treats the theme of "death in love." The Tristan play follows the structure of the opera, but the treatment is more psychological than metaphysical.[69] Tristan is a weakling; Iseult, the prototype of modern liberated and passionate women. Iseult "would rather be myself than be queen" and scorns marriages that are arranged primarily for the purposes of international diplomacy.[70] When the two lovers drink the potion, Symons combines both Swinburne's sunlit and Wagner's nocturnal imagery. First, Iseult experiences a feeling of being "as universal as the sun" and "a cup for an immense thirst of light."[71] Next she becomes afraid that death has taken hold of her and that her soul is returning to night.[72] Symons also makes a point of Tristan's singing:

> I made a song once, all men sing it now,
> The song of Iseult, Tristan's life and death,
> And women weep to hear it, and men too.
> I made it with the sorrow of the world
> And with the sorrow in the hearts of men.[73]

In his critical writings Symons presents his view of Wagner's works directly. "The Ideas of Richard Wagner" in *Studies in the Seven Arts* (1906) summarizes the main points of Wagner's *Opera and Drama.* Symons's "Notes on Wagner at Bayreuth" comments on the Bayreuth and Munich opera houses, on *Parsifal,* and on Wagner's art in general. His impression of the atmosphere at the Prinz-Regenten Theatre in Munich is illustrative:

> As at Bayreuth, the solemnity of the whole thing makes one almost nervous, for the first few minutes of each act; but, after that, how near one is, in this perfectly darkened, perfectly quiet theatre, in which the music surges up out of the 'mystic gulf,' and the pic-

ture exists in all the ecstacy of a picture on the other side of it, beyond reality, how near one is to being alone, in the passive state in which the flesh is able to endure the great burdening and uplifting vision. There are thus now two theatres in the world in which music and drama can be absorbed, and not merely guessed at. [74]

Of *Parsifal* Symons writes that Wagner had composed religious music that gave expression to "the unsatisfied desire of a kind of flesh of the spirit" and that rendered "mysticism through the senses." [75] It is unimportant to Symons how far Wagner's intentions were technically Christian, or even religious in the orthodox sense.

His music, his acting, are devout, because the music has a disembodied ecstacy, and the acting a noble rhythm, which can but produce in us something of the solemnity of sensation produced by the service of the Mass, and are in themselves a kind of religious ceremonial. [76]

Symons rightly describes the "continuous unresolved melody" as the expression of subconscious life and the leitmotive as symbols of an inner life guiding and having a spiritualizing effect upon both music and action. When Symons compares Wagnerian with other opera, he finds that there is no comparison:

And now turn from this elemental music, in which the sense of all human things is expressed with the dignity of the elements themselves, to all other operatic music (think of Glück, of Mozart, of Beethoven!) it is for the most part fettered to a little accidental comedy or tragedy, in which two lovers are jealous, or someone is wrongly imprisoned, or a libertine seduces a few women. Here music is like a god speaking in the language of savages, and lowering his supreme intellect to the level of their speech. The melodious voice remains, but the divine meaning has gone out of the works. Only in Wagner does God speak to men in his own language. [77]

Among the lesser decadents upon whom Wagner left an imprint was the poet Theodore Wratislaw, an Englishman of Polish origin, who was an admirer of Swinburne and a friend of Beardsley and Symons, as well as of others of the same circle. The title poem of *Orchids,* his collection, is distinctly reminiscent of *Les Fleurs du mal.* His Wagnerian poems include "Tannhäuser," "Songs to Elizabeth," "Bryhildr," and "Siegfried." The first stanza of his "Tannhäuser" depicts the minstrel in the grip of the "Black Venus of the nether gulfs," while the second stanza heralds the "pilgrims' stately song." "Songs to Elizabeth" describes Tannhäuser's unsuccessful struggle to free himself from Venus; the first stanza is introduced by a quotation from Wolfram's apostrophe to the evening star: "O du mein holder Abenstern." "Bryhildr" describes the encirclement of the Valkyrie by fire and the loss of her godhood. "Siegfried" is also the Siegfried of the opera: "Leuchtende Liebe, Lachender Tod."

Now that the glow of scandal surrounding the decadents[78] has faded, some recent criticism has reassesed their contributions; for example:

> The end of the nineteenth century in England released in artists a kind of rage for experience. . . . It was prevailingly iconoclastic, partly out of a delight in the pure gesture of revolt, but also from a very real need to transcend the stale conventionality, the hermetic smugness and hypocrisy of a society immured in bourgeois values.[79]

Their daring found a hero in Wagner and their confusion, their alternation between extremes of eroticism and religion, even their uniting of the two, found expression in Wagner's operas, particularly in *Tannhäuser, Tristand und Isolde,* and, to a lesser extent, *Parsifal.* Their stylistic inspiration came partly from French symbolism and thus also, but much more indirectly, from Wagner.

Perhaps the last word on the subject of Tannhäuser to come from a poet of the period was written by John Davidson (1857–1900) in "A New Ballad of Tannhäuser." Davidson was not one of the decadents: he came to Wagner through Nietzsche. In a footnote to his ballad he acknowledges that the best-known story of Tannhäuser is "the sophisticated version of Wagner's great opera."[80] His intention is to submit a modern and more humane interpretation of the world legend in which the idea of the inherent impurity of nature is finally laid to rest. Davidson's "Ballad" is a praise of free love:

> The undivined, eternal God
> Looked on him from highest heaven
> And showed him by the budding rod
> There was no need to be forgiven.

Though un-Wagnerian in its ending, the poem does seem to embrace Wagner's music. Davidson's Tannhäuser is lured by music to the Venusberg initially, and "the ceaseless dulcet music" insures his return.

> The air, a world-enfolding flood
> Of liquid music poured along;
> And the wild cry within his blood
> Became at last a golden song.

Davidson, a great admirer of Nietzsche's philosophy, apparently shared some of Nietzsche's initial attraction to Wagner's music.

Among English novelists, the influence of Wagner is most pronounced in the case of George Moore (1852–1953). Moore left his home in Ireland as soon as he was twenty-one and headed for Paris and the life of art. Discovering that he was an inferior painter, he began to write and, at the same time, to taste French literary society. He became acquainted with Zola, Verlaine, Mallarmé, Villiers dé L'Isle-Adam, and cultivated Édouard Dujardin, later to become editor of the *Revue Wagnérienne*. Here he learned the vocabulary of French literary Wagnerism, but as yet he had heard little Wagnerian music.[81] In 1890 his lack of funds forced him to return to London.

At least five of Moore's works are autobiographical: *The Confessions of a Young Man* (1880); *Memoirs of My Dead Life* (1906); *Hail and Farewell* (1911–13); *Avowals* (1919); and *Conversations in Ebury Street* (1924). With these may be included the published *Letters to Dujardin* (1929). *Memoirs* is a satirical catalogue of Moore's real and imagined love affairs, in which he maintains a pagan attitude throughout. The Wagnerian passage best worth mentioning comes from a section called "Sunday Evening in London," wherein Picadilly Circus is viewed as Klingsor's garden.

This street is like Klingsor's garden; here, too, are flower-maidens, patchuli, jessamine, violet. Here is the languorous atmosphere of *Parsifal,* Come, let us go. . . . The circus on a sultry summer night under a full moon is very like Klingsor's garden. Come, if you be not Parsifal. [82]

In 1901 Moore left England for Dublin. He was motivated largely by his disgust over England's participation in the Boer War.

Hail and Farewell is at once Moore's autobiography and a memoir of the Celtic Renaissance, to which Moore contributed in a minor way. In this memoir he reminisces about the first time that he had heard the *Ring,* in the nineties:

> In London literature and poverty absorbed me for several years and I had forgotten music altogether when Edward asked me if I would go to hear *The Rhinegold.* I had consented, regretting my promise almost as soon as it was given, for Wagner was reputed unmelodious and difficult to all except the most erudite. . . . But the moment the horns gave out the theme of the Rhine my attention was arrested and a few minutes after it was clear that a new birth awaited me. [83]

A few days later he heard *Tristan,* and that same year he embarked on the first of his trips to Bayreuth. According to Moore, so essentially human is Wagner that there

> is something in his art for everybody, something in his music for me, and a great deal for musicians; and besides the music some part of which everybody except the tone-deaf can hear, there are the dramas, wonderful in conception and literary art; for him gifted with imagination there are scenes in *The Ring* as beautiful as any in Shakespeare. [84]

While in Bayreuth Moore visited Wahnfried and was introduced to Frau Wagner. She was then nearly seventy; nevertheless, Moore found her so charming he playfully contemplated running off with her. [85] *Hail and Farewell* is by no means an ordinary or simple autobiography. Not only does it contain many references to Wagner, but it is also Wagnerian in scope. It consists of three parts—"Ave," "Salve," and "Vale—" introduced by what Moore calls an overture announcing the mood and themes of the succeeding sections. These themes are developed and reappear as literary leitmotives. Toward the close he summarizes his lifelong preoccupation with religious doubt, Irish nationalism, and Wagner:

> Ireland has lain too long under the spell of the magicians, without will, without intellect, useless and shameful, the despised of nations. I have come into the most impersonal country in the world to preach personality—personal love and personal religions, personal art, personality for all except God; and I walked across the greensward afraid to leave the garden, and to heighten my inspiration I looked toward the old apple-tree, remembering that many had striven to draw forth the sword that Wotan had struck into the tree about which Hunding had built his hut. Parnell, like Siegmund, had drawn it forth, but Wotan had allowed Hunding to strike him with his spear. And the allegory becoming clearer I asked myself if I were Siegfried, son of Siegmund slain by Hunding, and if it were not my fate to reforge the sword that lay broken in halves in Mimi's cave. It seemed to me that the garden filled with tremendous music, out of which came a phrase glittering like a sword suddenly drawn from its sheath and raised defiantly to the sun.[86]

Following this passage in the text is a musical staff bearing the motive of Siegfried's sword sounded in the last scene of *Das Rheingold.* In *Avowals* of 1919 Moore again acknowledges his debt to Wagner, and in *Conversations in Ebury Street* in 1924 he alludes to the exultant pleasure that he had experienced upon hearing *Lohengrin* for the first time, to the joy of living he sensed in Wagner, to Dujardin's Wagnerism, and to Verlaine's Parsifal poem. Disappointed in the attempt to revive Irish literature, Moore had returned in 1911 to England and Ebury Street, where he resided until his death in 1933.

Moore considered himself the youngest of the naturalists and the oldest of the symbolists. His earlier efforts, such as *A Mummer's Wife* (1885) and *Esther Waters* (1894) owe much to Zola.[87] The novel *Spring Days* (1888) contains a passage reminiscent of *Tristan und Isolde* in which the lovers drink a love-potion and proclaim their delirium of passion in Wagnerian imagery.[88] In later works such as *The Brook Kerith* (1916) and *Héloïse and Abélard* (1912) Moore attempted, as did the symbolists, to create a musically nuanced prose and to develop a dignified, melodious language with which to tell his stories.

The novels *Evelyn Innes* (1898) and *Sister Teresa* (1901) are transitional and most explicitly Wagnerian in content. Moore remained a religious skeptic and an admirer of the pagans to the end of his life. However, these two novels demonstrate his concern, in Wagnerian terms, with the problems of sensuality and spirituality that so occupied English artists.

Evelyn Innes is a Wagnerian singer who regards each of the roles she studied—Elizabeth, Isolde, Brünhilde, and Kundry—as part of her own developing personality. As the only child of a Catholic organist devoted to reviving the church music of Palestrina, Evelyn seems destined to sing antique music in quiet country churches. Her life is utterly changed by Sir Owen Asher. Asher, a wealthy aristocrat, the consummate "man-of-the-world," and owner of the periodical *Wagnerian Review,* intends to write a criticism of Mr. Innes's concerts but instead induces Evelyn to run off to Paris with him, ostensibly in search of adequate musical training for her unusually good voice. As Owen rationalizes his position, Wagner's finest female roles have never really been sung before; they have "merely been howled." [89] Therefore Evelyn should be the first to sing them. Her extraordinary talent is duly recognized by Madame Savelli, the best teacher in Paris, and Evelyn prepares to sing and at the same time yields to Asher, sexually, emotionally, and intellectually: "It was a sort of delicious death, a swooning ecstacy, an absorption of her individuality into his." [90] Central to Moore's first volume of *Evelyn Innes* is a dream of Evelyn's in which two Tristans appear—a fair and a dark. Asher is the first. She sees herself as Isolde to Asher's Tristan.

> Her pious girlhood found expression in the Elizabeth and what she termed the other side of her character she was going to put on the stage in the character of Isolde. . . . No one whom she had seen had attempted to differentiate between Isolde before she drinks and after she had drunk the love potion, and, to avoid this mistake she felt she would only have to be true to herself. [91]

There follows Evelyn's description of her fateful relationship with Asher. Elsewhere Moore repeats it: "The story of *Tristan and Isolde* seemed to be their own story." [92] Somewhat later in the novel Evelyn goes on to the role of Brünhilde, played to Asher's Siegfried.

> Her Elizabeth was a side of her life that now existed only on the stage. Brunhilde was her best part, for into it she poured all her joy of life, all her enthusiasm for life and for the hero who came to awaken her to life and love.[93]

And she remembered "how Owen, like Siegfried, had come to release her, and all the exhausting passions of that time."[94] The second Tristan of her dream, the dark Tristan, is Ulick Dean, a character Moore modeled partly on his friend William Butler Yeats. Dean, a poet, opera libretto in hand, is much the opposite of Asher.[95] Asher is an atheist, a positivist; Dean, while not precisely a Christian, is interested in all religions, mysticisms, and mythologies. He likes *Tannhäuser,* which he thinks is the most sincere of Wagner's operas, and dislikes *Parsifal,* except for the scene in Klingsor's garden in the second act. He knows that Wagner attempted to write a libretto with either Christ or Buddha as the subject. But, as Dean says: "In neither Christ nor Buddha did the question of sex arise, and that was the reason that Wagner eventually rejected both. He was as full of sex—mysterious, subconscious sex—as Rossetti himself."[96]

Evelyn never entirely repudiates her Catholic moral and religious upbringing. First, she suffers remorse for having deserted her father. Everytime she sings in *Die Walküre* she pictures her father as Wotan, and when eventually she seeks her father's forgiveness, she is acutely aware of acting the scene just as she had in the opera.[97] Next, she notices herself becoming dissatisfied with "the blankness" of Owen's positivist creed. The fundamental worry for Evelyn is the problem of her own deeply experienced eroticism, without benefit of marriage ties, and the ideal of chastity she also believes in. Central to the second volume is a passage in which Evelyn explains to herself that, although there may possibly be as many different moralities as there are individuals, "the restriction of sexual intercourse is the moral ideal of Western Europe," the one point on which all Christians agree and that she finds at the

root of her conflicting emotions.[98] While Evelyn never plays
Kundry on the stage, at the end of the novel she endures a
crisis of personality not unlike Kundry's, as she is torn cruelly
between two differing views of life. She decides to enter a convent.

In Moore's sequel Evelyn has become Sister Teresa. At first
she seems content with her new life. Then she undergoes a final
period of doubt and resolution. Each stage of her mounting
doubt is marked by an increased interest in playing and especially in daydreaming about Wagner's music.[99] When in the
end she has resolved to remain forever in the convent, she discovers, as a consequence, that she has also lost her voice.
Curiously, for the second edition Moore wrote another ending
to the story. Here Evelyn emerges from the convent to do social
work.[100] What Moore carefully accomplished in the novels
was to create a new and candid psychic understanding of sexual passion with the help of Wagnerian opera.

D. H. Lawrence's *Trespasser,* published in 1912, is an un-
gainly early novel by a man who was to produce much greater
works. Nevertheless, it is of interest precisely because the crude
outlines of Wagnerian influence in this novel had not yet been
smoothed and shaped or integrated into the author's mature
style. The story, which may also have been influenced by
Moore's *Evelyn Innes,* was originally titled *The Saga of Siegmund.*[101] It concerns an adulterous, although unconsummated,
love affair between a violinist and her teacher and takes place
during their brief sojourn on the Isle of Wight.[102] Its hero, Siegmund, commits suicide at the end. Many references to Wagnerian opera accompany the plot's unfolding. As Siegmund
sets off for the Isle of Wight, his old life "dissipates like mist,"
and he finds himself in the world of "romance, going back to
Tristan."[103] When Siegmund and Helen hear the sound of a
fog horn, they discuss whether it most resembles the note of
Wotan's wrath, Siegfried's dragon, or the call of the horn across
the sea to Tristan.[104] The grail music of *Lohengrin* "holds the
best interpretation of the sunset."[105] As they lose their way in
a wood, Siegmund whistles the bird music from *Siegfried* and
pieces from *Tristan.*[106] When at last they must leave the Isle and

Siegmund must return to his family, Helen withdraws to Tintagel on the Cornish coast:

> When Helen was really rested, she took great pleasure in Tintagel. In the first place, she found that the cove was exactly, almost identically the same as the Valhalla scene in *Walküre*; in the second place, "Tristan" was here, in the tragic country filled with the followers of a late Cornish summer, and everlasting reality. . . . It was the enchanted land of divided lovers. Helen forever hummed fragments of *Tristan*. As she stood on the rocks, she sang, in her little half-articulate way, bits of Isolde's love, bits of Tristan's anguish to Siegmund.[107]

It is clear that Wagner's *Tristan*, not Arnold's or Tennyson's, has become the symbolic expression of modern lovers' travail. Possibly Wagner's "mysticism of the senses" may have appealed strongly to Lawrence in his youth and may have contributed to his revolt against rationalism. Traces of Lawrence's Wagnerism remain in one of his best novels, *Women in Love* (1920). The novel has something of a Norse mythological framework, and images of *Götterdämmerung* are interwoven in the closing chapters. Possibly, also, Lawrence was using "rather loosely the symbolism G. B. Shaw found implicit in Wagner's musical version of the myth, the symbolism of modern capital and industry," since there is much in the novel concerning the stifling effect of modern economic life.[108]

Topical allusions to Wagner in other novels of the late nineteenth century are plentiful. These include *Robert Elsmere* (1888) by Mrs. Humphrey Ward, *During a Long Night* (1888) by Eliza Lynn-Linton, *The Wages of Sin* (1891) by Lucas Malet, *Philistia* (1884) by Grant Allen, and *The Mirror of Music* (1895) by Stanley Makower. In three other minor novels the plot hinges upon a Wagnerian theme. Arnold Bennett published *Sacred and Profane Love* in 1905. In it a young woman falls in love with a great pianist at a performance in her hometown. Inevitably they meet, play the second act of *Tristan* on the piano together, and enjoy one night of love that changes their lives completely.[109] The girl makes her way to London, becomes a famous novelist, and ten years later meets her pianist, now an alcoholic living in Paris, and "redeems" him. Finally the two compose a fantastically successful opera, complete with leitmotives. They are on their way to America when the heroine suddenly dies of appendicitis and the novel abruptly ends. The second novel to employ a Wagnerian theme, *The Rubicon* (1894), was written by E. F. Benson, author of ninety-three published books. The Wagnerian opera utilized in this work is *Tannhäuser*. A lovely young married woman engages in a flirtation with an already affianced young man. Though a *Tannhäuser* performance alerts him to the dangers of his position, he plunges ahead to his doom.[110] The third Wagnerian novel, *The Nature of a Crime*, was a collaboration by Ford Madox Ford and Joseph Conrad. It appeared serialized in the *English Review* in April and May of 1909, but it was not published in book form until 1924. Consisting of a series of letters written to a married woman for whom the writer cherishes an unconsummated and obsessive love, it contains a *Liebestod* motif and prominent references to *Tristan und Isolde*. After having attended a performance of the opera, the lover writes to his lady:

> We are held . . . simply by the idea of a love philtre—it's that alone that interests us, that performs the miracle. . . . We see a vision of a state of mind in which morality no longer exists: we are given a respite, a rest: an interval in which no standard of conduct oppresses us.[111]

Actually, it would seem that the medieval myths, particularly those of Tristan and Isolde and Tannhäuser, were transformed by Wagner into modern myths, and so in Wagnerian dress became part of the public domain.

Of course, not all authors cared for or were concerned with Wagner. Some were interested only in passing. George Gissing regretted his ignorance of music, though he does mention having heard and immensely enjoyed the overture to *Tannhäuser*.[112] Thomas Hardy remarked that Wagner's music was "weather and ghost music," with its wind and storm effects, capable of expressing emotion but not the subject of or reason for that emotion.[113] George Meredith attended Wagner concerts and was grieved at his death.[114] Rudyard Kipling apparently made no mention of Wagner, perhaps because he disapproved of decadence and long-haired poets. Robert L. Stevenson and W. E. Henley, also counterdecadents, flourished without Wagner, and Venon Lee (Violet Paget) thought that Wagner's music was degenerate. Lastly, George du Maurier's very successful *Trilby* contains a thinly disguised passage against "Blagnerismus."[115]

Since this chapter began with Edward Robert Bulwer Lytton and Julian Fane, both diplomats and men of letters, it might conclude with Maurice Baring (1874–1945) also a diplomat and author, but of a generation that was adolescent when Wagnerism reached its height in the 1890s. When Baring was at Cambridge, for instance, he and others published one issue of a little magazine called *ABC* and invited Aubrey Beardsley to design its cover. Beardsley acquiesced, but no one really believed that what resulted was his drawing. According to Baring's autobiography, *The Puppet Show of Memory,* Baring's parents disliked modern German opera: "Wagner was thought noisy, and *Faust* and *Carmen* alone of more modern operas really tolerated.[116] Baring had no knowledge of Wagner until he was sent abroad to Germany for language training:

> One night I went to hear *Tannhäuser.* Wagner was only a name to me, and meaning something vaguely noisy. . . . I had no idea of what *Tannhäuser* was about. I went expecting a tedious evening of dry and ultra-classical, unintelligible music. As soon as the orchestra began the overture, I was overwhelmed. I did not know that music was capable of so tremendous an effect. The Venusberg music and the Pilgrims' Chorus opened a new world, and I was so excited afterwards that I could not sleep a wink. I was stunned by these magnetic effects of sound.[117]

Eventually Baring went to Bayreuth. He remarked that it was marvelous to hear the operas for the first time without any preconceived ideas. Every note and every scene "were a revelation and a surprise."[118] He heard *Die Meistersinger, Parsifal,* and *Tristan und Isolde* three times each on a single trip. By comparison with these, *Tannhäuser* seemed "tawdry and thin."[119] The next time that he was at Bayreuth he heard the *Ring.* He left little comment on his reaction to the music, but he said a great deal about the audience.

But of all that sound fury, the only thing that remains in my mind is a French lady who sat next to me and who, when Siegfried's body was carried by to the strains of the tremendous funeral march, burst into sobs, and said to me "Moi, aussi, j'ai un fils, monsieur." [120]

He described himself at that time as "a fervent Wagnerite" in frequent discussion with doubting friends. [121]

More of his impressions may be found in his autobiographical novel, *C.* Like the Maurice Baring of *The Puppet Show of Memory,* C. learns about Wagnerian music from his French and German tutors. Also, he is told by a poet friend that Wagner's music in a certain epoch of one's life annihilates everything else: "You must get through it like the measles. . . . It's poisonous, neurotic stuff, and it's all wrong; but you'll have to experience the disease." [122] C. then goes to hear *Tannhäuser:*

> Never did he receive a more violent electric shock. . . . He did not follow all of it, but he was swept away. . . . There was no difficulty in following the story and when he was transported to the Venusberg, he felt he was witnessing a poem of Swinburne's in action. . . . He would like, he thought, a crashing, thunderous Venusberg song to be sung before all his aunts, which would cause their conventions, creeds, prejudices, morals and ideals to come crashing to the ground. [123]

If C. believes *Tannhäuser* to be a poem of Swinburne's in action, then the story of Wagnerian influence has come to a full circle. C., being unmusical and "too innately classical," does not become a Wagnerite, but Wagner's music heard for the first time, nevertheless, hypnotises him, raises his sensitivity to artistic impressions, and is "a fresh landmark in his progress of emancipation." [124] Next he hears *Tristan und Isolde.* Though the Tristan is nearly senile and the Isolde massive, he is

> utterly spellbound, intoxicated, shipwrecked on an ocean of ecstacy, and yet oppressed; he felt at one moment as if he were drowning in heavy seas, at another as if he were alone in a sultry desert, and always in a stifling twilight. [125]

He also says that he, too, feels as if he has drunk of a fatal cup. Furthermore, C. attends Bayreuth with several of his wellborn friends. Of his two ladies, Leila, who makes him miserable for

many pages, cannot appreciate any but Wagner's music. [126]
Beatrice, who rejects him for a convent, likes only the Pilgrims'
Chorus in *Tannhäuser*. Baring himself later converted to Roman
Catholicism.

In conclusion, though there are many and varying references
to Wagner and to Wagnerian themes scattered throughout
English literature, it seems correct to say that Shaw was most
taken with the *Ring* for its social and economic implications
and Irvine with the *Ring* and *Parsifal* for highly intellectual
and philosophical reasons. On the other hand, the poets and
novelists responded most extravagantly to *Tannhäuser* and
Tristan und Isolde for their psychological and metaphysical
insights into sex. Thus many of them also sympathetically
appreciated the religious aspirations or conflicts of Wagner's
heros. Above all, they agreed with Maurice Baring "that someone should sing the Venusberg song all over England and
shatter the walls of Philistinism." [127]

5

Parsifal, Religion, and the English

In 1888 Mrs. Humphrey Ward published her three-volume novel, *Robert Elsmere*. The book contains several topical references to Wagner of the sort that had become clichés by that time.[1] What is unusual and important is that this novel, an instantaneous best-seller, has a clergyman for its hero. Robert Elsmere rejects the church and the theology by which he was raised, but he retains the desire to follow the good example of Jesus the man. As he sees it, "The problem of the world at this moment is—*how to find a religion?*—some great conception which shall be once more capable, as the old was capable, of welding societies, and keeping man's brutish elements in check."[2] The task is to avoid the pitfalls of positivism while getting rid of what no longer seems reasonable in Christian thought and practice. William Gladstone, although he disapproved of the novel, thought that it was "eminently an offspring of its time."[3] and that its popularity was an indication that conscientious Englishmen were struggling with the same problem as Elsmere.[4]

Many Wagnerians thought that they had the answer to this problem. The Wagnerian movement in England was conducted by those who experienced not only the charm of Wagner's music but also the charm of a religious revival. David Irvine in his eight volumes was the movement's theologian. George Bernard Shaw in *Back to Methusaleh* was the movement's prophet. George Moore in his *Evelyn Innes* created, if not a saint's life, at least a spiritual Odyssey. William Ashton Ellis in the *Meister* preached the gospel of spiritual growth to counter scientific materialism. The last of Wagner's operas, *Parsifal*, was particularly gratifying to religiously minded Wagnerians of various persuasions, and they accorded it a special welcome. In fact, *Parsifal*, far more than the *Ring*, caught the interest of the general public as well.

In *Parsifal* the last of Wagner's innocent heroes encounters some knights of the brotherhood of the Holy Grail in a forest near the castle of Monsalvat. The knights are preparing a morning bath for their ailing king, Amfortas, who has an in-curable wound. The knights rebuke Parsifal for having just shot and killed a swan. It is the first of his lessons in suffering and compassion. The knights also explain how Amfortas had been betrayed by a beautiful woman into the hands of Kling-sor, a sorcerer, who seized the sacred spear from Amfortas and inflicted upon him a wound that could be healed only by a guileless fool. Klingsor had been denied admittance to the brotherhood because of his lust, which he had then tried to remedy by self-castration. Now he had become a powerful magician unencumbered by any desire but that for power and revenge. The beautiful woman is Kundry, who appears in a dual role as temptress in thrall to Klingsor and as abject servant of the Grail community. This community is failing through the growing inability of Amfortas to perform the communion service. The rest of the opera concerns the awaken-ing of Parsifal to the knowledge of the world's suffering, his temptation by Kundry and Klingsor, his retrieval of the sacred spear, and the redemption of the Grail brotherhood.

To some interpreters the opera is a Christian allegory.[5] All the familiar symbols and rituals—the chalice, the spear that pierced Christ's side, baptism and communion—are present. To this day *Parsifal* is often performed on Good Friday to de-vout audiences. To others it embodies both Buddhist and Christian doctrine.[6] Parsifal's spiritual education resembles that of the Buddha. Both he and Kundry also seem to have lived previous lives, past incarnations. This theory gains some credence from the fact that Wagner actually contemplated operas on the lives of both Buddha and Christ. The basic universal message of both religions remains "enlightenment through compassion brings salvation." To humanists,[7] Parsifal is *self*-redeemed, and the opera may be considered Wagner's last address to a moribund Christian society, perfectly in keeping with his views in the earlier operas. On the other hand, Parsifal may be neither religious nor humanistic but "a structure plainly exhibiting the nihilistic, authoritarian, and racial concepts of Nazi ideology."[8] In this interpretation the Grail community is seen as an Aryan society in need of redemption from blood pollution. Finally, Nietzsche, the most astute of Wagner's critics, suggests that *Parsifal* is a cunning alliance of "beauty and sickness."[9] He views Wagner himself as the Klingsor of all Klingsors.

Apart from a few initial qualms concerning the propriety of using Christian symbols on the stage, most of the English of the nineteenth century believed that *Parsifal* was a respectable and edifying opera. They objected neither to the concept as a whole, nor to any particular part. Compared with the earlier outcry against the incest of Siegmund and Sieglinde, there was silence on the subject of Klingsor's self-castration. Perhaps Victorian prudery intervened, or, more likely, the English did not fully understand the German text. Nor did the English understand *Parsifal* as a lesson in blood pollution, although the theosophists were pleased that Wagner had been inspired partly by the religions of the "Aryan" East. Only a few critics, like John Runciman and Robert Trevelyan, took the Nietzschean point of view.

The first group of *Parsifal* enthusiasts, including Charles Gatty, Hugh Reginald Haweis, Alfred Gurney, and Peter Taylor Forsyth, most of them clergymen, viewed *Parsifal* either as presenting a Christian message or, at least in some way, as assisting the Christian cause.[10] Charles Gatty interprets it as an allegorical and symbolic drama demonstrating "the secret of redeeming love."[11] *Parsifal* exhibits two communities: the ideal mystic community of the knights of the Holy Grail, which hints at a spiritual utopia or kingdom of God among men, and the enchanted domain of Klingsor. Klingsor manifests the "Pagan pride of life," and his garden contains temptations designed to "turn the soul away from God."[12] In this garden Amfortas is disfigured by the lasting stigmata of sin: "As Titurel is a type of the past golden age of loving faith, so Amfortas represents the present age of loveless doubt. . . . Parsifal is the divinely appointed deliverer."[13] Parsifal's innocence allows him to be open to divine sympathy. Parsifal is divinely guided: "The story of Parsifal's life may also be taken as an allegory of the wonderful designs of Providence concerning the soul of man in relation to the mystery of existence, its concealed purpose, and its hidden God."[14] As a child assigned to lead the wise, Parsifal's strength lies in his sympathy with suffering. Particularly, he turns his pity to Amfortas and thence "to the crucified God upon the hill of Calvary."[15] Parsifal's cry of anguish echoes the "Wail of God" for sinful man. The ultimate message of the opera is that men should become pure like Parsifal and renounce worldly pursuits. Renunciation of this world is a precondition to "cooperation with redemption":

> The virtue of self-renunciation, a means of closer union with God, as a release from the limitations of the flesh, and by way of expiation for sin, is a necessary condition of heroic co-operation with divine redemption. It is embodied in our Lord's words, "whosoever shall lose his life for My sake and the gospel shall save it." This is the secret of redeeming Love. . . . By the power of Christ's Great Renunciation God and man are reconciled, the dead are raised to life, the lost are found, and the wounded are made whole.[16]

Thus, Parsifal is a Christ figure and hero of the Great Renunciation. The effect of the music drama is to expand the moral vision of men: "The fetters of selfish habit are melted by the compunction occasioned by this work of art, and the soul hovers towards heaven."[17]

Hugh Reginald Haweis was a popular clergyman—pastor of St. James, Westmoreland St., Marylebone—who tried to keep up with the latest developments in theology. He wrote the preface to Ward's 1891 edition of *Robert Elsmere*. At the time of his death the *Times* wrote that his sermons would probably have scandalized his grandfather, another well-known clergyman, and that he deserved to be remembered not only as a versatile writer and speaker, but also "as an indication of the vast comprehensiveness of the Anglican Church."[18] Haweis showed perhaps as much interest in music as in religion, having originally been trained as a violinist. He organized musical Sunday evenings at his church, and orchestral music and oratorio performances were made part of the regular church services. In fact, "his soundest and most original literary work was on music, though his theological writings were bulkier."[19] In *Music and Morals,* published in 1871, he wrote of his respect for Wagner's genius, although he did not completely agree with Wagner's theories.[20] In 1883, as music critic of *Truth,* Haweis asserted that to the time of his death that year Wagner had been "the greatest composer and most impressive art-personality then alive in the world."[21] Haweis's interpretation of *Parsifal* seems to lie within the framework of conventional Christianity. Actually, his descriptions of Bayreuth, the *Ring,* and *Parsifal* concentrate on the emotional rather than the intellectual content. He was an example of a person upon whom Wagner's operas had "more effect on the nervous system than on the intellect."[22]

Haweis was present in 1876 at the opening of Bayreuth. Later he recorded his impressions of that happy occasion: "I confess I came fully under Wagner's spell—I spent a delightful evening at his house in 1876. It was at the close of the first Bayreuth festival."[23] He perceived Bayreuth "to be given over to a kind of idolatry of Wagner," of which he thoroughly approved, and he found the *Ring* indescribably beautiful.[24] Haweis saw Wagner again in England, heard him read one act of *Parsifal,* and received Wagner's embrace: "He advanced toward me as I suddenly entered the room, with 'Ach mein lieber Herr Haweis, was haben Sie den [sic] über mich schön geschrieben!' and so saying, taking me by both elbows, he saluted me on both cheeks in the orthodox manner."[25]

The musical clergyman attended two crowded performances of *Parsifal* at Bayreuth in 1888. In the morning he visited Wagner's grave and then returned to his room to prepare himself "by reading and meditation for the great religious drama" he was about to witness.[26] Though he recalled that some religious people were uneasy over the possibility of finding the sacraments imitated upon the stage, he commented: "Yet no one who has seen *Parsifal* comes away without the most reverent sympathy for this ideal representation of all that was most pure and elevating in medieval Roman Catholicism."[27] Indeed, the music drama became for him an act of worship.

> Every thought of the stage had vanished—nothing was further from my own thoughts than play-acting. I was sitting as I should sit at an oratorio, in devout and rapt contemplation. Before my eyes had passed a symbolic vision of prayer and ecstasy, flooding the soul with overpowering thoughts of the divine sacrifice and the mystery of unfathomable love.[28]

At the conclusion of act one Haweis thought to himself that Bayreuth was truly the Monsalvat of modern drama, sacred to the highest aims of art. During the intermission between the second and third acts he noticed how awed and subdued the audience appeared:

> Not a heart there but could interpret that struggle between the flesh and the spirit from its own experiences. Not one but knew the desperately wicked and deceitful temptations that come like enchantresses in the wizard's garden, to plead the cause of the devil in the language of high-flown sentiment or even religious feeling. Praise and criticism seemed dumb; we rather walked and spoke of what we had just witnessed like men convinced of judgement, and righteousness, and sin.[29]

The visit to Bayreuth was a pilgrimage that cost him time, trouble, and money; the effect was totally hypnotic. "When I came out they asked me who was Amfortas. I did not know. I said 'the wounded king'."[30] At the music drama's end Haweis was at a loss to express "the beatific vision of God's eternal love and Real Presence" as it was restored to the Grail community: "Words can add nothing to the completeness of the drama, and no words can give any idea of the splendor and complexity of that sound ocean upon which the drama floats from beginning to end."[31] Haweis was not alone on the Wagnerian ocean of sound. Others experienced the same narcosis:

> We float along with the music without conscious effort . . . and we are borne hither and thither on the waves of sound, which descend

at one moment to the depths of sorrows and mysteries never before explored, and now rise to heights of bliss never before attained. And here and there, when we have reached the highest pitch of excitement in the personages of the drama, some stately march or simple phrase comes to still the troubled waters, and we lose ourselves once more in the calm of the eternal sea of thought.[32]

Thus Wagner's music cast its spell on clergymen and counttesses in the nineteenth century as it enchanted Adolf Hitler in the twentieth.[33]

Alfred Gurney was the vicar of St. Barnabas, Pimlico. Son of a well-known hymn writer, Gurney himself was the author of highly praised religious verse, including *The Vision of the Eucharist, Day Dreams,* and *A Christmas Faggot.* The *Times* referred to him as a High Churchman, although his most famous lecture, "Our Catholic Inheritance in the Larger Hope," might have been charged with Universalism.[34] The vicar was a friend of the Beardsleys and was among the many Englishmen to visit Bayreuth. In 1888 he wrote *"Parsifal": A Study.* Rather coyly he denied any desire to take sides in the contest between Wagner's admirers and detractors. However, he would venture to urge that "no one be over-confident in this controversy until he was heard *Parsifal."*[35]

Gurney comments that at certain golden periods in history art has been truly inspired and that this point might suggest itself to anyone who had been to Bayreuth to hear *Parsifal.* He praises *Parsifal* as salutary, soothing, and elevating: "It is the high vocation of Art, and especially of music, not only to stimulate, but also to tranquilize"[36]—presumably, to assuage men's savage instincts. Most particularly, he reminds his readers: "It is a joy to remember as we follow the sublime story of *Parsifal,* that in one of his last published letters Wagner makes an earnest and unhesitating profession of allegiance to Christ."[37] There follows an unexceptional description of the plot, in which Titurel is represented as an illustration of the ministry of old age; Amfortas, the unabsolved sinner; Klingsor, the hardened miscreant; and Kundry, the follower in the footsteps of Mary Magdalene. In delineating the character of Parsifal, however, Gurney seems to sense that Wagner was perhaps less interested in the God who became a man than preoccupied with the man who became like God. Considering act 3, Gurney says that in Parsifal, and in Kundry as well, "we may discern the evolution of the New Man—the gradual upgrowth and development of that which springs from an incorruptible seed, and attains at length, fostered by salutary resistance, to the full measure of Christ."[38] In the last scene, when Parsifal heals Amfortas by touching his wound with the sacred spear and presides over the communion service, according to Gurney

> the kingdom of love, joy, peace, and righteousness is established. . . . It is the apocalyptic doxology, indicating that the Saviour is Himself saved—a Divine work only completed and concluded when all whom His love has created and redeemed at great length conformed to his likeness, and are partakers of His perfection.[39]

Concluding his study with one of his own poems, Gurney represents *Parsifal* as the story of the evolution of God in humanity:

> Deep calleth unto deep—God's deep
>   To God-created depths in man;
> The hands that sow the hands that reap,
>   Complete what His began.
>
> For His the seed, and His the fruit
>   And His the life at every stage;
> In God humanity strikes root,
>   Evolved from age to age.
>
> From age to age the vision grows;
>   Discerning eyes with wonder see
> The desert blossoms as the rose
>   God in humanity.
> . . . .
> Deep answers deep—an antiphon
>   More clearly heard from age to age
> For God and man, in Christ are one
>   and God man's heritage.[40]

Thus were Darwin, Wagner, and Christianity blended in Gurney's poetry.

The most astute religious analysis of Wagner and *Parsifal* came from the pen of Peter Taylor Forsyth (1848–1921), a Scottish Congregationalist minister. Having studied at Göttingen, he was familiar with German theology and Biblical scholarship. At first he appeared to be in the liberal Protestant camp. Later he lost much of his confidence in the goodness of man and his ability to follow the ethical example of Jesus and "developed a deepening sense of sin in the face of the holiness of God."[41] His theology emphasized the grace of God, who had taken upon himself the consequences of man's sinfulness, and the "good news" of the gospel proclaiming the forgiveness of man. Forsyth enjoyed a second vogue in the 1950s after two tragic world wars had taken place.

Forsyth's *Religion in Recent Art,* published in 1911, is a collection of lectures on Dante Gabriel Rossetti, Edward Burne-Jones, Theodore Watts, Holman Hunt, and Wagner. Wagner appealed to Forsyth because he "was not only a musician, but a poet and thinker" as well, with a systematic view of life— almost a theology.[42] Wagner was "the most gifted and passionate expositor of that semi-religious philosophy and semi-Christian atheism which is associated with the names of Schopenhauer and Pessimism."[43] In producing a great master in art, pessimism had done what neither positivism nor agnosticism "had enough human nature" to do. Forsyth finds pessimism, while atheistic, nevertheless deeper and nearer to Christianity than philosophies of naturalism and evolution:

> There are features in this strange philosophy which raise it almost to a religion having no few points of contact with our own. . . . It rises from a burdened world, from a disjointed time, from lands where thought is too much divorced from action, and where the pressure of militarism upon industry cooperates with the ecclesiastical destruction of vital faith to reduce the value, the reasonableness, the sanctity of life. It bears the cross, it sups full of sorrow; but it sees no Resurrection. . . . It is one side of Christianity, nevertheless, because it is not pure Naturalism, because it is a creed of sorrow, because it distrusts the easy optimism of the merely happy creeds, because it has a heart for the world-pain, something like a sense of sin. . . . It is Christian, furthermore, in that pessimism is not absolute.[44]

Forsyth finds that there was a certain magnificence about the vision of atheistic pessimism that was actually lacking in popular contemporary Christianity.

According to Forsyth, Wagner seized on the thin strain of redemption in Schopenhauer's thought. "It is doubtful if any artist since the great medieval painters has worked under such a sense of the redemptive idea as Wagner."[45] Forsyth does not care that Wagner was theologically not the orthodox Christian. Doubtless the time would come, he says, when theologians would be worthy of theology,

> but while this good time is on the way let us learn whatever strong teaching is to be found, and yield to us the spell of the Lord wherever his Spirit breathes. Art which is saturated with Christian ideas and aspirations cannot be quite outside the kingdom of heaven, even if it misread some of the Christian realities.[46]

Forsyth praises Wagner for having transcended Schopenhauer's pessimism:

> Love, in philosophical Pessimism, does not really conquer death. In Wagner it does—if not always in theory yet always like *King Lear* in the aesthetic effect. The last darkness—and he makes it dark enough—is glorified and warmed by a passion of persistent and all-commanding love, which never lets us go without the sense that salvation hovers about the blackest woe and the most dismal confusion of failure.[47]

This to Forsyth is the message of *Tristan und Isolde* and also of the *Ring*. The last lines of *Die Götterdämmerung* sound to him "like Scripture, and one reads them over and over and over again with new delight and cheer."[48]

Forsyth considers *Parsifal* the highest example of pessimism transcended and the greatest religious art creation since the Greeks. He praises *Parsifal* for returning to European culture its sense of sin, its need for forgiveness, and the faith in salvation.[49]

Forsyth's interpretation of *Parsifal,* of course, is related to his own understanding of Christ's experience. Christ was not sent merely to clear away outward obstacles to forgiveness, to provide a sacrifice in order to release the mercy of God, nor, on the other hand, was he sent simply to announce impending forgiveness, as a prophet might. Rather, "he actualised in human nature when He actualised in Himself, the forgiving presence of God"; that is, Christ revealed God "by bearing Him in upon us, leavening us with Him practically, and consciously, not metaphysically."[51] True to his pietistic leanings, Forsyth claims that redemption is a matter of the soul's inner struggle, rather than of ecclesiastical ritual. Expressed in contemporary terms, "redemption is a psychological process within a universal soul."[52] Hence, Forsyth might have resolved Robert Elsmere's dilemma by urging him to take heart, by reassuring him that it is neither by physical science nor by biblical criticism that the traditional theories of the Gospel shall be tested, but rather existentially by the modern soul. Traditional theories were "not so much in collision with the truth of nature as inadequate to the aspirations of the heart, foreign to the modern conscience."[53] Forsyth thought, as did Thomas Mann, that Schopenhauer and Wagner were masters of psychology. He concludes his study of *Parsifal* by stating that Wagner was not the founder or prophet of a new religion but an artist with a message for the soul. He could not bring redemption itself. But

> if too little stress has been laid by the Church upon Christ's conquest of man's sin in his spiritual history; if His life-long temptation and victory have been neglected as the real work of Redemption; if Christian people have been too easily satisfied to have such a work done for them instead of repeated in them; if the Christian conflict has been too un-moral, too legal, fanciful, or sentimental, and if it has thus been severed from the great Art of the spiritual imagination, we may gladly submit to be recalled to one neglected truth of Scripture by an artist and thinker who is not singular, but the hierophant of God's spirit of the age.[54]

Among Christian interpreters of *Parsifal*, Peter Taylor Forsyth seems the most thoughtful and the best able to explain just how a "Christian atheist" might possibly have created—without being cynical or degenerate—a Christian drama. *Parsifal* shows Christians how the drama of redemption can take place within themselves.

A second group of enthusiasts, the Theosophists, attacked metaphysical problems from quite a different vantage point. Theosophy originated in the seventeenth century as a kind of speculation that sought to derive from the knowledge of

God found in secret books such as the Jewish cabala or in the Scriptures, mystically and symbolically interpreted, a deeper knowledge and control of nature than that offered by then current philosophies. A Theosophical Society was founded in New York in 1875 by H. S. Olcott, W. Q. Judge, and Helena P. Blavatsky. Its professed goals were to create a universal brotherhood, to promote the study of Eastern religion and philosophy—especially Aryan—and to investigate the unfamiliar laws of nature and faculties latent in man. Theosophy was one of many popular metaphysical or spiritualist movements that claimed communication with unseen spirits and combined pyschic research with an interest in oriental religions. One historian goes so far as to say that "nearly all the intellectuals of the seventies and eighties gave Spiritualism some attention."[55] Despite appearances, the theosophists did not actually believe in the supernatural. They considered their philosophies to be scientific as well as religious. God was impersonal and immanent in nature. "The metaphysical sects arrived at a type of humanism in which man becomes the master of his fate. He is believed capable of creating his conditions for his progression through the knowledge and utilization of God's laws."[56] They tended to avoid creeds and organized churches, searching instead for arcane clues in the holy writings of East and West or in mystical experiences artificially induced. W. Q. Judge illustrates the Theosophical point of view, in particular, in his description of the aims of Madame Blavatsky:

> The aims and object of her life were to strike off the shackles forged by priestcraft for the mind of man. She wished all men to know that they are God in fact, and that as men they must bear the brunt of their own sins, for no one else can do it. Hence she brought forward to the West the old Eastern doctrines of Karma and reincarnation. . . . She also desired that science should be brought back to the true ground where life and intelligence are admitted to be within and acting on and through every atom in the universe. Hence her object was to make religion scientific and science religious, so that the dogmatism of each might disappear.[57]

Blavatsky is most remembered now for her alleged communication with the mahatmas or masters, who were neither angels nor gods, but beings who had reached a higher and more nonmaterial stage of existence.[58] All this is understandable in an age when orthodox religion and deterministic science apparently had separately reached dead ends.

Perhaps the most famous Theosophist in England was William Butler Yeats. In 1917 he wrote *A Vision,* which describes his own theosophical system. Yeats was a member of the London Rhymers' Club in the nineties, a time when interest in the symbolists reached a high point. He includes Wagner among them and implies that Wagner, like Gerald de Nerval, Maeterlinck, Villiers de l'Isle-Adam, and Verlaine, was a contributor to a new sacred book that all the arts were seeking to create.[59] Though he also shared with Wagner an interest in the creation of a national art—Celtic in Yeats's case— he does not seem to have been directly influenced by Wagner's operas.[60] George Moore speaks of Yeats as being unmusical, alleging that he would place *Tristan* and *Madame Butterfly* in the same class.[61] Although this may be a matter of taste, the fact that Yeats was tone-deaf may have had something to do with it!

The less well known Alice Leighton Cleather is a better example of theosophical Wagnerian. She was the daughter of an Anglican clergyman, whose "natural bent of mind" soon led her "to discover the limitations of orthodox Christianity."[62] Finding Western philosophy inadequate, she turned to A. P. Sinnett's *Occult World* and *Esoteric Buddhism.* These impelled her to join the London Lodge of the Theosophical Society. On first meeting Blavatsky, she "experienced a distinct shock as her extraordinarily penetrating blue eyes literally bored a hole through my brain."[63] She became one of Blavatsky's Inner Group of twelve personal pupils. Interestingly enough, Cleather was never enthusiastic about tabletapping, hypotism, and the like. She resigned from the society when, after Blavatsky's death, it was taken over by Annie Besant and A. P. Sinnett, who relied increasingly on chelas, psychics, and clairvoyants. Cleather was convinced that after Blavatsky's death there was no possibility of direct communication with the mahatmas, "except, of course, for individuals who were capable of rising to their plane by interior effort or aspiration."[64] Thereafter, she carried on her work privately, and she left England just before World War I. She traveled with her son and Basil Crump, a barrister who had joined the Theosophical Society and who collaborated with Cleather on her books.[65] In 1918 she went to India, and in 1920 she was accepted into the Buddhist laity. She and Crump judged the internecine warfare and charlatantry within the Theosophical Society in Wagnerian terms:

> Richard Wagner, who had considerable knowledge of magic, gives an exact and terrible illustration of this process in his symbolical music-drama *Parsifal*. The plastic elemental female principle is there personified in Kundry. Awake she is the humble serving messenger of the Grail Brotherhood; but, unknown to them, the black magician, Klingsor, can throw her into a hypnotic trance and compel her to serve his nefarious ends. . . . The terrible danger to sensitive and hysterical women of being subjected to this process by an unscrupulous male hypnotiser cannot be exaggerated; and men like Sinnett, who have recourse to such evil practices in the pursuit of their selfish ends are black magicians of the worst description, and are a menace to humanity. . . . The whole may be taken as a drama of the Theosophical Society, which may now be said to be under the dominion of Klingsor, and still waiting the coming of its Parsifal who can shatter the vast fabric of psychic illusion.[66]

The new Parsifal supposedly was due in 1975.

Cleather apparently lectured on "Wagner as a Pioneer of Humanitarianism," as Samuel Butler recalled in his letters,[67] and she also produced, with Basil Crump, several books on Wagner, including *"Parsifal," "Lohengrin" and the Legend of the Holy Grail* (1904) and *"The Ring of the Nibelung": An Interpretation Embodying Wagner's Own Explanations* (1909). She attended the Bayreuth festival and examined, with Cosima's permission, Wagner's library at Wahnfried. Impressed by "the extraordinary scope of his studies," she noted that "all of the sacred books of the East are there."[68] She mentioned the Buddhism expressed in Wagner's letters to Liszt, Röckel, and Wesendonck,[69] and quoted a friend who had heard Gobineau state that Wagner had called himself a Buddhist at heart. Characteristically, she sought esoteric meanings in the operas: "We make a special point of the inner meaning of each work, treating them as symbolical dramas."[70] Generally speaking, for Cleather Parsifal is "the hero of a mystery-play in which the essential elements of the great religions of the Eastern and Western worlds—Christianity and Buddhism—are blended in a form especially adapted to the western world of today."[71] Her book deals with *Parsifal* and *Lohengrin* together because she was very interested in the location of the Holy Grail. She concludes that there is "one important point . . . much more clearly stated by Wagner" than by other authorities that she consulted—

> namely, that the Grail came originally from the East, and that it was brought from its mountain fastness in India (probably the Himalyas) and placed in the sanctuary of Monsalvat, in the Pyrenees, in order to spread its light and wisdom in western lands. When the mission was concluded, the Brotherhood returned once more with the sacred vessel.[72]

The Grail brothers appear to her to be theosophical mahatmas. Cleather interprets all Wagner's drama to "represent different phases of the complex struggles undergone by the human being in the course of its evolution towards perfection."[73] In *Tristan und Isolde,* for instance, the demons of the lower mind are finally defeated, and the two make peace with themselves and enter into a conscious union with the World-Soul. *Parsifal* is the culmination of Wagner's interrelated operas. Parsifal alone is "a perfect being; there is no female figure on, or near, his level."[74] In him intellect and intuition are united, as they must be of necessity in the perfect human being. Only such a person can attain the power to redeem. In *Parsifal* the main theme is compassion, as Cleather believes was the keynote of Wagner's own life. Cleather finds the entire conception simple and beautiful, yet immensely grand and almost impossible to describe.[75]

Parsifal was the first opera that William Ashton Ellis chose to explicate in the Meister, in 1888. Having been Madame Blavatsky's physician during her serious illness in 1886, Ellis knew the Theosophists. But his views seem even more eclectic than theirs. Seemingly, he was aware of multiple occult, theosophical, Christian, and humanistic possibilities in Wagner, all of which he took seriously. A clue to Ellis's orientation may be found in his "Richard Wagner as Poet, Musician, and Mystic," a paper he read to the Society for the Encouragement of the Fine Arts on 3 February 1887. Speaking of mysticism, Ellis quotes extensively from Thomas Carlyle, who, while abandoning his parents' Calvinism, had retained a transcendentalist belief in the reality of the unseen world. Ellis is particularly fond of using Carlyle's statement that "the invisible world is near us." In this paper he notes how in reacting against materialism men were banding together,

> some attempting to deal with the question from the side of ghostly manifestations, as the Spiritualists; some from that of thought-transference and allied phenomena, as the Society for Psychical Research; and some from the side of the ancient, and till lately almost inaccessible store of occult wisdom, as the Theosophical Society. The object in all, however, is the same: to shake off this great pall of gross matter that shuts men off into separate prison cells of personal egoism, and to reach forth, however feebly at first, into a realm, the nearness to us of which Carlyle thus set forth.[76]

Ellis maintains that such too was the purpose of Wagner, at first unconsciously, but later systematically expanded in his mature works.

In his article on *Parsifal* Ellis denies that this opera was a work of Wagner's declining years; rather it is the necessary outcome of the "psychological studies" that had preceded it. The secret of its charm lies in its "subtle mysticism . . . streaming over every bar of the music" and stealing away "our senses from this earth."[77] In answer to the question What do the Grail and Spear signify? Ellis states that their exoteric meaning is Christian but that they also have an esoteric meaning that underlies all religion: "The inner essence that no terms of intellect can convey." For instance, astrologists regard the circle and the straight line as archetypal religious symbols and understand them to mean "the dual aspect of the universe, the union of the eternal Motherhood and Fatherhood."[78] Ellis is also quick to point out traces of Buddhism in Wagner's description of Parsifal's early life and possible previous lives, that is, the hero's possible incarnations.

According to Ellis, in the second-act temptation of Parsifal by Kundry, Wagner has condensed into a single episode a whole world tragedy. It is the core of the music drama, for at that point Parsifal becomes

> the conscious Redeemer of his race. Upon himself he has taken the sins of Amfortas, as the higher principle in man,—the true *Ego,* the *daimon* of Plato and Socrates, the *higher self* of the Eastern philosopher—must take upon itself the experience of its earthly vehicle. [79]

By the close of the drama Parsifal has completed the act of renunciation, the final aim of the teaching of both Jesus and Siddhartha. Contrary to Cleather's interpretation, Kundry has achieved spiritual union with Parsifal, equality at last: "Thus has Matter, brought to rest, passed from the illusory form, the *Maya* of the Vedas, of which Kundry in her protean external appearance was the type, into the divine essence of the Spirit." [80] As a result of Parsifal's renunciation, the golden age and the brotherhood of man return to earth in the last scenes. To Ellis *Parsifal* is the most remarkable drama of modern times. Thus, in Ellis's interpretation, ideas of Christianity, Buddhism, Carlylean idealism, the golden age, evolution, astrology, and hope for human brotherhood cluster together in an attempt to fill the spiritual vacuum of the late nineteenth century. [81]

By contrast, Moncure Conway started out as a Methodist clergyman and ended as a pure rationalist. He said he had "spent his life decorating one Bambino after another—the Messiah, the Redeemer, the Martyr, the prophet, the typical man, the reformer, the altruist, the free-thinking teacher." [82] Born in Virginia, he journeyed to England during the American Civil War. Conway was both an abolitionist and a pacifist. From 1864 to 1897 he was the pastor of South Place Chapel, Finsbury in London, a fellowship of liberal thinkers, and there in 1883 he held a memorial service for Wagner. [83] His study of Thomas Paine is still read, though his autobiography, his literary and philosophical studies, and his fiction are less well known. Conway shared with other Wagnerites a high esteem for art. He called the artist "the forerunner of the Christ to be." [84] The ministry of art was "the highest because, when true, it awakens in man the emotions which lift him to the highest possibilities of his existence."[85] It was the mission of art to redeem man and to lead the spiritual evolution of humanity. This was "the gospel of art," and he lamented that, unfortunately, art was still considered so profane that it had to wear a veil on Sundays. But Conway would have nothing to do with Schopenhauer or pessimism—the philosophy of, as he put it, "all is for the worst." Nor was he a theosophist. Rather, like Bernard Shaw, he stressed man's ability to improve his own lot in a new "era of conscious and purposed selection."[86]

Conway commented on two Wagner operas. Characteristically, he chose the least mystical: *Rienzi* and *Die Meistersinger*. He heard *Rienzi* in Munich in 1871 just after his tour of the battlefields of the Franco-Prussian War. Of all the Wagner operas, he confessed that he liked *Rienzi* best, even though he knew that most Wagnerians would not have made that choice. What appealed to him was "the spell woven about me by the Messengers of Peace. The nightmares that followed my journalistic tramp on the battlefields had been revived by the apotheosis of War at Berlin, but they were dispelled by the troop of beautiful olive-bearers and their wondrous *Frauenchor.*"[87] In another scene he "recognized in the composer a Prospero creating a fairer world than that hard and heartless imperial realm whose barbaric splendors I had seen in Berlin."[88] Wagner has seldom been so praised for his pacifism! *Die Meistersinger* Conway welcomed as a tribute to art; he was particularly moved by Eva's admiration for Hans Sachs. "It is a fine expression of the magic of pure art, whereby it not only stills danger, but calms the tumult of passion,—the pains of the past, anxieties of the future, last and forgotten in a present joy that holds no sting."[89] Of *Parsifal* this clergyman said not a word.

The vogue for *Parsifal,* particularly for its asceticism and its redemptive message, took an unusual turn in the work of Robert C. Trevelyan (1872–1951).[90] Trevelyan was a classicist, poet, and author of several "operatic fables." Maurice Baring knew him at Cambridge, where Trevelyan was elected to The Society, an elite discussion group. Among its members in the 1890s were Alfred North Whitehead and Bertrand Russell.

Russell later described Trevelyan as the most bookish man he ever knew.[91] Politically, Trevelyan became a Fabian and a pacifist. In *The Birth of Parsival* (1905) he did for Wagner's last work what John Davidson had done for *Tannhäuser:* he rewrote (and also expanded) the story as Nietzsche might have. Next, in *The New Parsifal* (1914), he wrote a comedy in which neither Nietzsche nor Wagner are taken very seriously.

In *The Birth of Parsival* Titurel's son and heir, Fritmutel, travels to a distant kingdom in the service of the Grail and there falls in love with and possesses Herzeloida, the king's daughter, in defiance of his vows. Kundry, as messenger of the Grail, denounces him and predicts his doom. Frimutel (Amfortas) refuses to repent and breaks the magic sword of the Grail into pieces. Thereupon he becomes afflicted with horrible delusions impelling him to enter the tent of the king's sons, Herzeloida's brothers, and slay them while they sleep. Then, driven by the frenzy of his violence and lawlessness, he goes to dwell like a beast in the forest. Meanwhile, a son, Parsival, is born to Herzeloida. She conceals him until she is compelled to confess to her father, who, prompted by the malicious priest Thaddeus, commands that she and the child be exposed to the mercies of the wilderness. There Frimutel discovers them and is cured of his insanity. But Frimutel never repents of his rebellion against the Grail in the name of love, and despite Herzeloida's pleas, does not forsake his views. Thus Herzeloida departs with Kundry to bring up her son Parsival in a place appointed by the Grail.

Obviously, Frimutel is not at all like the sin-laden and weary Amfortas of the opera. Initially, Frimutel bids Herzeloida to forget sin, to believe that reason does not condemn love:

> But, wouldst thou know what God would have us do
> Rather give ear to Reason, whose clear voice bids
>   make much of life, while yet we may,
> Redeeming and enhancing with some joy,
> Some brightness for Love's fact, time's weary waste
> Of barren hours; so may we serve him best.[92]

He regards himself as having "dared to cast off the bonds of superstition and base fear," and he believes that his mission is to deliver the Grail by the strength of love "from ignoble superstition, / From joyless and loveless worship, / Ignorant and irrational and vain."[93] In particular he condemns the priestcraft and false religion that holds the Grail captive. Frimutel's destruction of the Grail sword concludes the first act. Herzeloida is the center of the second and third acts. She, too, although more traditional in religious outlook, discovers the heartlessness of priests and even the heartlessness of simple but ignorant country people in trying her utmost to protect her child. In the second act, she defends the child from shepherds who, fearing he is unnatural, try to kill him. In the third act Herzeloida defends the child against Thaddeus, the King's priest, who believes that the child houses Satan's spirit. She and the child are banished. In the concluding act Frimutel, Parsival, and Herzeloida are temporarily reunited. Frimutel unsuccessfully urges that Herzeloida and the child remain with him. When Herzeloida bids him seek pardon, Frimutel replies adamantly:

> Whereof should I repent?
> For what seek pardon? and from whom? Can
>   that
> Which is not just pardon? Can he repent
> Whose mind is conscious of no guilt?[94]

At the end Fritmutel is prepared to endure, believing that Parsival, "first-born of hope and freedom," will in turn abjure the Grail, even as he had inherited something of his father's disposition.[95]

The New Parsifal may be considered a sequel to the *Birth of Parsival*, yet it was hardly written in the same tone of stoical, freethinking defiance. In this play, Parsifal is portrayed as Percy Smith, an "Anglo-Philistine" in a flying-machine! Wagner first appears as an irate ghost in the middle of a prefatory discussion between the Lord Chamberlain and a censor of plays. Wagner's ghost declares that the play was "a blasphemous foul plot / Against my majesty, and the sanctitude / of the Bayreuthian Grail."[96] In this play Klingsor, "this abhorred Nietzschean imposter," together with the knights and flower maidens, has kidnapped the Grail and set off for Dionysiac orgies on Circe's isle. The Lord Chamberlain has not the faintest idea as to the identity of the ghost, and the shade of Wagner is forced to introduce himself. Wagner is immediately

recognized, ironically, as the composer of *Lohengrin's* Wedding
March, whereupon, outraged and insulted, the ghost vanishes.
Meanwhile, in this highly fanciful work, Circe has changed
the knights and flower maidens into asses. Klingsor himself
is protected by the Grail "from dreamland of ascetic gloom
rescued to gladsome light",[97] but Circe loses the power to
change the asses back into human beings. The Grail points
to the coming of the Phoenix to rescue them. Suddenly, out
of the air drops Percival Smith, "the bold cloud-cruising
Philistine," in a monoplane. He shoots the Phoenix. The bird
tumbles onto the Grail. As in Egyptian mythology, the Phoenix
bursts into flame and rises again anew from its own ashes.
Percy zooms off to chase it. The blazing Phoenix has puri-
fied the Grail of its Christianity, and a pagan celebration
ensues. Klingsor curses all "professorial owls and clerical
moles, bookworms, loud puritan asses,/All they who believe
not in Pater's prose, nor in Max Beerbohm's revelations."[98]
In the midst of the orgy Percy Smith returns with two friends,
an archeologist, and a literary critic, editor of the *Daily Pill.*
Smith has drunk from the Grail, and seeing what a Philistine
he has been, he decides to buy it or to seize it, and also to con-
vince Circe to run away with him. Klingsor, aware of the plot,
brings out two Grails to fool "those who wish to sell it to Christ
or Mammon."[99] There follows a contest to choose the true
Grail. Percy's friends, but not Percy, choose the wrong Grail.
Klingsor then flies away with the true Grail, but, immobilized
just a few feet off the ground, he has to jettison that which is
weighing him down—the *Oxford Treasury of Victorian Verse,* the
score of *Parsifal,* the *Mona Lisa,* etc. The Phoenix then inter-
venes and judges that Percy should have the Grail, but he
refuses it because the responsibilities that it entails are too
great. The Phoenix acknowledges that Percy has acted rightly:
"Unwholesome for mankind and perilous how are proved /
Religious and aesthetic grails alike."[100] The Grail is then removed to "a prig's paradise" of cultural-mandarin holiness
by the angels, Goethe, Pater, and, Nietzsche. At this critical
juncture, however, Wagner's ghost reemerges from the earth,
snatches the Grail, and returns it to the earth forever. Circe
comments that there is no reason to worry, for "deep down in

the earth is another nobler land of bliss / Where Orpheus, Dionysius, Tristan, Tannhäuser, Osian, Blake and Aeschylus dwell, / And thither from all sacerdotal taint Hellenized and cleansed, the Grail shall Wagner bear."[101] Circe sets off for this region, and the chorus boards Percy's yacht "from Graildom and culture-Brahminism," delivered to the common workaday world "yet with dreams still." Perhaps Wagner, rightly understood, had won the day. Rarely do Wagnerians have a sense of humor. Shaw and Trevelyan were among the exceptions.

By 1914 in England Wagner's music drama had supported and sustained many seekers for metaphysical truth. The operas had inspired a socialist interpretation of good and evil, a five-part drama of the evolution of human beings into purely spiritual creatures, proselytizing of Schopenhauer's pessimism, and literary researches into the psychology of erotic and religious passion. *Parsifal,* in particular, provided a spiritual experience for many listeners. Its theme of love and compassion appealed to the religious mind. Its music bathed the listener in a soothing wash of inchoate and luxurious pious emotion. Only a few, like Trevelyan, found the opera amusing or vulnerable to criticism.[102] With Trevelyan's version of *Parsifal,* however, it may be said that the vogue for *Parsifal* had descended from the purely metaphysical regions. World War I would soon be upon Europe, and Wagner the German suddenly seemed more prominent than Wagner the artist of salvation.

6

Conclusion: 1914

E. F. Benson spent June of 1914 at Capri, which he often visited in the summer. In July he expected to return to London to see friends and play golf, and in August he intended to view the second cycle of Wagner operas at the Bayreuth festival.[1] In September and October he was to be again in Capri. He had heard that there were troubles in Ireland and serious strikes threatened at home, but then there were always troubles in Ireland, and threats of strikes were not new. He heard too of the assassination at Sarajevo, but this event also made little impression. He knew nothing about Sarajevo or the archduke. Until the end of July, Benson still felt secure. After all, Serbia was far away and, as for the Kaiser, he was "a mere figure of fun . . . a Valkyrie with a fierce moustache." Thus Benson and many others approached the war that shook a civilization.

In England the Great War brought a caesura to cosmopolitanism as far as Germany was concerned. The Saxe-Coburgs became the Windsors, and many lesser persons also repudiated their Germanic ties. Ford Madox Hueffer, for instance, became Ford Madox Ford. Likewise, in musical circles empathy with German culture received a severe shock. For years, foreigners, many of them German, had dominated English music. This was true not only of composers but also of performers, conductors, and teachers. "Right up to the outbreak of the First World War liberal opinion was biased in favor of the large number of Germans who had settled in England and made positive contributions to English cultural life."[2] Some of these included Carl Engel, music historian; Joseph Mainzer, music publisher; Alfred Jaeger, music consultant to the Novello publishing house and close friend of Elgar; pianoforte teachers Ernest Pauer, Wilhelm Ganz, Wilhelm Kuhe; conductors Franz Rodewald, August Manns, and Charles Hallé; and Carl Rosa, opera impressario. Even in the provinces, effective control of musical affairs "often passed into the cousinly hands of the expatriate *Kapell-* or *Konzertmeister.*"[3]

At the outset of the war many orchestral and choral societies had difficulty deciding the propriety of continuing performances of any music at all during the national emergency. However, in keeping with policy adopted in other areas of national life, most music societies soon agreed to resume "business as usual," although on a limited scale. Thus, eleven days after the declaration of war, the Promenade Concerts opened the season in London. Unfortunately for Wagnerism, the main enthusiasm was for patriotic selections. Among these was "Land of Hope and Glory," which, Lady Elgar recalled, received a standing ovation.[4] The usual weekly Wagner nights were now superseded by a night given to French and Russian music. For the duration of the war and even afterwards a controversy raged over the question of whether to continue to perform "enemy music" and to employ "enemy" performers. A "Music in Wartime" committee was set up to consider the problem of enemy aliens in the music profession.[5] Soon the *Internationale Musikgesellschaft*, of which the Royal Music Association had been a member, became defunct. Articles in the newspapers urged the exclusion of German music from all concert programs. To be sure, Ernest Newman in the *Musical Times* doubted the sanity of prohibiting German music, and the directors of the Promenade Concerts later rescinded their decision. They agreed that a complete boycott of music originating in Germany would be impossible. Nevertheless, as the organization for war gradually became "total," popular attitudes hardened. Although C. Villiers Stanford argued in the *Musical Standard* during 1917 for the retention of Wagner and

Brahms on the grounds that these composers had always been opposed to the spirit of Prussianism, choral conductor Henry Coward vehemently rejected any music written in Germany after 1870. The enmity was, of course, reciprocal. Eugene d'Albert had repudiated his British citizenship in 1882, renounced his repudiation after a successful concert tour in 1902, and repudiated it again during the war. He became a German subject. Houston Stewart Chamberlain, the son of a British admiral and the son-in-law of Wagner, also became a German in a public ceremony. In England he was denounced as a raving renegade.[6] The conductor Hans Richter, who had resided in England from 1897 to 1911, repudiated his honorary doctorates from Manchester and Oxford.[7] The temporary collapse of German influences in 1914 closed the primary episode of Wagnerism in England. Only toward the end of 1919 did "enemy music" return to the programs, "two enthusiastically received performances of Schönberg's String Sextet, at the end of December, being considered to mark the turning point."[8] Schönberg, an Austrian, may have appeared slightly less of an enemy than Wagner. More importantly, his mature style represented a decisive departure from Wagnerian music. Schönberg's experiments in dodecaphony had actually begun as early as 1908 with *Das Buch der hängenden Garten* and were continued in 1912 with *Pierrot Lunaire.* Thus the blackout of Wagner during the Great War for reasons of patriotism only made total what was already a partial eclipse of Wagner brought about by the growing popularity of Schönberg, Stravinsky, Bartok, Satie, all youthful composers competing for the limelight before the war. Even the rising vogue of the cinema was producing a decline in audiences for traditional music.

By 1914 Wagner had become his own Wotan: a god in music whose genius had to be reckoned with even if it were now to be superseded. In England Wagner had obviously made a strong impression on a society that, on the whole, believed that music was no proper pursuit or interest for a gentleman. His way prepared by earnest disciples and his reputation preceded by the fame of the Bayreuth opening in 1876, Wagner became the lion of the London season in 1877. Han Richter's concerts, featuring Wagner's music, opened in 1879 and became regular and popular events of the London scene. Eighteen eighty-eight was an even bigger year for Wagner—perhaps London's greatest Wagner year—when the entire *Ring* cycle was performed four times at Her Majesty's Theatre and *Tristan und Isolde* was given at Drury Lane. These were premieres in London, and they created a new standard and a new mental perspective for a rising generation of operagoers and critics.[9] The 1890s' saw productions of most of Wagner's music dramas in the English language, the bourgeoning of the London Wagner Society, and the publication of an extensive literature on Wagner, testifying to the strength of his public. These works included the complete translation of Wagner's prose; the first of Ernest Newman's books on the master, *Study of Wagner;* and the limited edition of Mary Burrell's *Richard Wagner's Life and Works, 1813–1834*, copies of which soon sold for fifty pounds each.[10] Critics complained that, while there was a Handel festival only once every three years, Wagner "nights" seemed to come three times a week and that even in the provinces Wagner had displaced the older masters. Franz Liszt had once written a series of articles protesting the subordinate position of the artist in the social world. By the end of the century Liszt's friend Wagner, with ego brazen enough for ten artists, had enrolled the Bavarian king, the German nation, and the city of Bayreuth in his cause. In England in 1897, the year of the Queen's Diamond Jubilee, Victoria's son-in-law, the Marquis of Lorne (later Duke of Argyll), wrote the libretto for *Diarmid,* produced by Carl Rosa and composed by Hamish MacCunn. The success of the work was marred only by its lack of originality. The plot closely resembled *Tristan und Isolde.* In the next two decades the *Ring* was produced in English; Wagner's autobiography was published—also in English; and *Parsifal* opened at Covent Garden in January 1914.

In the literature of music Wagner developed important innovations in harmony and orchestration that by 1914 had become quite commonplace. As Bernard Shaw said, "Who now cares about unprepared major ninths, or elevenths, or thirteenths?[11] Then, too, Wagner inspired admirers and musical imitators among the lesser British composers. Rutland Boughton and Reginald Buckley together wrote their own *Music-Drama of the Future* in 1911, praising Wagner's idea of the synthesis of the arts, to which they added English-style choral singing. In 1914 they opened the Glastonbury Festival as an English Bayreuth. Though interrupted by the war, the festival clung to existence until 1926. Arthur Sullivan attended Wagnerian opera at Covent Garden and observed that *Die Meistersinger* was the greatest comic opera ever written.[12] Hubert Parry studied with Edward Dannreuther and, like Dannreuther, acknowledged Wagner as his hero. Villiers Stanford utilized the principle of leitmotives in operas written in his youth, and he owed much to Wagner in his later orchestration as well. Alexander Mackenzie, sent to Germany at the age of ten to study music, absorbed many Wagnerian ideas and composed the music for several librettos by Francis Hueffer. Among the greater British composers, Wagner inspired the early work of Elgar and Holst. Elgar displayed his enthusiasm for the Wagnerian leitmotiv in *The Dream of Gerontius*. Gustav Holst deeply admired Wagner, and Wagner influenced the texture of his harmonic thinking, particularly in *The Mystic Trumpeter*. But these are technical matters best left to the musicologist.

What remains unusual and controversial is that the popularity of Wagner amounted to a "mania" that exceeded the honor due to his musicianship. It is impossible to explain on artistic grounds alone why Wagner was considered worthier than other great composers by so many nineteenth-century Englishmen. Why should there have been Wagnerism but not an *ism* for Mozart or Beethoven? The fact is that Wagner was a cultural phenomenon; his music dramas seemed to offer philosophic and pyschic inspiration to late Victorians in a changing and challenging era.

In the first place, many persons climbed on the Wagnerian raft in order to cross a sea of religious anxiety. Intellectual developments in the nineteenth century had struck a severe blow against religious orthodoxy. These developments included the Darwinian critique of the teleological notion of God and the impact of historical scholarship upon Bible studies. Thus, men strove to retain their inherited or instinctive beliefs and at the same time to accept the conclusions of natural and social science. Tennyson, as poet laureate, argued poignantly for "believing where we cannot prove." The Metaphysical Society debated for ten years the question of whether or not Christianity was a degrading superstition, and came to no conclusion.

By the end of the 1870s a new philosophic idealism, associated with J. N. Stirling, T. H. Green, F. H. Bradley, and others, was emerging from the academic world. However, this scholarly neo-Hegelianism was not to become the property of the common man or the educated layman. Instead, many turned to less intellectual substitutes, including Wagnerism. Almost all of Wagner's operas exhibit a preoccupation with redemption and a hunger for the infinite. Sometimes redemption comes through sexual love, as in *Tristan und Isolde,* and sometimes through selfless renunciation, as in *Parsifal.* The leitmotives, in addition, provide a glossary of moral attitudes and religious symbols to follow in the music. For instance, there are the themes of the Eucharist, the Holy Grail, and faith in *Parsifal,* and the themes of the curse and love's redemption in the *Ring.* Furthermore, Wagner sidestepped the knotty issues raised by biblical criticism. By relying on myth, which needs neither historical nor scientific verification, Wagner offered the listener the experience of religious emotion without requiring him to bother about its intellectual authenticity. By flirting with Buddhism and oriental mysticism via Schopenhauer, Wagner again avoided the rigors and dilemmas of Christian theology, while retaining religious concern. English Wagnerians were most grateful. Alfred Forman and John Payne thought that they lived in a world governed by blind will and deplored it. They found solace both in Wagner's music and in his poems. David Irvine acknowledged that the most radical evil of his day was "the lack of a religion to suit the intellectual requirements of the age." He believed that he lived in a world where man was both God and the Devil. In as much as he saw the Devil dwelling primarily in the Establishment, Irvine invoked Wagner to exorcise him. George Bernard Shaw found Darwinism unsatisfactory. He then created "a metabiological pentateuch," which, together with the *Ring,* he believed was an important addition to vitalist art. William Ashton Ellis insisted that Wagner's music dramas were an acceptable alternative to the "custom-dulled rites of the Church," as well as a release from scientific materialism and a liberal education. The various authors represented in the *Meister* echoed Ellis's sentiments. Progressive-minded Protestant clergymen, Theosophists, and decadents converted to Roman Catholicism, alike, rallied to Wagnerism. Ford Madox Ford even claimed to have heard Wagner mentioned favorably in a sermon at the Wesleyan chapel in D. H. Lawrence's Nottingham.[13] Thus the composer gladdened the hearts of many on a perilous metaphysical passage.

Wagnerism also drew on another deeply experienced need of the late Victorian era—the need for social justice. Victorians lived in an age of unprecedented prosperity. Their enthusiasm for the products of business and industry was bounded only by their perception that not everyone benefited. Herbert Spencer and Samuel Smiles may have explained how God and mammon could be reconciled in a laissez-faire economic system, but their explanations did not always suffice. Wagner in 1848 had participated in a complex European revolution and was for a time thought to be a political as well as an artistic revolutionary. Bernard Shaw seized upon this possibility in Wagner and interpreted the *Ring* as a socialist allegory that included proletarians, capitalists, and corruption of wealth. Again in *Widowers' Houses* he connected Wagnerian symbols with social problems. David Irvine, accusing the church of theft and self-interest, attacked it as a social as well as a spiritual despotism. He hoped his new Wagner-Schopenhaurian philosophical synthesis would further democracy. D. H. Lawrence, though far from being a socialist or a democrat, nevertheless produced a searing condemnation of the quality of life in an industrial society. He cast the antihero of *Women in Love* as a modern Nibelung. George Moore imagined himself the Siegfried of Irish anticlericalism. Lastly, even the skeptical Ernest Newman, for whom the word "redemption" meant a feature of the pawnbroking business, experienced *Parsifal* as "an artist's dream of an ideally innocent world, purged of the lust, hatred, and cruelty that deface the world we live and groan in."[14] Only a few Wagnerians were active political rebels, but many shared a concern for social ethics.

Hence, they deplored materialism in its popular as well as its philosophical meaning.

If the Victorian temper signified materialism, Darwinism, and positivism to the generation of the 1880s and 1890s, it also evoked the image of prudery. The aesthetes of the eighties began a rebellion against prudery by declaring themselves uninterested in morals. The decadents followed in the nineties by studiously probing into the bizarre and unwholesome world of "unnatural" sensation. Havelock Ellis carried out a major scientific and literary inquiry into the psychology of sex, and in politics and family life "the woman question" emerged. If many Wagnerians sought liberation from confining materialist philosophies, so others delighted in publicly exploring the sexual realm of life. Wagner had provided in his music dramas deeply moving interpretations of fundamental human passions. In *Tannhäuser* he pitted lust against chastity, Venus against the pure Elizabeth, with Tannhäuser caught between. In *Tristan und Isolde* he created a concentrated study of erotic passion stripped of most of its medieval framework. In *Parsifal* he belabored the theme of sexual betrayal and ascetic overcoming. Opera lovers labeled his music voluptuous, sensuous, and infernal, terms more emotive than aesthetic in their frame of reference. Wagner haters declared him immoral as man and artist. It is possible that Wagner's placing of the sexual in the context of the mystical provided a barely socially acceptable means by which eroticism might be frankly displayed. Wagnerian and theologian Peter Taylor Forsyth recognized the greatness of the operas and commented that "the passion of sex is the deepest passion of the race, except the passion to be delivered in God from the abuse of passion."[15] For praising Venus in his Tannhäuser poem, Swinburne was pilloried as a "fleshly" poet. Irvine discussed neither *Tristan* nor *Tannhäuser,* yet he approvingly alluded to radical Swedenborgian ideas of sex in the Divinity. Shaw blithely celebrated *Tristan und Isolde* as "universal in its appeal to human sympathy" and asserted that in order to enjoy the opera one need not be a philosopher or a fanatic but only need have had a serious love affair.[16] He, too, in many of his plays, was preoccupied with the meaning of sexuality. The decadents, who relished being pagan and pious, erotic and abstemious at the same time, also loved the *Tristan* opera.[17] Beardsley sketched Tristan, Isolde, and Tannhäuser, wrote a pornographic Tannhäuser novel, and praised the *Ring* as a kind of Black Mass. Oscar Wilde's Dorian-Tannhäuser linked the spiritual esctacies of medieval saints with the morbid confessions of modern sinners. George Moore conjured Wagnerian music in the temptation scenes of his heroine. Other writers followed suit. In short, at the century's end, most literate adolescents, upon whom sexual consciousness was beginning to dawn, knew Tristan, Isolde, and Tannhäuser—primarily through Wagner's operas.

Thus it was that the Wagnerians took their place among the advocates of new attitudes—in the company of anarchists, socialists, spiritualists, "free lovers," "simplelifers," antivivisectionists, Theosophists, vegetarians, jingoists, and suffragettes.[18] By 1914, before the war closed the curtain on German music, many Wagnerians remained faithful to the cause; however, much of the public had turned to new sensations in the arts and to a Sybaritic and unphilosophic enjoyment of what was left of the nineteenth century.

In sum, many intellects of the nineteenth century had lost their faith in Christianity, together with their belief in the rational validity of any metaphysical knowledge. Thus bereft, they had to rely increasingly upon the word of science. Science, particularly scientific determinism, however, could not provide complete and satisfactory answers to the questions of what is the nature of man, how ought human beings treat one another, and how ought they to behave sexually. English Wagnerians sensed this dilemma and to a great extent participated in the revolt against positivism late in the century. In Wagner's music dramas and prose essays, some Wagnerians found the elements with which to revitalize their interest in traditional Christian concepts of love, compassion, and redemption, while others used Wagnerism to restore a spiritual dimension to liberalism or to transcend Darwinism. Still others, in their enjoyment of Wagner's music, participated in the rediscovery of the nonlogical, inexplicable, and erotic aspects of human experience. Of course, English Wagnerians did not produce a consistent system of belief in reaction to scientism, nor, on the other hand, did the entire movement plunge headlong over the cliff of irrationalism. But Wagner was not far wrong when he cursed the English for being a nation of oratoriolovers. For many of them the Bayreuth *Festspielhaus* was a new church.

Notes

Introduction

1. G. K. Chesterton, *Heretics* (London: John Lane, 1905), p. 291.

2. So much so that Paul Henry Lang, when music critic of the *Herald Tribune,* "used to fly into imposing rages every Eastertime when productions of *Parsifal* at the Met were greeted by the audience with reverential silence as though they were attending church services." John Simon, "The Boo Taboo," *New York,* 24 June 1968, p. 47.

3. The important exception is Houston Stewart Chamberlain. However, though born an Englishman, he received his education abroad, wrote his books in German or French, married Wagner's daughter, and became a German citizen. The subject of his first book in 1892 was Wagner's *Lohengrin.* A study of Wagnerian drama appeared in 1892 and a biography of Wagner in 1895. His well-known and controversial work *The Foundations of the Nineteenth Century* appeared in English in 1911, after the height of "Wagnermania" had been reached. His anti-English war essays, entitled *The Ravings of a Renegade Englishman,* were published in England in 1915. He joined the Nazi Party in his last years.

4. Jessie L. Weston, *The Legends of the Wagner Drama: Studies in Mythology and Romance* (London: Nutt, 1900), p. 2.

5. Jacques Barzun, *Darwin, Marx, and Wagner,* 2d ed., rev. (Garden City, N.Y.: Doubleday Anchor, 1958), p. 328.

Chapter 1: The Introduction of Wagner to England: Resistance and Acceptance

1. The Philharmonic returned the score by mail in 1840. Wagner was unable to pay the postage due and refused the parcel. It was returned to London, where it turned up in 1894 in the possession of a broken-down music conductor in a Welsh workhouse. The value of the manuscript was discovered by a buyer in 1904. See Ernest Newman, *The Life of Richard Wagner,* 4 vols. (New York: Knopf, 1933–46), 1:294.

2. Percy A. Scholes, *The Mirror of Music,* 2 vols. (London: Novello, 1947), 1:251.

3. Ibid., p. 252.

4. Johanna sang the music of Meyerbeer, not of Wagner. Her manager, who was also her father, preferred certain financial success to experimentation with new music.

5. Henry Davison, comp., *Music during the Victorian Era. From Mendelssohn to Wagner:*

being the memoirs of J. W. Davison. . . (London: Reeves, 1912), pp. 69–70. This book contains reprints of some of Davison's articles in full and pieces of his articles and conversation stitched together in the main text.

6. Scholes, *Mirror of Music,* 1:85.

7. Davison, *From Mendelssohn to Wagner,* p. 145.

8. Ibid., p. 146.

9. Pierson returned to Germany and there spent the rest of his days.

10. Prosper Sainton (1813–1890) came to England from Toulouse in 1844. Reviews of his farewell concert at the Albert Hall in June 1883 praised him for his contributions to English music.

11. Wagner to Otto Wesendonck, 21 March 1855, in *Letters of Richard Wagner,* ed. Wilhelm Altman, trans. M. M. Bozman, 2 vols. (London: J. M. Dent & sons, 1927), 1:278. Hereafter cited as *Letters.*

12. He discovered that he did not even have the copyright to *Lohengrin,* owing to the decision of the House of Lords to deprive foreign composers of copyright on any works not written for or in England and not having first been published there.

13. On the following day he moved to 22 Portland Terrace, near the north gate of Regent's Park.

14. Praeger wrote a memoir, *Wagner as I Knew Him* (New York: Longmans, Green & Co., 1892).

15. See Davison, *From Mendelssohn to Wagner,* p. 141; Carl Friedrich Glasenapp, *The Life of Richard Wagner,* trans. William Ashton Ellis, 6 vols. (London: Kegan Paul, Trench, Trübner & Co., 1900–1908), vols. 4–6, *The Life of Richard Wagner, by William Ashton Ellis,* by Ellis, 5:41–100. Two, *passim;* Francis Hueffer, *Half a Century of Music in England, 1837–1887* (Philadelphia: Gebbie, 1889), pp. 40–42.

16. Newman, *Life of Wagner,* 2:454.

17. Ibid., p. 264.

18. Ellis, *Life of Wagner,* 5:116. Volume 5, written by Ellis, contains the most complete account of Wagner's reception by the London press.

19. Ibid., p. 118.

20. Praeger, *Wagner as I Knew Him,* p. 221.

21. Ibid.

22. Ellis, *Life of Wagner,* 5:120.

23. Henry Fothergill Chorley, *Modern German Music,* 2 vols. (London: Smith, Elder & Co., 1854), 1:360. See pp. 348–71 passim.

24. *Athenaeum,* no. 1422, 27 January 1855, p. 120, and no. 1423, 3 February 1855, p. 153.

25. Ellis, *Life of Wagner,* 5:166.

26. Glover was also known as a composer, mainly of cantatas.

27. Ellis, *Life of Wagner,* 5:168.

28. He was the father-in-law of Charles Dickens.

29. Ellis, *Life of Wagner,* 5:170.

30. *Times* (London), 14 March 1855, p. 11.

31. *Athenaeum,* no. 1429, 17 March 1855, p. 329.

32. Ellis, *Life of Wagner,* 5:186.

33. Ibid., p. 208.

34. Ibid., p. 213.

35. Ibid., p. 216.

36. Ibid., p. 296.

37. Newman, *Life of Wagner,* 2:463.

38. *Morning Post* (London), 27 June 1855, as quoted in Ellis, *Life of Wagner,* 5:355.

39. *Sunday Times* (London), 1 July 1855, as quoted in Ellis, *Life of Wagner,* 5:356.

40. *Musical World,* 30 June 1855, as quoted in Ellis, *Life of Wagner,* 5:363.

41. George Hogarth, *The Philharmonic Society of London, 1813–1862* (London: Bradbury and Evans, 1862), p. 110.

42. Robert W. Gutman, *Richard Wagner* (New York: Harcourt, Brace & World, 1968), p. 172.

43. Ellis, *Life of Wagner,* 5:304.

44. Richard Wagner, *The Letters of Richard Wagner: The Burrell Collection,* ed. John N. Burk (New York: Macmillan Co., 1950), p. 358 (hereafter cited as *Letters: Burrell Collection*). Before meeting the queen, Wagner was certain that her taste was "trivial to the last degree." Wagner, *Letters,* 1:278.

45. It is interesting to consider how many thousands of modern couples have been married to the strains of the Wedding March.

46. This translation was inept. William Archer later remarked in the *Magazine of Music,* April 1866, that "a schoolboy translating Goethe with a dictionary and grammar, and retaining the exact order of words would produce a sufficiently ludicrous result. This was the procedure adopted by the translator of Wagner, who seems, however, to have made scant use of the Grammar." Quoted in William Ashton Ellis, "Richard Wagner's Prose," *Proceedings of the Royal Music Association* 19 (13 December 1892): 15.

47. Scholes, *Mirror of Music,* 1:252. Manns (1825-1907) originally came over from Germany with a Herr Schallehn's brass band. He conducted the Crystal Palace Orchestra from 1855 to 1901.

48. Constance Bache, *Brother Musicians* (London: Methuen & Co., 1901), p. 200.

49. Ibid., p. 198.

50. Mehlig was a well-known London pianist.

51. Bache, *Brother Musicians,* p. 199.

52. Thomas Wright, *The Life of John Payne* (London: T. F. Unwin, 1919), p. 154. See also chap. 4 of this dissertation.

53. "Lyric Feuds," *Westminster Review* 88 (July 1867): 67.

54. Ibid., p. 69.

55. Hueffer, *Music in England,* pp. 65–66.

56. Francis Hueffer, *Musical Studies* (Edinburgh: A. and C. Black, 1880), p. 135. This is a collection of Hueffer's articles.

57. Davison, *From Mendelssohn to Wagner,* p. 330.

58. Davison died in 1885. His *Musical World* became defunct in 1891. Hueffer died in 1889. G. B. Shaw paid tribute to him in *London Music in 1888–1889, As Heard by Corno di Bassetto (later known as Bernard Shaw)* (London: Constable & Co., (1938), pp. 23–24.

59. *Athenaeum,* no. 2366, 1 March 1873, p. 288.

60. Ibid., no. 2408, 20 December 1873, p. 823.

61. *Athenaeum* reported that many anti-Wagnerians were converted because *Die Meistersinger* seemed close to more orthodox forms of opera.

62. Edward Dannreuther, *Richard Wagner: His Tendencies and Theories* (London: Augener & Co., 1873), p. 19.

63. Ibid., pp. 11–12.

64. Ibid., p. 20.

65. Ibid., p. 71.

66. Scholes, *Mirror of Music*, 1:253. Music critic Hermann Klein in his memoirs agreed with the assessment of the *Musical Times*. In addition, Klein reported that "the opera was received with a warmth that grew and grew till it culminated in a tremendous climax of enthusiasm. The 'tooth-and-nail' opponents of Wagner, who flourished exceedingly in London at this time, were simply dumbfounded." Hermann Klein, *Thirty Years of Musical Life in London, 1870–1900* (New York: Century Co., 1903), p. 44.

67. *Times* (London), 29 August 1876.

68. *Times* (London), 23 August 1876.

69. *Times* (London), 24 August 1876.

70. Joseph Bennett, *Letters from Bayreuth* (London: Novello, Ewer, 1877), p. 23.

71. Ibid., pp. 146–47.

72. Ibid., pp. 36, 43.

73. Ibid., p. 50.

74. Ibid., p. 63.

75. Ibid., p. 77.

76. Ibid., pp. 98–99.

77. Shaw, *London Music*, p. 309.

78. Bache, *Brother Musicians*, p. 246.

79. Ibid., p. 250.

80. The concerts took place on 7, 9, 12, 14, 16, and 19 May and 28 and 29 May.

81. Scholes, *Mirror of Music*, 1:250.

82. *Athenaeum*, no. 2585, 12 May 1877, p. 618.

83. Quoted in Max Moser, *Richard Wagner in der englischen Literatur des XIX Jahrhunderts* (Bern: A. Franke, 1938), p. 12.

84. Charles L. Graves, *Mr. Punch's History of Modern England*, 4 vols. (New York: Frederick A. Stokes Co., n.d.), 3:357.

85. Moncure Daniel Conway, *Autobiography*, Memories, and Experiences, 2 vols. (London: Cassell & Co., 1904), 2:337.

86. Hueffer, *Music in England*, p. 72.

87. Conway, *Autobiography*, 1:388–89. Conway could remember Dannreuther, as a boy, playing the organ in Conway's Unitarian Church in Cincinatti.

88. George Eliot, *The Writings of George Eliot: Life, Letters*, and *Journals*, 25 vols. (New York: AMS Press, 1970), 23:271.

89. Charles L. Graves, *Hubert Parry*, 2 vols. (London: Macmillan & Co., 1926), 1:176.

90. Ibid., p. 177.

91. Ibid., p. 178.

92. Ibid., p. 168.

93. "Parry relates that he had difficulty finding someone to escort Cosima to a soirée at the Grosvenor Gallery on the 9th. He at last secured a lady of high rank 'who to my surprise was quite willing, and I thought rather pleased to have a lioness in tow, notwithstanding the inclination of Society to taboo a person who puts "frau Richard Wagner, geb. Liszt" on her cards, and who was as long as the humour lasted, the wife of Bülow. But I put it to my friend that she would be escorting the daughter of her "old friend Liszt" and that bait took.' " Graves, *Hubert, Parry,* 1:278.

94. Herbert Spencer, *An Autobiography,* 2 vols. (New York: Appleton, 1904), 1:350. Spencer's remarks about Wagner resemble Wagner's remarks about his rival Meyerbeer.

95. The *Ring* was presented at Her Majesty's Theatre under Angelo Neumann; *Die Meistersinger* and *Tristan und Isolde* were presented at Drury Lane under Richter.

96. Hueffer, *Music in London,* p. 80.

97. Ibid., p. 79.

98. *Times,* (London), 14 February 1883, p. 9.

99. *Saturday Review,* 17 February 1883, pp. 205–6.

100. *Athenaeum,* 2886, 17 February 1883, pp. 224–25.

101. The parent society (Allgemeine Wagner Gesellschaft) was founded in 1878 in Bayreuth and claimed eight thousand members and three hundred branches.

102. *Meister* 1, no. 4 (1888):149.

103. According to Louis N. Parker in "Lettre D'Angleterre," *Revue Wagnérienne* 2, no. 4 (8 May 1887): 114–119, Moseley was one of the founders of the society.

104. Quoted in Moser, *Richard Wagner,* p. 13.

105. He defended his rights to the Twickenham Ferry after another had set up a rival in the early years of the twentieth century. He took the case to the House of Lords and lost in 1915. He occupied Ham House in London

106. Ellis, *Life of Wagner,* 5:376. Ellis qualified as a physician in 1878. He was assistant medical officer at the Western Dispensary, a life member and lecturer of the British Red Cross Society, secretary of the Association of Members of the Royal College of Surgeons, and assistant demonstrator in anatomy at St. George's General Hospital. He also wrote on the reform of the Royal College of Surgeons in the late nineties. He died on 2 January 1919. *Times* (London), 4 January 1919, p. 3.

107. Stephen E. Koss, *Lord Haldane* (New York: Columbia University Press, 1969), p. 54.

108. *Meister* 1, no. 1 (1888): 3.

109. There were five thousand English at Bayreuth in 1894.

110. *Meister* 1, no. 1 (1888): 4.

111. By Percy Anderson, described as a well-known artist and steadfast admirer of Wagner's dramas.

112. Shaw, *London Music,* p. 17.

113. *Meister* 1, no. 2 (1888): 38.

114. Bernard Shaw, *Music in London, 1890–1894,* 3 vols. (London: Constable & Co., 1931), 114, 2:21, 3:111–12.

115. *Meister* 2, no. 8 (1889): 109.

116. Ibid., no. 5 (1889): 5.

117. Ibid. 3, no. 9 (1890): 3.

118. Ibid., p. 6.

119. Ibid. 4, no. 16 (1891): 123.

120. Cyriax died on 29 September 1892.

121. *Meister* 5, no. 20 (1892): 103.

122. Ibid., pp. 100–101.

123. Ibid. 2, no. 6 (1893): 71.

124. Hueffer, in *Music in England,* pp. 42–43, had already hinted at this.

125. Ellis, *Life of Wagner,* 5:385.

126. See William Ashton Ellis, *Wagner Sketches: 1849, A Vindication* (London, Kegan Paul, Trench, Trübner & Co., 1892).

127. Ellis, *Life of Wagner,* 5:384.

128. Ibid., p. 381.

129. Ibid., pp. 415, 417. Ellis suspected that Praeger's widow was the instigator.

130. Dysart owned the manuscripts of Praeger's work.

131. C. A. Barry, "Introductory to the Study of Wagner's Comic Opera *Die Meistersinger von Nurnburg,"* *Proceedings of the Royal Music Association* 7 (7 March 1881): 91.

132. They concluded that Wagner's music was not noisy.

133. H. F. Frost, "Some Remarks on Richard Wagner's Music-Drama *Tristan und Isolde,"* *Proceedings of the Royal Music Association* 8 (1 May 1882): 148.

134. Ibid., p. 160–61.

135. Ibid., p. 165.

136. J. S. Shedlock, "Wagner and Liszt Correspondence," *Proceedings of the Royal Music Association* 14 (2 April 1888): 119–20.

137. Ibid., p. 132.

138. Ibid., p. 134.

139. Henry Cart, "Richard Wagner," *Proceedings of the Royal Music Association* 16 (3 February 1890): p. 73.

140. Ibid., p. 77.

141. Ellis, "Richard Wagner's Prose," p. 29.

142. Ibid., p. 24.

143. Ibid., p. 26.

144. In 1892 and 1893, respectively. Naylor was also a composer of opera.

145. H. W. L. Hime, *Wagnerism: A Protest* (London: Kegan Paul, Trench & Co., 1882), p. 22.

146. Ibid., p. 37.

147. Edmund Gurney, "Wagner and Wagnerism," *Nineteenth Century* 13 (March 1883): 451.

148. Ibid., p. 444.

149. J. F. Rowbotham, "The Wagner Bubble," *Nineteenth Century* 24 (October 1888): 501–12 passim.

150. C. Villiers Stanford, "The Wagner Bubble: A Reply," *Nineteenth Century* 24 (November 1888): 27.

151. J. Cuthbert Hadden, "The Wagner Mania," *Nineteenth Century* 44 (July 1898): 131.

Chapter 2: Bernard Shaw, Wagnerite

1. Charles Archer, *William Archer* (New Haven, Conn.: Yale University Press, 1931), p. 119.

2. W. H. Auden (himself a Wagnerite) has claimed that Shaw "was probably the best music critic who ever lived." See his article "The Fabian Figaro," in *George Bernard Shaw: A Critical Survey*, ed. Louis Kronenberger (New York: World Publishing Co., 1953), p. 156. See also the article on Shaw in Grove's. *A Dictionary of Music and Musicians* ed. Eric Blom, 10 vols., 5th ed. (London: Macmillan & Co., 1954), 7:743, and an article by George S. Barber entitled "Shaw's Contribution to Music Criticism," PMLA 72 (December 1957): 1005–17.

3. Jacques Barzun, "Bernard Shaw in Twilight," in *George Bernard Shaw: A Critical Survey*, ed. Louis Kronenberger (New York: World Publishing Co., 1953), p. 165.

4. Shaw to Hueffer, 7 January 1883, in *Collected Letters of Bernard Shaw, 1874–1897*, ed. Dan Laurence (New York: Dodd, Mead & Co., 1965), p. 55.

5. Bernard Shaw, *London Music in 1888–1889, As Heard by Corno di Bassetto (Later Known as Bernard Shaw)* (London: Constable & Co., 1938), p. 244.

6. *Musical Review*, 10 and 17 March 1883.

7. Shaw *London Music*, p. viii.

8. Ernest Belfort Bax. *Reminiscences and Reflexions of a Mid and Late Victorian* (New York: T. Seltzer, 1920), p. 66.

9. G. B. Shaw, *Music in London, 1890–1894*, 3 vols. (London: Constable & Co., 1931), 2:259.

10. Shaw, *London Music*, p. 322.

11. Ibid., p. xxx.

12. Ibid., p. xxxi.

13. Ibid., p. 156.

14. Ibid., p. 152.

15. Ibid., p. 153.

16. Ibid., p. 162.

17. Ibid., p. 151.

18. Ibid., p. 163.

19. Ibid., pp. 162–63.

20. Shaw, *Music in London*, 2:120.

21. Ibid., 1:141–42.

22. Ibid., 2:280.

23. Unlike many Wagnerites, Shaw appreciated Verdi; however, his blind spot was Brahms.

24. Max Nordau, *Degeneration*, 8th ed. (New York: Appleton, 1896), p. 194.

25. Bernard Shaw, *The Sanity of Art* (New York: B. R. Tucker, 1908), pp. 88–89.

26. Stephen Winsten, ed., *G. B. S. at 90: Aspects of Bernard Shaw's Life and Work* (New York: Dodd, Mead & Co., 1946), p. 26. According to Winsten: "Nordau visited us many years afterwards and confessed himself a convert. . . . He had brought his daughter with him whom he wanted to train as an artist and he sat down and read to us from Shaw's *The Sanity of Art.*"

27. New editions appeared in 1902–13 and 1922.

28. Bernard Shaw, *The Perfect Wagnerite: A Commentary on the Niblung's Ring* (New York: Dover Publications, 1967), p. 2.

29. Ibid., p. 9.

30. Ibid., p. 11.

31. Ibid.

32. Ibid., p. 17.

33. Ibid., p. 44. Shaw's own spelling and translation.

34. Ibid., p. 63.

35. Ibid., p. 67.

36. Ibid., p. 87.

37. Ibid., p. 101.

38. Ibid., pp. 28–29.

39. Oswald Mosley, leader of the British Fascist Union and also a Wagnerite, attempted to reconcile Shaw and Wagner by suggesting that Parsifal was the next stage in the evolution of human life. Parsifal achieved a synthesis of life and love: "He does not deny life but, through his final renunciation fulfills life's creative purpose. . . . That is what man must aim at becoming; this, I believe, is the message of the *Ring.*" Mosley, *Wagner and Shaw: A Synthesis* (London: Sanctuary Press, 1956), p. 61.

40. Shaw, *Perfect Wagnerite,* p. xii.

41. G. B. Shaw, "Memoranda," Appendix 1 of Edward R. Pease, *The History of the Fabian Society* (London: F. Cass, 1963), pp. 278–79.

42. Only H. M. Hyndman of the Social Democratic Federation told Shaw concerning Wagner: "I was playing his overtures in the orchestra before you were breeched." Henry Mayer Hyndman, *Further Reminiscences* (London: Macmillan & Co., 1912), p. 211.

43. Bernard Shaw, *Immaturity* (London: Constable & Co., 1938), pp. 161–62.

44. Bernard Shaw, *Cashel Byron's Profession, The Works of Bernard Shaw* (London: Constable & Co., 1938), 4:91.

45. Ibid., p. 92.

46. Archer, *William Archer,* p. 118.

47. William Irvine, *The Universe of G. B. S.* (New York: Russell and Russell, 1968), p. 155.

48. Shaw, *Collected Letters,* pp. 175, 188.

49. Bernard Shaw, *Man and Superman, The Theatre of Bernard Shaw,* ed. Alan S. Downer (New York: Dodd, Mead & Co., 1969), p. 421.

50. Martin Meisel, *Shaw and the Nineteenth-Century Theatre* (Princeton, N.J.: Princeton University Press, 1963), p. 60. Meisel's sources were manuscript letters of Shaw to Siegfried Trebitsch, 20 July 1919 and 15 September 1920. See also Bryan Magee, *Aspects of Wagner* (New York: Stein and Day, 1969), p. 94.

51. Bernard Shaw, *Back to Methusaleh, Complete Plays, with Prefaces,* 6 vols. (New York: Dodd, Mead & Co., 1962), 2:lxxiv.

52. Ibid., p. xix.

53. Ibid., 2:lxxxi.

54. Ibid., p. lxxii.

55. Ibid., Postscript after Twenty-five Years, p. cv.

56. Ibid., p. lxxxii.

57. Shaw first heard the name Nietzsche from a German mathematician in 1891. At that time he complained of his lack of training in the German language. English translations of the philosopher's works began to be available only after 1896. See David S. Thatcher, *Nietzsche in England, 1890-1914* (Toronto: University of Toronto Press, 1970), pp. 176–77; see also James W. Groshong, "George Bernard Shaw and Germany" (Ph.D. diss., Stanford University, 1957).

58. Janice Henson, "Bernard Shaw's Contribution to the Wagner Controversy in England," *Shaw Review* 4, no. 1 (January 1961): 26. Also Richard Wagner, *Richard Wagner's Prose Works,* trans. William Ashton Ellis, 8 vols. (New York: Broude, 1966), 46–68. It has also been argued that the portrait of Louis Dubedat in this play is partially based on Wagner's character "R" in the same source. See Elsie B. Adams, *Bernard Shaw and the Aesthetes* (Columbus: Ohio State University Press, 1971) pp. 127–29.

59. Bernard Shaw, *Androcles and the Lion, Complete Plays, with Prefaces,* 6 vols. (New York, 1962), 5:387.

60. Meisel, *Shaw and Nineteenth-Century Theatre,* pp. 38–61 passim.

61. Shaw's rehearsal notes included sharps, flats, clefs, and key signatures.

62. Quoted in Gerald Weales, *Religion in Modern English Drama* (Philadelphia: University of Pennsylvania Press, 1961), p. 51.

63. Meisel, *Shaw and Nineteenth-Century Theatre,* p. 61.

64. Edmund Wilson, "Bernard Shaw at Eighty" in *George Bernard Shaw: A Critical Survey,* ed. Louis Kronenberger (New York: World Publishing Co., 1953), p. 141.

65. Groshong, *"George Bernard Shaw and Germany,"* p. 141.

66. Bernard Shaw, *How to Become a Music Critic,* ed. Dan H. Laurence (New York: Hill & Wang, 1961), p. 147.

67. Quoted in Magee, *Aspects of Wagner* p. 60.

68. G. K. Chesterton, "The Critic," in *George Bernard Shaw: A Critical Survey,* ed. Louis Kronenberger (New York: World Publishing Co., 1953), p. 30.

Chapter 3: David Irvine, Schopenhauer, and Wagner

1. *Westminster Review* 59 (April 1853): 202–12.

2. See articles by James Sully in *Cornhill Magazine* 33 (April 1876): 431–43 and by Francis Hueffer in the *Fortnightly Review,* 26 (December 1876): 773–92. See also Helen Zimmern, *Schopenhauer: His Life and His Philosophy* (London: Longmans, 1876), and James Sully, *Pessimism* (London: Henry S. King, 1877).

3. Thomas Mann, *Essays of Three Decades* (New York: Knopf, 1965), p. 394.

4. Victor Plarr, *Ernest Dowson, 1888-1897* (New York: L. J. Gomme, 1914), p. 48. See also John A. Lester, Jr., *Journey through Despair, 1880-1914* (Princeton, N.J.: Princeton University Press, 1968), p. 65 and pp. 55–80 passim.

5. See Francis Hueffer, "Arthur Schopenhauer," *Fortnightly Review* 26 (December 1876): 773–92, and William Ashton Ellis, "Wagner and Schopenhauer," *Fortnightly Review* 71 (March 1899): 413–32.

6. After Forman heard his first Wagner concert in 1873, he purchased Wagner's collected writings and set about translating his poetry. Forman and Dannreuther secured the stage props for the first *Ring* performance in 1876, a humorously exasperating task described by W. Courtope Forman in the *Daily Telegraph,* 12 July 1930. Forman met Wagner in London in 1877. He was a member of the refounded Wagner Society of 1884 and of the *Schopenhauer Gesellschaft.*

7. Alfred Forman, *Sonnets* (London: Privately printed, 1886), p. 10.

8. Ibid., p. 50.

9. Ibid., p. 31.

10. Ibid., p. 20.

11. R. B. Haldane, also a Wagnerite, translated Schopenhauer but admired Hegel more.

12. David Irvine, *Wagner's "Ring of the Nibelung" and the Conditions of Ideal Manhood* (London: H. Grevel & Co., 1897), *A Wagnerian's Midsummer Madness* (London: H. Grevel & Co., 1899), *"Parsifal" and Wagner's Christianity* (London: H. Grevel & Co., 1899), *Philosophy and Christianity* (London: Watts & Co., 1905), *Metaphysical Rudiments of Liberalism* (London: Watts & Co., 1911), *Wagner's Bad Luck* (London: Watts & Co., 1911), *The Badness of Wagner's Bad Luck* (London: Watts & Co., 1912), and a translation of Schopenhauer's *Transcendent Speculations on Apparent Design in the Fate of the Individual,* in memory of Wagner (London: Watts and Co., 1913).

13. Bernard Shaw, *Collected Letters of Bernard Shaw, 1874–1897,* ed. Dan H. Laurence (New York: Dodd, Mead & Co., 1965), p. 815.

14. Carl Friedrich Glasenapp, *The Life of Richard Wagner,* trans. William Ashton Ellis, 6 vols. (London: Kegan Paul, Trench, Trübner & Co., 1900–1908), vols. 4–6, *The Life of Richard Wagner, by William Ashton Ellis,* by Ellis, 6:448.

15. Death Certificate, District of Warringah at Mosman, New South Wales, Australia.

16. Irvine, *Metaphysical Rudiments,* p. viii.

17. Ibid., p. xxi.

18. Irvine, *Wagner's "Ring,"* p. 225.

19. Irvine, *Metaphysical Rudiments,* p. xiii.

20. Irvine, *Wagner's "Ring,"* p. 8.

21. Ibid., p. 42.

22. Ibid., p. 44.

23. Ibid., p. 66.

24. Ibid., p. 67.

25. Ibid., p. 69.

26. Ibid., p. 70. If Irvine believed in a Trinity, it would have consisted of Oliphant, Wagner, and Schopenhauer, for he bracketed these three frequently. Oliphant had several careers, culminating in his discipleship to T. L. Harris, founder of the Brotherhood of the New Life.

27. Ibid., p. 71.

28. Ibid., p. 72.

29. Ibid., p. 210.

30. Ibid., p. 171.

31. Ibid., p. 161.

32. Ibid., p. 223.

33. Ibid.

34. Ibid., p. 15.

35. Ibid., p. 226.

36. Irvine, *Wagnerian's Midsummer Madness,* p. 232.

37. Ibid., p. 241.

38. Ibid., p. 247.

39. Ibid., p. 255.

40. Irvine, *Philosophy and Christianity,* p. 7.

41. Irvine, *Parsifal,* p. 26.

42. Ibid., p. 136.

43. Ibid., p. 152.

44. Ibid., p. 301.

45. Oliphant believed in an arcane meaning of the Bible and Kabbala. Irvine often quoted Oliphant on the nature of symbolical and metaphorical meanings.

46. Ibid., p. 313.

47. Ibid., p. 332.

48. Ibid., p. 302.

49. Ibid., p. 337.

50. Ibid., p. 351.

51. Robert W. Gutman, *Richard Wagner* (New York: Harcourt, Brace & World, 1968), p. 431.

52. Irvine, *Parsifal,* p. 223.

53. Ibid, pp. 224, 228.

54. Ibid., p. 225.

55. Ibid., p. 209.

56. Gutman, *Richard Wagner,* p. 241.

57. Irvine, *Parsifal,* p. 233.

58. Ibid., p. 243.

59. Ibid., p. 229.

60. Ibid., p. 243.

61. Ibid., p. 245.

62. Ibid.

63. Ibid., p. 246.

64. Gutman, *Richard Wagner,* p. 424.

65. Ibid., p. 425.

66. Irvine, *Parsifal,* p. 262.

67. Ibid., pp. 264, 270.

68. Ibid., p. 218, and Irvine, *Metaphysical Rudiments,* pp. 98–99.

69. Irvine, *A Wagnerian's Midsummer Madness,* p. 13.

70. Ibid., p. 44.

71. Irvine, *Wagner's Bad Luck,* p. 116.

72. Ibid., p. 5.

73. Gutman, *Richard Wagner,* pp. 224–25.

74. Irvine, *Badness of Wagner's Bad Luck,* p. 15.

75. Ibid., p. 42.

76. *Spectator,* 26 August 1911, p. 315.

77. Ibid., p. 316.

78. Irvine, *Badness of Wagner's Bad Luck,* p. 25.

79. Ibid., p. 33.

80. Ibid., p. 34. Irvine much preferred the liberal Roman Catholic Hilaire Belloc's *Eye Witness.* He hoped for a similar but non-Catholic journal in the liberal camp and regretted that no wealthy Wagnerian patron had been found to finance such a paper.

81. *Saturday Review,* 24 June 1911, p. 773.

82. Irvine, *A Wagnerian's Midsummer Madness,* pp. 127–28.

83. Ernest Newman, "Wagner and His Autobiography," *Fortnightly Review* 96 (July 1911),: pp. 75–85 passim.

84. Ibid., p. 85.

85. Ibid., p. 81.

86. Irvine, *Badness of Wagner's Bad Luck,* pp. 86–87.

87. Ibid., p. 100.

88. Ibid., p. 119.

89. Ibid., p.121.

90. Irvine, *Philosophy and Christianity,* p. 11.

91. Irvine, *Parsifal,* pp. 417–18.

92. This book was originally undertaken to correct William Ashton Ellis's interpretation of Schopenhauer in volume 6 of his and Glasenapp's *Life of Wagner.* Ellis attributed Schopenhauer's pessimism to eye strain and migraine headaches.

93. Irvine, *Metaphysical Rudiments,* p. 13.

94. Ibid., p. 25.

95. Ibid., p. 280.

96. Irvine, *A Wagnerian's Midsummer Madness,* p. 89.

Chapter 4: Wagner among the Literati

1. W. Somerset Maugham, *Of Human Bondage* (New York: Modern Library, 1915), p. 229.

2. Matthew Arnold, *Letters of Matthew Arnold, 1848–1888,* ed. G. W. E. Russell, 2 vols. (Grosse Point, Mich.: Scholarly Press, 1968), 2:374.

3. Edward Robert was the son of Sir Edward George Bulwer-Lytton, who wrote the novel *Rienzi,* from which Wagner's first successful opera was derived. Perhaps his best-known work was *The Last Days of Pompeii.* The younger Edward's pseudonym was Owen Meredith.

4. Robert Lytton, *Julian Fane: A Memoir* (London: John Murray, 1872), p. 136.

5. Ibid., p. 114.

6. *Westminster Review* 76 (October 1861): 366.

7. See Georgiana Macdonald Burne-Jones, *Memorials of Edward Burne-Jones,* 2 vols. (New York: Macmillan Co., 1904); William Bell Scott, *Autobiographical Notes,* ed. W. Minto (New York: Harper & Bros., 1892); J. W. Mackail, *The Life of William Morris,* 2 vols. (New York: B. Blom, 1968); May Morris, *William Morris: Artist, Writer, Socialist,*

2 vols. (Oxford: B. Blackwell, 1936). Scott was responsible for a limerick about Hueffer:

> There's a solid fat German called Hueffer:
> Who of anything funny's a duffer:
> To proclaim Schopenhauer
> From the top of a tower
> Will be the last effort of Hueffer.

8. William Gaunt, *The Pre-Raphaelite Dream* (New York: Schocken Books, 1966), p. 31.

9. Philip Henderson, *William Morris: His Life, Work, and Friends* (New York: McGraw-Hill, 1967), pp. 91–92.

10. Henderson, *William Morris,* p. 169.

11. Mackail, *Life of Morris,* 1:300.

12. Ibid.

13. Robert W. Gutman, *Volsunga Saga,* trans. William Morris (New York: Collier Books, 1962), p. 72.

14. Henderson, *William Morris,* p. 170.

15. Namely, "A Dead Friend," "Past Days," and "Autumn and Winter."

16. Mollie Painter-Downes, "Algernon Charles Swinburne and Theodore Watts-Dunton," pt. 2, *New Yorker,* 30 January 1971, p. 42.

17. When in 1869, Powell and Swinburne contemplated hearing *Die Walküre* in London, they may have planned to attend a private recital of this society. The opera's first public performance took place in Munich in 1870.

18. Algernon C. Swinburne, *The Swinburne Letters,* ed. Cecil Y. Lang, 6 vols. (New Haven, Conn.: Yale University Press, 1952), 1:99.

19. Ibid., 2:11, 38.

20. Ibid., p. 183.

21. Ibid., p. 231.

22. Ibid., 1:250. Paragraph from a letter dated 13 July 1867. This letter is puzzling since the *Ring* was not yet complete and the proposed Wagner Theatre in Munich never begun. Possibly, the original editor, Edmund Gosse, mistakenly united two different letters. Or perhaps Gosse (or Swinburne) reversed digits and wrote "67" when he meant "76." *Lohengrin* was first performed in London in May 1875. Swinburne went abroad with Nicol in the spring of 1876. Perhaps they intended to stop at Bayreuth for the premiere of the *Ring.* In any case, the originals of the letters are said to have been destroyed.

23. Georges Lafourcade, *Swinburne: A Literary Biography* (New York: Russell and Russell, 1967), p. 184.

24. See Léon Guichard, *La Musique et les lettres en France au temps du Wagnérisme* (Paris: Presses Universitaires de France, 1963), for a discussion of Baudelaire, French poetry, and Wagner.

25. Baudelaire entrusted the letter to Felix Nadar, who forgot to deliver it.

26. John A. Cassidy in *Algernon C. Swinburne* (New York: Twayne Publishers, 1964), p. 103, argues that Swinburne in his *Notes* deliberately lied about not receiving the pamphlet before writing the poem, that *Laus Veneris* is an allegory of his unhappy love affair with Mary Gordon, terminated early in 1864, and that Swinburne, troubled

by the mounting notoriety of his poem, wished to conceal any autobiographical references. Cassidy states:

> If we imagine London as the Horselberg, the life of abnormal sexual excesses there as Venus, Swinburne as Tannhäuser, Mary Gordon's rejection as the Pope's and Swinburne's return to the vile life as Tannhäuser's re-entry into the Venusberg, the parallel is almost perfect—almost, except for the belated forgiveness that comes with the blossoming of the Pope's staff.

Georges Lafourcade, *Swinburne,* pp. 99–100, also mentions an unhappy and obscure love affair during 1863–64.

27. Lionel Stevenson, *The Ordeal of George Meredith* New York: Scribner, 1953), pp. 113–14.

28. Francis Jacques Sypher, Jr., "Swinburne and Wagner," *Victorian Poetry* 19 (Summer 1971):171.

29. Such as Gautier's account of *Tannhäuser,* in *Le Moniteur,* 29 September 1857.

30. Samuel Chew, *Swinburne* (Hamden, Conn.: Archon Books, 1966), p. 89.

31. Sypher, "Swinburne and Wagner," p. 170.

32. Algernon C. Swinburne, *Poetical and Dramatical Works* (New York: John D. Williams, 1887), p. 14.

33. Chew, *Swinburne,* p. 168.

34. Swinburne, *Letters,* 1:xxxi.

35. John R. Reed, "Swinburne's *Tristram of Lyonesse:* The Poet-Lover's Song of Love," *Victorian Poetry* 4, no. 2 (Spring 1966): 100.

36. Quoted in Lafourcade, *Swinburne,* p. 185.

37. Max Moser, *Richard Wagner in der englischen Literatur des XIX Jahrhunderts* (Bern: A. Franke, 1938), p. 43.

38. Francis Fergusson, *The Idea of a Theatre* (Garden City, N.Y.: Doubleday & Co., 1949), p. 87.

39. Richard Wagner, *Tristan and Isolde,* trans. Stewart Robb (New York: E. P. Dutton & Co., 1965), p. 150.

40. Wagner, *Tristan und Isolde,* p. 63.

41. Swinburne, *Poetical and Dramatical Works,* p. 729.

42. Ibid., p. 673.

43. Ibid., p. 811.

44. John Payne, *Autobiography* (Olney, near Bedford: Thomas Wright, 1926), pp. 11–12.

45. Moser, *Richard Wagner* pp. 45–46.

46. Payne, *Autobiography,* p. 21.

47. Members of Payne's Featherstone Club included J. T. Nettleship the painter, Arthur O'Shaughnessy the poet, E. B. Baxter, Sir H. S. Cotton, Sir Edmund W. Byrne, and Sir C. J. Lyall. Without offering any other evidence, Thomas Wright goes on to say of Payne: "Indeed, it was largely owing to his efforts that Wagner eventually obtained vogue in this country." Thomas Wright, *The Life of John Payne* (London: T. F. Unwin, 1919), p. 154.

48. John Payne, *"The Masque of Shadows" and other Poems* (London: B. M. Pickering, 1870), pp. 145–222.

49. Ibid., pp. 59–141.

50. John Payne, *Intaglios* (London: B. M. Pickering, 1871), p. 59.

51. John Payne, *Songs of Life and Death* (London: H. S. King & Co., 1872), p. vi.

52. R. C. K. Ensor, *England, 1870–1914* (Oxford: Clarendon Press, 1960), p. 304.

53. Ibid., p. 333, and Moser, *Richard Wagner*, p. 53.

54. Ernest Belfort Bax, *Reminiscences and Reflexions of a Mid and Late Victorian* (New York: T. Seltzer, 1920), pp. 63–64.

55. Arthur Symons, *Dramatis Personae* (Indianapolis, Ind.: Bobbs-Merrill Co., 1923), p. 97.

56. Arthur Symons, *Aubrey Beardsley* (London: At the Sign of the Unicorn, 1898), as quoted in Stanley Weintraub, *Beardsley* (New York: G. Braziller, 1967), p. 140.

57. Aubrey Beardsley, *Letters from Aubrey Beardsley to Leonard Smithers* (London: First Edition Club, 1937(, Letters 62, 64.

58. Reproductions may be found in Aubrey Beardsley, *The Early Work of Aubrey Beardsley* (New York: Dover Publications, 1967), and in *The Later Work of Aubrey Beardsley* (New York: Dover Publications, 1967).

59. Beardsley, *Letters to Smithers*, Letter 60. Emphasis added.

60. Ibid., Letters 21, 58.

61. Edmund Wilson, *The Shores of Light* (New York: Vintage, 1961), p. 71.

62. Aubrey Beardsley and John Glassco, *Under the Hill* (New York: Grove Press, 1959), p. 60. Glassco used the unexpurgated version and added his own ending to the incomplete story.

63. Shaw modeled Louis Dubedat in *The Doctor's Dilemma* partially on the character of Beardsley.

64. French novels frequently were covered in yellow. This was one of the reasons why the editors chose the color in the first place. Beardsley's sole connection with Wilde was his illustrations for Wilde's *Salome*.

65. It was said that Wilde's model for Dorian was John Gray, a homosexual poet of decadence and later the convert to the Roman Catholic priesthood who received Beardsley into the church when Beardsley was on his deathbed. Gray at the time denied any connection with the book, but a letter to Wilde survives in which he signed himself "Dorian." In his *Silverpoints*, a collection of poems, a translation of Verlaine's "Parsifal" appears. Charles Ryskamp, ed., *Wilde and the Nineties* (Princeton, N.J.: Princeton University Press, 1966), p. 45.

66. Oscar Wilde, *The Picture of Dorian Gray* (New York: Tudor, 1930), p. 185.

67. Ibid., p. 200. For other Wagnerian references, see pp. 65–66.

68. "During Music," a poem by Arthur Symons in his *Silhouettes* (London: John Lane, 1892), may also owe something to Wagner.

> The music had the heat of blood,
>   A passion that no words can reach;
> We sat together, and understood
>   Our hearts' speech,

We had no need for word or sign,
The music spoke for us, and said
All that her eyes could read in mine
Or mine in hers had read.

69. Acts 2, 3, 4 follow Wagner's opera. Act 1 takes place in the court of Iseult of Ireland. Symons also reintroduces Iseult of Brittany, that is, Iseult of the White Hands.

70. Arthur Symons, *Tristan and Iseult* (New York: Brentanos 1917), p. 20.

71. Ibid., p. 43.

72. Ibid., p. 44.

73. Ibid., p. 92.

74. Arthur Symons, *Plays, Acting, and Music* (New York: E. P. Dutton & Co., 1909), p. 299.

75. Ibid., pp. 300–301.

76. Ibid., pp. 306–7.

77. Ibid., p. 314.

78. Ernest Dowson, author of "Cynara," often called *the* poem of English decadence, frequently attended performances of Wagnerian opera, according to his friend and biographer, Victor Plarr. Plarr, *Ernest Dowson, 1888–1897* (New York: L. J. Glomme, 1914), p. 27.

79. Ryskamp, ed., *Wilde and the Nineties*, p. 27.

80. John Davidson, *New Ballads* (London: John Lane, 1897), p. 117.

81. Moser, *Richard Wagner*, p. 91.

82. George Moore, *Memoirs of My Dead Life* (New York: Boni & Lireright, 1920), p. 278.

83. George Moore, *Hail and Farewell*, 2 vols. (New York: Appleton-Century-Crofts, 1925), 1:177. His friend Edward Martyn, Irish playwright and founder of the Irish Literary Theatre, was also a Wagnerite, as was Annie Horniman, who subsidized the Abbey Theatre. On Irish Wagnerites, see William Blissett, "George Moore and Literary Wagnerism," *The Man of Wax: Critical Essays on George Moore*, ed. Douglas A. Hughes (New York, 1971), pp. 185–215.

84. Moore, *Hail and Farewell*, 1:178–79.

85. Ibid., p. 193.

86. Ibid., 2:390.

87. Zola and Cézanne were members of the Marseilles Wagner Society.

88. George Moore, *Spring Days* (London: Vizetelly & Co., 1888), pp. 313–14.

89. George Moore, *Evelyn Innes*, 2 vols. (London: T. F. Unwin, 1898), 1:93.

90. Ibid., 106.

91. Ibid., p. 195.

92. Ibid., 2:41–42.

93. Ibid., 1:211.

94. Ibid., 2:7.

95. In the novel Dean writes "Grania." The opera manager comments that he is glad "Grania" is based on a legend. "Wagner had shown that an opera could

not be written except on a legendary basis. The Irish legends were just the thing the public was prepared to take an interest in." Ibid., 1:245. Moore and Yeats collaborated on a play, *Diarmuid and Grania,* for the Irish stage, based on Irish legend and Wagnerian motifs.

96. Ibid., p. 248.

97. Ibid., p. 260.

98. Ibid., 2:106–7.

99. George Moore, *Sister Teresa* (London: T. F. Unwin, n.d.), pp. 309, 311–12, 320–21.

100. He also eliminated some of the Wagnerian references.

101. Graham Hough, *The Dark Sun: A Study of D. H. Lawrence* (New York: Macmillan Co., 1957), p. 41.

102. It is also in part the story of an incident in the life of Helen Corke, a friend of Lawrence's, who later published her own Wagnerian novel. See Helen Corke, *D. H. Lawrence: The Croydon Years* (Austin: University of Texas Press, 1965), pp. 4–10. Lawrence taught her German so that she could read Wagner's librettos.

103. D. H. Lawrence, *The Trespasser* (London: Heinemann, 1961), p. 14.

104. Ibid., p. 17.

105. Ibid., p. 21.

106. Ibid., p. 75.

107. Ibid., p. 166.

108. Harry T. Moore, *D. H. Lawrence: His Life and Works,* rev. ed. (New York: Twayne Publishers, 1964), p. 139. For example, the villain, Gerald Crich, is likened to a Nibelung. D. H. Lawrence, *Women in Love* (New York: Viking Press, 1971), p. 40.

109. Arnold Bennett, *Sacred and Profane Love* (New York: George H. Doran Co., [1905]), pp. 45–55.

110. Benson also wrote a modest retelling of *Die Walküre* in English prose.

111. Joseph Conrad and Ford Madox Ford, *The Nature of a Crime* (Garden City, N.Y.: Doubleday, Page & Co., 1924), pp. 32–34.

112. George Gissing, *The Letters of George Gissing* (London: Constable & Co., 1927), pp. 193–94.

113. Florence Hardy, *The Life of Thomas Hardy, 1840–1928,* (New York: St. Martins, 1962), p. 181. See also p. 329. Hardy seems akin to Swinburne in his appreciation of Wagnerian music as the sound of the elemental forces of nature.

114. George Meredith, The *Letters of George Meredith,* ed. C. L. Cline, 3 vols. (Oxford: Clarendon Press, 1970), 2:688. See also 2:705, 715, 745. There is also mention of Wagner in idem, *One of Our Conquerors, The Works of George Meredith,* 29 vols. (New York: Constable & Co., 1909–12), 17:139.

115. *Trilby* concerns a tone-deaf Parisian grisette who becomes a famous singer through the hypnotic efforts of her tutor, Svengali. Du Maurier also wrote for *Punch.*

116. Maurice Baring, *The Puppet Show of Memory* (Boston: Little, Brown and Co., 1922), p. 52.

117. Ibid., p. 120.

118. Ibid., p. 134.

119. Ibid.

120. Ibid., p. 168.

121. Ibid., p. 186.

122. Maurice Baring, *C* 2 vols. (Garden City, N.Y.: Doubleday, Page & Co., 1924) 1:141.

123. Ibid., p. 195.

124. Ibid.

125. Ibid., p. 204–5.

126. Ibid., 2:113.

127. Ibid., p. 206.

Chapter 5: *Parsifal,* Religion, and the English

1. Mrs. Humphrey Ward, *Robert Elsmere,* ed. Clyde L. Ryals (Lincoln: University of Nebraska Press, 1967), pp. 54, 89, 162, 176–77, 188, 220.

2. Ibid., p. 410.

3. William E. Gladstone, "*Robert Elsmere* and the Battle of Belief," *Nineteenth Century* 23 (May 1888): 767.

4. See L. E. Elliott-Binns, *The Development of English Theology in the Later Nineteenth Century* (London: Longmans, Green & Co., 1952). He also notes "the displacement in the popular mind of the official guardians and exponents of the faith by literary guides" (p. 4).

5. For instance, Oliver Huckel, *Parsifal* (New York: Crowell, 1903). Huckel (d. 1940) was a Congregationalist minister. Also see Anton Orel, "The Blind Prophet," discussed in Martin Cooper, *Ideas and Music* (Philadelphia: Chilton, 1967).

6. See Albert Ross Parsons, "*Parsifal*": *The Finding of Christ Through Art* (New York: Metaphysical Publishing Co., 1893).

7. See Robert Raphael, *Richard Wagner* (New York: Twayne Publishers, 1969).

8. Robert W. Gutman, *Richard Wagner* (New York: Harcourt, Brace & World, 1968), p. 452. Hermann Rauschning in an account of a conversation with Hitler in 1934 showed that Hitler believed that he, and only he, fully understood Wagner's ideas and that these ideas were completely in agreement with his own. See George G. Windell, "Hitler, National Socialism, and Richard Wagner," *Journal of Central European Affairs* 22 (January 1963): 491.

9. Friedrich Nietzsche, *The Birth of Tragedy* and *The Case of Wagner,* trans. Walter Kaufmann (New York: Vintage, 1967), p. 184.

10. Since the tenets of Christianity are sometimes still a source of debate, by Christianity here is meant elements of belief in the transcendent God, the divinity of Christ, the Crucifixion and Resurrection, the soul, miracles, the exclusivity of Christianity, antipathy of the flesh and the spirit, and emphasis on the Scriptures.

11. Charles Tindal Gatty, *The Sacred Festival-Drama of "Parsifal"* (London: Schott & Co., 1894), p. 136. Gatty is the author of *Christian Art* (1890) and *The Revival of the Catholic Faith in England* (1910), for the Catholic Truth Society.

12. Ibid., p. 138.

13. Ibid., pp. 139, 141.

14. Ibid., p. 143.

15. Ibid., p. 144.

16. Ibid., pp. 150–51.

17. Ibid., p. 151.

18. *Times* (London), 30 January 1901, p. 7.

19. Ronald Bayne, *Dictionary of National Biography*, S.V. "Haweis, Hugh Reginald."

20. Hugh Reginald Haweis, *Music and Morals* (New York: Harper & Bros., 1872), p. 424.

21. "Scrutator. Wagner.—In Memoriam" *Truth*, 13 (22 February 1883): 254.

22. H. Heathcote Statham, *My Thoughts on Music and Musicians* (London: Chapman and Hall, 1892), p. 409.

23. Hugh Reginald Haweis, *My Musical Memories* (New York: Funk & Wagnalls, 1884), p. 182.

24. With the exception of the scenes of Fafner, "whose tail stuck half-way on the wag."

25. Haweis, *My Musical Memories*, p. 184.

26. Ibid., p. 199.

27. Parsons, *Parsifal*, p. 112.

28. Haweis, *My Musical Memories*, p. 211.

29. Ibid., p. 217.

30. Ibid., p. 218.

31. Ibid., pp. 222–23.

32. M. A. A. Galloway, "Wagner at Bayreuth," *Nineteenth Century* 36 (October 1894): 511.

33. Windell, "Hitler, National Socialism, and Richard Wagner," pp. 479–97.

34. *Times* (London), 2 December 1898, p. 6.

35. Alfred Gurney, *"Parsifal": A Study* (London: Kegan Paul, Trench & Co., 1888), p. 3.

36. Ibid., p. 6. This is Haweis's view also in *Music and Morals*.

37. Gurney, *"Parsifal": A Study*, p. 10.

38. Ibid., p. 55.

39. Ibid., pp. 64–66.

40. Ibid., pp. 66–67.

41. Kenneth Scott Latourette, *Christianity in a Revolutionary Age*, 5 vols. (New York: Harper, 1959–63), 2:327.

42. Peter Taylor Forsyth, *Religion in Recent Art* (London: Hodder and Stoughton, 1911), p. 212.

43. Ibid., p. 210. For treatment of the secular pessimists see chap. above.

44. Ibid., p. 221.

45. Ibid., p. 236.

46. Ibid., p. 238.

47. Ibid., p. 239.

48. Ibid., p. 240.

49. Ibid., pp. 258–59.

50. Ibid., p. 253.

51. Ibid., p. 260.

52. Ibid., p. 262.

53. Ibid., p. 263.

54. Ibid., p. 315.

55. Warren Sylvester Smith, *The London Heretics, 1870–1914* (New York: Dodd, Mead & Co., 1968), p. 144. A few of the interested persons were George Eliot, W. T. Stead, A. Conan Doyle, W. E. Henley.

56. J. Stillson Judah, *The History and Philosophy of the Metaphysical Movements in America* (Philadelphia: Westminster Press, 1967), pp. 14–17.

57. Quoted in Smith, *London Heretics,* p. 159.

58. One is reminded of Shaw's nonmaterial human beings of the future in the last play of the *Back to Methusaleh* pentology.

59. William Butler Yeats, *Ideas of Good and Evil* (London: A. H. Bullen, 1903), p. 294.

60. Except for a play, *Diarmuid and Grania,* written with George Moore. The play was performed only once, and neither Yeats nor Moore liked it.

61. George Moore, *Hail and Farewell,* 2 vols. (New York: Appleton-Century-Crofts, 1925), 1:56.

62. Alice Leighton Cleather, *H. P. Blavatsky* (Calcutta: Thacker, Spink & Co., 1922), p. 1.

63. Alice Leighton Cleather, *H. P. Blavatsky as I Knew Her* (Calcutta: Thacker, Spink & Co., 1923), p. 4.

64. Cleather, *H. P. Blavatsky,* p. 27.

65. Basil Crump was editor of the *Law Times* for eleven years. He resigned because of a nervous breakdown brought on by overwork (according to Cleather).

66. Cleather, *H. P. Blavatsky as I Knew Her,* pp. 64–66.

67. Henry Festing Jones, *Samuel Butler, Author of Erewhon (1835–1902): A Memoir,* 2 vols. (London: Macmillan & Co., 1919), 2:373, and Philip Henderson, *Samuel Butler* (New York: Barnes & Noble, 1967), p. 228. Jones says "Mr." Cleather; Henderson says "Mrs."

68. Alice Leighton Cleather and Basil Crump, *"Parsifal," "Lohengrin," and the Legend of the Holy Grail* (London: Methuen & Co., 1904), p. 181.

69. Wagner to Liszt, 7 June 1855, in *Correspondence of Wagner and Liszt,* ed. William Ashton Ellis, trans. Francis Hueffer, 2 vols. (London: H. Grevel & Co , 1888), 2:91– 100; Wagner to Mathilde Wesendonck, 30 April 1855, and Wagner to August Röckel, 23 August 1856, in *Letters of Richard Wagner,* ed. Wilhelm Altman, trans. M. M. Bozman, 2 vols. (London: J. M. Dent & Sons, 1927), 1:280, 310.

70. Cleather and Crump, *"Parsifal," "Lohengrin," and Holy Grail,* p. 5.

71. Ibid., p. 103.

72. Ibid., pp. 35–36.

73. Ibid., p. 99.

74. Ibid., p. 101.

75. Ibid., p. 106.

76. William Ashton Ellis, "Richard Wagner as Poet, Musician, and Mystic" (Paper delivered before the Society for the Encouragement of the Fine Arts, 3 February 1887), p. 26.

77. *Meister* 1, no. 2 (1888):39.

78. Ibid., p. 44.

79. Ibid., p. 117.

80. Ibid., no. 4 (1888): 123.

81. Ellis' heavy-handed eclecticism is most apparent in his description of the closing scene of *Parsifal:*

Whereas the final scene of the drama has been here regarded as the return of the golden age on earth, it may with equal consistency be viewed as the attainment of that state which Christians call Heaven, or, with even more propriety, the *Nirvana* of the Buddhists,—that state in which the desires of individual egoism are stilled in the great peace of the Renunciation of Self, attained by Parsifal only after he had learned compassion by suffering. As in Parsifal himself the evolution of the individual soul is depicted, so in the history of the Holy Spear is pictured the great cycle of the universe, from its First Emanation from the Great Unknown (brought down by an angel host), through the depths of material degradation (in the power of Klingsor) to its reabsorption in the infinite where Time and Space are not; from action to rest, from Manvantara to Pralaja. None who have witnessed *Parsifal* at Bayreuth but must have felt its moral influence, its echo from the days when Faith was yet a living factor in the world and its promise of a time when the Love of Mankind united in the bonds of a Universal Brotherhood shall fulfill the last words of the drama: *Erlösung dem Erlöser.* [Ibid., p. 124].

82. *Times* (London), 19 November 1907, p. 6.

83. Recall that Conway knew Dannreuther and met Wagner in 1877.

84. Moncure Daniel Conway, *Lessons for the Day* (London: Watts & Co., 1907), pp. 31–23.

85. Ibid.

86. Ibid., p. 30.

87. Moncure Daniel Conway, *Autobiography, Memories, and Experiences,* 2 vols. (London: Cassell & Co., 1904), 2:226–27.

88. Ibid., p. 227. Conway does not specify the scene.

89. Moncure Daniel Conway, *Addresses and Reprints, 1850–1907* (Boston: Houghton Mifflin Co., 1909), p. 260.

90. Son of G. O. Trevelyan and brother of historian G. M. Trevelyan.

91. Bertrand Russell, *The Autobiography of Bertrand Russell, 1892–1914* (New York: Bantam Books, 1968), p. 79.

92. R. C. Trevelyan, *The Birth of Parsival* (London: Longmans, Green & Co., 1905), pp. 8–9.

93. Ibid., pp. 10, 12.

94. Ibid., p. 99.

95. Ibid., p. 182.

96. R. C. Trevelyan, *The New Parsifal* (London: Chiswick Press, 1914), p. 23.

97. Ibid., p. 14.

98. Ibid., p. 43.

99. Ibid., p. 44.

100. Ibid., p. 71.

101. Ibid., p. 73.

102. John F. Runciman, otherwise a Wagnerian, found *Parsifal* "disgusting."

Saturday Review, 7 May 1904, pp. 582–83. On the other hand, the normally skeptical Newman found *Parsifal* one of the three or four most moving spiritual experiences of his life. *Saturday Review,* 12 September 1970, p. 80.

Chapter 6: Conclusion: 1914

1. E. F. Benson, *As We Were: A Victorian Peep Show* (London: Longmans, Green & Co., 1931), p. 293.

2. E. D. Mackerness, *A Social History of English Music* (London: Routledge & Kegan Paul, 1964), p. 220.

3. Percy M. Young, *A History of British Music* (New York: Benn, 1967), p. 419.

4. Percy M. Young, *Elgar, O. M.* (London: Collins, 1855), p. 172.

5. Mackerness, *A Social History,* p. 237.

6. See Lewis Melville, Introduction to *The Ravings of a Renegade Englishman: War Essays by Houston Stewart Chamberlain,* trans. Charles H. Clarke (London: Jarrold & Sons, 1915).

7. Such gestures may have been largely for public consumption. Richter had a son-in-law in London, Sydney Loeb, to whom he wrote on several occasions during the war. In these private letters he continued to show his admiration for Elgar and his own devotion to the encouragement of music in England. Young, *Elgar, O. M.,* pp. 176–77.

8. Percy A. Scholes, *The Mirror of Music, 1844–1944,* 2 vols. (London: Novello, 1947), 2:892.

9. Hermann Klein, *Thirty Years of Musical Life in London, 1870–1900* (New York: Century Co., 1903), p. 124.

10. Mary Banks Burrell was the first important English collector of Wagner archives. Her life of Wagner reached his 25th year before she died in 1898. She was the wife of the Hon. Willoughby Burrell and the daughter of Sir John Banks, prominent physicist.

11. George Bernard Shaw, "The Reminiscences of a Quinquagenarian," *Proceed-*

12. Klein, *Thirty Years,* p. 197.

13. Edward Nehls, ed., *D. H. Lawrence: A Composite Biography,* 3 vols. (Madison:

14. Ernest Newman, *Wagner as Man and Artist* (New York: Vintage, 1960), p. 379.

15. Peter Taylor Forsyth, *Religion in Recent Art* (London: Hadder and Stough-

16. Bernard Shaw, *London Music in 1888-1889, As Heard by Corno di Bassetto (Later*

17. See Edmund Wilson, *The Shores of Light* (New York: Vintage, 1961), pp. 68-72.

18. This list owes much to Samuel Hynes, *The Edwardian Turn of Mind* (Princeton, N.Y.: Princeton University Press, 1968), pp. 132-71. Wagner was also recognized in England for his vegetarianism and anti-vivisectionist beliefs.

Selected Bibliography

Primary Sources

These include poems, novels, letters, memoirs, collected articles, and other materials belonging to the period of Wagnerism before 1914.

Books

Allen, Grant. *Philistia*. London: Chatto and Windus, 1888.

Archer, Charles. *William Archer*. New Haven, Conn.: Yale University Press, 1931.

Arnold, Matthew. *Letters of Matthew Arnold, 1848–1888*. Edited by G. W. E. Russell. 2 vols. Grosse Point, Mich.: Scholarly Press, 1968.

Bache, Constance. *Brother Musicians*. London: Methuen & Co., 1901.

Baring, Maurice,. *C*. Garden City, N.Y.: Doubleday, Page & Co., 1924.

_____. *The Puppet Show of Memory*. Boston: Little, Brown and Co., 1922.

Bax, Ernest Belfort. *Reminiscences and Reflexions of a Mid and Late Victorian*. New York: T. Seltzer, 1920.

Beardsley, Aubrey. *The Early Work of Aubrey Beardsley*. New York: Dover Publications, 1967.

_____. *Last Letters of Aubrey Beardsley*. Introduction by John Gray. London: Longmans, Green & Co., 1904.

_____. *The Later Work of Aubrey Beardsley*. New York: Dover Publications, 1967.

_____ . *Letters from Aubrey Beardsley to Leonard Smithers.* London: First Edition Club, 1937.

Beardsley, Aubrey, and Glassco, John. *Under the Hill.* New York: Grove Press, 1959.

Bennett, Arnold. *Sacred and Profane Love.* New York: George H. Doran Co., [1905].

Bennett, Joseph. *Letters from Bayreuth.* London: Novello, Ewer, 1877.

Benson, E. F.. *As We Were: A Victorian Peep Show.* London, Longmans, Green & Co., 1931.

_____ . *The Rubicon.* New York: D. Appleton & Co., 1894.

_____ . *The Valkyrie.* Boston: L. C. Page & Co., 1905.

Burne-Jones, Georgiana Macdonald. *Memorials of Edward Burne-Jones.* 2 vols. New York: Macmillan Co., 1904.

Burrell, Mary B. *Thoughts for Enthusiasts at Bayreuth.* London: Pickering and Chatto, 1888.

Chorley, Henry Fothergill. *Modern German Music.* 2 vols. London: Smith, Elder & Co., 1854.

_____ . *Thirty Years' Musical Recollections.* New York: Alfred A. Knopf, 1926.

Cleather, Alice Leighton. *H. P. Blavatsky.* Calcutta: Thacker, Spink & Co., 1922.

_____ . *H. P. Blavatsky as I Knew Her.* Calcutta: Thacker, Spink & Co., 1923.

Cleather, Alice Leighton, and Crump, Basil. *"Parsifal," "Lohengrin," and the Legend of the Holy Grail.* London: Methuen & Co., 1904.

_____ . *"The Ring of the Nibelung": An Interpretation Embodying Wagner's Own Explanations.* London: Methuen & Co., 1909.

Conrad, Joseph, and Ford, Ford Madox. *The Nature of a Crime.* Garden City, N.Y.: Doubleday, Page & Co., 1924.

Conway, Moncure Daniel. *Addresses and Reprints, 1850–1907.* Boston: Houghton Mifflin Co., 1909.

_____ . *Autobiography, Memories, and Experiences.* 2 vols. London: Cassell & Co., 1904.

_____ . *Lessons for the Day.* London: Watts & Co., 1907.

Corke, Helen. *D. H. Lawrence: The Croyden Years.* Austin: University of Texas Press, 1965.

Dannreuther, Edward. *Richard Wagner: His Tendencies and Theories.* London: Augener & Co., 1873.

————. *Wagner and the Reform of Opera.* 2d ed. rev. London: Augener & Co., 1904.

Davidson, John. *New Ballads.* London: John Lane, 1897.

Davison, Henry, comp. *Music during the Victorian Era. From Mendelssohn to Wagner: being the memoirs of J. W. Davison* . . . London: Reeves, 1912.

Dowson, Ernest. *The Letters of Ernest Dowson.* Edited by Desmond Flower and Henry Maas. Rutherford, N.J.: Fairleigh Dickinson University Press, 1967.

du Maurier, George. *Trilby.* London: J. M. Dent & Sons, 1956.

Elgar, Edward. *Letters to Nimrod, 1897–1908.* Edited by Percy M. Young. London: D. Dobson, 1965.

Eliot, George. *The Writings of George Eliot: Life, Letters, and Journals.* 25 vols. New York: AMS Press, 1970.

Ellis, William Ashton. *Wagner Sketches: 1849, A Vindication.* London: Kegan Paul, Trench, Trübner & Co., 1892.

Forman, Alfred, trans. *The Nibelung's Ring.* London: Schott & Co., 1877.

————. *Sonnets.* London: Privately printed, 1886.

Forsyth, Peter Taylor. *Religion in Recent Art.* London: Hodder and Stoughton, 1911.

Gatty, Charles Tindal. *The Sacred Festival-Drama of "Parsifal."* London: Schott & Co., 1894.

Gissing, George. *The Letters of George Gissing.* London: Constable & Co., 1927.

Glasenapp, Carl Friedrich. *The Life of Richard Wagner.* Translated by William Ashton Ellis. 6 vols. London: Kegan Paul, Trench, Trübner, & Co., 1900–1908. Vols. 4–6, *The Life of Richard Wagner, by William Ashton Ellis,* by William Ashton Ellis.

Grand-Carteret, John. *Richard Wagner en caricatures.* Paris: Larousse, 1892.

Graves, Charles L. *Hubert Parry.* 2 vols. London: Macmillan & Co., 1926.

————. *Mr. Punch's History of Modern England.* 4 vols. New York: Frederick A. Stokes Co., n.d.

Gurney, Alfred. *"Parsifal": A Study.* London: Kegan Paul, Trench & Co., 1888.

Gutman, Robert W. *Volsunga Saga.* Translated by William Morris. New York: Collier Books, 1962.

Haldane, Richard Burdon. *R. B. Haldane: An Autobiography.* London: Hodder and Stoughton, 1929.

Harrison, Mary St. Leger Kingsley [Lucas Malet]. *The Wages of Sin.* London: S. Sonnenschein & Co., 1891.

Haweis, Hugh Reginald. *Music and Morals.* New York: Harper & Bros., 1872.

————. *My Musical Memories.* New York: Funk & Wagnalls, 1884.

Hime, H. W. L. *Wagnerism: A Protest.* London: Kegan Paul, Trench & Co., 1882.

Hogarth, George. *The Philharmonic Society of London.* London: Bradbury and Evans, 1862.

Huckel, Oliver. *Parsifal.* New York: Crowell, 1903.

Hueffer, Ford Madox [Ford]. *Memories and Impressions.* New York: Harper & Bros., 1911.

Hueffer, Francis. *Half a Century of Music in England, 1837–1887.* Philadelphia: Gebbie, 1889.

————. *Musical Studies.* Edinburgh: A. and C. Black, 1880.

————. (Franz). *Richard Wagner and the Music of the Future.* London: Chapman and Hall, 1874.

————. *Wagner's "Parsifal."* London: Schott & Co., n.d.

Hyndman, Henry Mayers. *Further Reminiscences.* London: Macmillan & Co., 1912.

Irvine, David. *The Badness of Wagner's Bad Luck.* London: Watts & Co., 1912.

————. *Metaphysical Rudiments of Liberalism.* London: Watts & Co., 1911.

————. *"Parsifal" and Wagner's Christianity.* London: H. Grevel & Co., 1899.

————. *Philosophy and Christianity.* London: Watts & Co., 1905.

————. *Wagner's Bad Luck.* London: Watts & Co., 1911.

————. *Wagner's "Ring of the Nibelung" and the Conditions of Ideal Manhood.* London: H. Grevel & Co., 1897.

————. *A Wagnerian's Midsummer Madness.* London: H. Grevel & Co., 1899.

Jones, Henry Festing. *Samuel Butler, Author of Erewhon (1835–1902): A Memoir.* 2 vols. London: Macmillan & Co., 1919.

Klein, Hermann. *Thirty Years of Musical Life in London, 1870–1900.* New York: Century Co., 1903.

Lawrence, D. H. *The Trespasser.* London: Heinemann, 1961.

_____ . *Women in Love.* New York: Viking Press, 1971.

Linton, Elizabeth Lynn. *Through the Long Nights.* New York: Harper & Bros., 1888.

Lytton, Robert. *Julian Fane: A Memoir.* London: John Murray, 1872.

_____ [Owen Meredith]. *Poems.* Boston, 1881.

Makower, Stanley. *The Mirror of Music.* London: John Lane, 1895.

Maugham, W. Somerset. *Of Human Bondage.* New York: Modern Library, 1915.

Meredith, George. *The Letters of George Meredith.* Edited by C. L. Cline. 3 vols. Oxford: Clarendon Press, 1970.

_____ . *One of Our Conquerors. The Works of George Meredith.* 29 vols. New York: Constable & Co., 1909–12. Vol. 17.

Moore, George. *Conversations in Ebury Street.* New York: Boni & Liveright, 1924.

_____ . *Evelyn Innes.* 2 vols. London: T. F. Unwin, 1898.

_____ . *George Moore in Transition: Letters to T. Fisher Unwin and Lena Milman, 1894–1910.* Edited by Helmet E. Gerber. Detroit, Mich.: Wayne State University Press, 1968.

_____ . *Hail and Farewell.* 2 vols. New York: Appleton-Century-Crofts, 1925.

_____ . *Letters from George Moore to Edward Dujardin, 1886–1922.* New York: Crosby, Gaige, 1929.

_____ . *Memoirs of My Dead Life.* New York: Boni & Liveright, 1920.

_____ . *Peronnik the Fool.* Mount Vernon, N.Y.: W. E. *Rudge.* 1926.

_____ . *Sister Teresa.* London: T. F. Unwin, n.d.

_____ . *Spring Days.* London: Vizetelly & Co., 1888.

Nietzsche, Friedrich. *The Birth of Tragedy* and *The Case of Wagner.* Translated by Walter Kaufmann. New York: Vintage, 1967.

Nordau, Max. *Degeneration.* 8th ed. New York: Appleton, 1896.

Paget, Violet [Vernon Lee]. *Gospels of Anarchy.* London: T. F. Unwin, 1908.

_____. *Laurus Nobilis.* London: John Lane, 1909.

Parry, C. Hubert. *Studies of Great Composers.* London: G. Routledge & Sons, 1902.

Parsons, Albert Ross. *"Parsifal": The Finding of Christ through Art.* 2d ed. New York: Metaphysical Publishing Co., 1893.

Payne, John. *Autobiography.* Olney, near Bedford: Thomas Wright, 1926.

_____. *Intaglios.* London: B. M. Pickering, 1871.

_____. *"The Masque of Shadows" and Other Poems.* London: B. M. Pickering, 1870.

_____. *New Poems.* London: Newman and Co., 1880.

_____. *Songs of Life and Death.* London: H. S. King & Co., 1872.

_____. *Vigil and Vision.* London: Villon Society, 1903.

Pease, Edward R., *The History of the Fabian Society.* 3d ed. London: F. Cass, 1963.

Plarr, Victor. *Ernest Dowson, 1888–1897.* New York: L. J. Gomme, 1914.

Praeger, Ferdinand. *Wagner as I Knew Him.* New York: Longmans, Green & Co., 1892.

Runciman, John F. *Old Scores and New Readings: Discussions on Musical Subjects.* London: At the Sign of the Unicorn, 1899.

Scott, William Bell. *Autobiographical Notes.* Edited by W. Minto. New York: Harper & Bros., 1892.

Shaw, Bernard. *Cashel Byron's Profession.* London: Constable & Co., 1938.

_____. *Collected Letters of Bernard Shaw, 1874–1897.* Edited by Dan H. Laurence. New York: Dodd, Mead & Co., 1965.

_____. *Complete Plays, with Prefaces.* 6 vols. New York: Dodd, Mead & Co., 1962.

_____. *How to Become a Music Critic.* Edited by Dan H. Laurence. New York: Hill & Wang, 1961.

_____. *Immaturity.* London: Constable & Co., 1938.

_____. *London Music in 1888–1889, As Heard by Corno di Bassetto (Later Known as Bernard Shaw).* London: Constable & Co., 1938.

_____. *Music in London, 1890–1894.* 3 vols. London: Constable, & Co., 1931.

————. *The Perfect Wagnerite: A Commentary on the Niblung's Ring.* New York: Dover Publications, 1967.

————. *The Sanity of Art.* New York: B. R. Tucker, 1908.

————. *Shaw on Music.* Edited by Eric Bentley. Garden City, New York: Doubleday & Co., 1955.

Spencer, Herbert. *An Autobiography.* 2 vols. New York: Appleton, 1904.

Statham, H. Heathcote. *My Thoughts on Music and Musicians.* London: Chapman and Hall, 1892.

Sully, James. *Pessimism.* London: Henry S. King, 1877.

Swinburne, Algernon C. *The Swinburne Letters.* Edited by Cecil Lange. 6 vols. New Haven, Conn.: Yale University Press, 1952.

————. *Poetical and Dramatical Works.* New York: John D. Williams, 1887.

Symons, Arthur. *Dramatis Personae.* Indianapolis, Ind.: Bobbs-Merrill co., 1923.

————. *Figures of Several Centuries.* Freeport, N.Y.: Books for Libraries Press, 1969.

————. *Images of Good and Evil.* London: Heinemann, 1899.

————. *Plays, Acting, and Music.* New York: E. P. Dutton & Co., 1909.

————. *Silhouettes.* London: John Lane, 1892.

————. *Studies in the Seven Arts.* New York: E. P. Dutton & Co., 1906.

————. *The Symbolist Movement in Literature.* New York: E. P. Dutton & Co., 1958.

————. *Tristan and Iseult.* New York: Brentanos, 1917.

Trevelyan, Robert C. *The Birth of Parsival.* London: Longmans, Green & Co., 1905.

————. *The New Parsifal.* London: Chiswick Press, 1914.

Wagner, Richard. *Correspondence of Wagner and Liszt.* Edited by William Ashton Ellis. Translated by Francis Hueffer. 2 vols. London: H. Grevel & Co., 1888.

————. *Letters of Richard Wagner.* Edited by Wilhelm Altman. Translated by M. M. Bozman. 2 vols. London: J. M. Dent & Sons, 1927.

————. *Letters of Richard Wagner: The Burrell Collection.* Edited by John N. Burk. New York: Macmillan Co., 1950.

_____ . *Letters of Richard Wagner to Emil Heckel.* Edited by William Ashton Ellis. London: Richards, 1899.

_____ . *Richard Wagner's Prose Works.* Translated by William Ashton Ellis. 8 vols. New York: Broude, 1966.

Ward, Mrs. Humphrey. *Robert Elsmere.* Edited by Clyde L. Ryals. Lincoln: University of Nebraska Press, 1967.

Wenley, R. M. *Aspects of Pessimism.* Edinburgh: W. Blackwood & Sons, 1894.

Weston, Jessie L. *The Legends of the Wagner Drama.* London: Nutt, 1900.

Wilde, Oscar. *The Picture of Dorian Gray.* New York: Tudor, 1930.

Winworth, Freda. *The Epic of Sounds.* Philadelphia: J. B. Lippincott, 1897.

Wratislaw, Theodore. *Orchids.* London: Smithers, 1896.

Wright, Thomas. *The Life of John Payne.* London, T. F. Unwin, 1919.

Yeats, William Butler. *Autobiography.* Garden City, N.Y.: Doubleday & Co., 1958.

_____ . *Ideas of Good and Evil.* London: A. H. Bullen, 1903.

_____ . *The Variorum Edition of the Plays of W. B. Yeats.* New York: Macmillan, 1966.

Articles and Periodicals

Barry, C. A. "Introductory to the Study of Wagner's Comic Opera *Die Meistersinger von Nurnberg.*" *Proceedings of the Royal Music Association* 7(7 March 1881): 75–97.

Baughan, E. Algernon. "The Development of Opera." *Proceedings of the Royal Music Association* 18 (9 February 1892): 71–91.

Cart, Henry. "Richard Wagner." *Proceedings of the Royal Music Association* 16 (3 February 1890): 63–78.

Ellis, William Ashton. "La théosophie dans les ouvrages de Richard Wagner." *Société nouvelle* 2 (1889): 258–65, 364–70, 442–57.

_____ . "Richard Wagner as Poet, Musician, and Mystic." Paper delivered before the Society for the Encouragement of Fine Arts, 3 February 1887.

_____ . "Richard Wagner's Prose." *Proceedings of the Royal Music Association* 19 (13 December 1892): 13–33.

_____ . "Wagner and Schopenhauer." *Fortnightly Review* 71 (March 1899): 413–32.

Frost, H. F. "Some Remarks on Richard Wagner's Music-Drama *Tristan und Isolde.*" *Proceedings of the Royal Music Association* 8 (1 May 1882): 147–67.

Galloway, M. A. A. "Wagner at Bayreuth." *Nineteenth Century* 36 (October 1894): 507–14.

Gladstone, William E. "*Robert Elsmere* and the Battle of Belief." *Nineteenth Century* 23 (May 1888): 766–98.

Gurney, Edmund. "Wagner and Wagnerism." *Nineteenth Century* 13 (March 1883): 434–52.

Hadden, J. Cuthbert. "The Wagner Mania." *Nineteenth Century* 44 (July 1898): 125–31.

Maitland, J. A. Fuller. "The Influence of Bayreuth." *Nineteenth Century* 40 (September 1896): 360–66.

Meister, vols. 1–8. London, 1888–95. London Branch of the Universal Wagner Society.

Parker, Louis N. "Lettre d'Angleterre." *Revue Wagnérienne* 2 (8 May 1887): 114-19. *Revue Wagnérienne*. Paris, 1855-88.

Rowbotham, J. F. "The Wagner Bubble." *Nineteenth Century* 24 (October 1888): 501–12.

Shaw, G. B. "The Reminiscences of a Quinquagenarian." *Proceedings of the Royal Music Association* 37 (6 December 1910): 17–27.

Shedlock, J. S. "Wagner and Liszt Correspondence." *Proceedings of the Royal Music Association* 14 (2 April 1888): 119–43.

Stanford, C. Villiers. "The Wagner Bubble: A Reply." *Nineteenth Century* 24 (November 1888): 727–33.

Publications occasionally useful include the *Academy, Athenaeum, Illustrated London News,* the *Times, Truth, Westminster Review, Saturday Review.* Most other articles on Wagner were collected and published in book form.

Secondary Sources

Books

Buckley, Jerome H. *The Victorian Temper.* Cambridge, Mass: Harvard University Press, 1951.

Cassidy, John A. *Algernon C. Swinburne.* New York: Twayne Publishers, 1964.

Chew, Samuel. *Swinburne.* Hamden, Conn.: Archon Books, 1966.

Cooper, Martin. *Ideas and Music.* Philadelphia: Chilton, 1967.

Dent, Edward J. *Opera.* Baltimore, Md.: Penguin Books, 1968.

Donington, Robert. *Wagner's "Ring" and Its Symbols.* London: Faber and Faber, 1963.

Elliott-Binns, L. E. *The Development of English Theology in the Later Nineteenth Century.* London: Longmans, Green & Co., 1952.

Ensor, R. C. K. *England, 1870–1914.* Oxford: Clarendon Press, 1960.

Fairchild, Hoxie Neale. *Religious Trends in English Poetry.* 4 vols. New York: Columbia University Press, 1939.

Faverty, Frederic E. *The Victorian Poets: A. Guide to Research.* Cambridge, Mass: Harvard University Press, 1968.

Fergusson, Francis. *The Idea of a Theatre.* Garden City, N.Y.: Doubleday & Co., 1949.

Gaunt, William. *The Pre-Raphaelite Dream.* New York: Schocken Books, 1966.

Guichard, Léon. *La musique et les lettres en France au temps du Wagnérisme.* Paris: Presses Universitaires de France, 1963.

Gutman, Robert W. *Richard Wagner.* New York: Harcourt, Brace & World, 1968.

Hardy, Florence. *The Life of Thomas Hardy, 1840–1928.* New York: St. Martins, 1962.

Henderson, Philip. *Samuel Butler.* New York: Barnes & Noble, 1967.

_____. *William Morris: His Life, Work and Friends.* New York: McGraw-Hill, 1967.

Hough, Graham. *The Dark Sun: A Study of D. H. Lawrence.* New York: Macmillan Co., 1957.

Hughes, Douglas A., ed. *The Man of Wax: Critical Essays on George Moore.* New York: New York University, 1971.

Hynes, Samuel. *The Edwardian Turn of Mind.* Princeton, N.J.: Princeton University Press, 1968.

Irvine, William. *The Universe of G. B. S.* New York: Russell and Russell, 1968.

Jackson, Holbrook. *The Eighteen Nineties.* New York: Mitchell Kennerley, 1913.

Jacobson, Anna. *Nachlänge Richard Wagners in Roman.* Heidelberg: C. Winter, 1932.

Judah, J. Stillson. *The History and Philosophy of the Metaphysical Movements in America.* Philadelphia: Westminster Press, 1961.

Kerman, Joseph. *Opera as Drama.* New York: Vintage, 1956.

Knust, Herbert. *Wagner, the King, and The Wasteland.* University Park: Pennsylvania State University Press, 1967.

Koss, Stephen E. *Lord Haldane.* New York: Columbia University Press, 1969.

Kronenberger, Louis, ed. *George Bernard Shaw: A Critical Survey.* New York: World Publishing Co., 1953.

Lafourcade, Georges. *Swinburne: A Literary Biography.* New York: Russell and Russell, 1967.

Latourette, Kenneth Scott. *Christianity in a Revolutionary Age.* 5 vols. New York: Harper, 1959–63.

Laver, James. *Manners and Morals in the Age of Optimism, 1848–1914.* New York: Harper Row: 1966.

Lester, John A., Jr. *Journey through Despair, 1880–1914.* Princeton, N.J.: Princeton University Press, 1968.

Mackail, J. W. *The Life of William Morris.* New York: B. Blom, 1968.

Mackerness, E. D. *A Social History of English Music.* London: Routledge & Kegan Paul, 1964.

Magee, Bryan. *Aspects of Wagner.* New York: Stein and Day, 1969.

Mann, Thomas. *Essays of Three Decades.* New York: Knopf, 1965.

Masur, Gerhard. *Prophets of Yesterday.* New York: Macmillan Co., 1961.

Meisel, Martin. *Shaw and the Nineteenth-Century Theatre.* Princeton, N.J.: Princeton University Press, 1963.

Merz, John Theodore. *A History of European Thought in the Nineteenth Century.* New York: Dover Publications, 1965.

Miller, J. Hillis. *The Disappearance of God.* Cambridge, Mass: Harvard University Press, 1963.

Moore, Harry T. *D. H. Lawrence: His Life and Works.* Rev. ed. New York: Twayne Publishers, 1964.

Morris May. *William Morris; Artist, Writer, Socialist.* 2 vols. Oxford: B. Blackwell, 1936.

Moser, Max. *Richard Wagner in der englischen Literatur des XIX Jahrhunderts.* Bern: A. Franke, 1938.

Mosley, Oswald. *Wagner and Shaw: A Synthesis.* London: Sanctuary Press, 1956.

Murphet, Howard. *When Daylight Comes: A Biography of Helen Petrevna Blavatsky.* Wheaton, Ill: Theosophical Publishing House, 1975.

Nehls, Edward, ed. *D. H. Lawrence: A Composite Biography.* 3 vols. Madison: University of Wisconsin Press, 1957–59.

Nethercot, Arthur. *Men and Supermen: The Shavian Portrait Gallery.* New York: B. Blom, 1963.

Newman, Ernest. *The Life of Richard Wagner.* 4 vols. New York: Knopf, 1933–46.

_____. *Testament of Music.* Edited by Herbert Van Thal. New York: Knopf, 1963.

_____. *Wagner as Man and Artist.* New York: Vintage, 1960.

The Nibelungenlied. Translated by A. T. Hatto. Hammondsworth, Middlesex., England: Penguin Books, 1965.

Plaine, H. L., ed. *Darwin, Marx, and Wagner.* Columbus: Ohio University Press, 1962.

Raphael, Robert. *Richard Wagner.* New York: Twayne Publishers, 1969.

Rougemont, Denis de. *Love in the Western World.* New York: Pantheon, 1956.

Russell, Bertrand. *The Autobiography of Bertrand Russell 1872–1914.* N.Y.: Bantam books, 1968.

Ryskamp, Charles, ed. *Wilde and the Nineties.* Princeton, N.J.: Princeton University Press, 1966.

Sans, Edouard. *Richard Wagner et la pensée schopenhauerienne.* Paris: C. Klincksieck, 1969.

Saurat, Denis. *Literature and Occult Tradition.* Translated by Dorothy Bolton. Port Washington, N.Y.: Kennikat, 1966.

Scholes, Percy A. *The Mirror of Music, 1844–1944: A Century of Musical Life in Britain as Reflected in the Pages of the Musical Times.* 2 vols. London: Novello, 1947.

Smith, Warren Sylvester. *The London Heretics, 1870–1914.* New York: Dodd, Mead & Co., 1968.

Stevenson, Lionel. *The Ordeal of George Meredith.* New York: Scribner, 1953.

Thatcher, David S. *Nietzsche in England, 1890–1914.* Toronto: University of Toronto Press, 1970.

Thompson, Paul. *The Work of William Morris.* New York: Viking Press, 1967.

Trilling, Lionel. *Matthew Arnold.* New York: Meridian, 1955.

Waddington, M. M. *The Development of British Thought, 1820–1890.* Toronto: J. M. Dent & Sons, 1919.

Weales, Gerald. *Religion in Modern English Drama.* Philadelphia: University of Pennsylvania Press, 1961.

Weintraub, Stanley, *Beardsley.* New York: G. Braziller, 1967.

Willey, Basil. *More Nineteenth Century Studies: A Group of Honest Doubters.* New York: Columbia University Press, 1956.

Wilson, Edmund. *The Shores of Light.* New York: Vintage, 1961.

Wingfield-Stratford, Esmé. *The Victorian Aftermath.* New York: W. Morrow & Co., 1934.

Winsten, Stephen, ed. *G. B. S. at 90: Aspects of Bernard Shaw's Life and Work.* New York: Dodd, Mead & Co., 1946.

Young, G. M. Portrait of an Age: *Victorian England.* London: Oxford University Press, 1961.

Young, Percy M. *Elgar, O. M.* London: Collins, 1955.

————. *A History of British Music.* New York: Benn, 1967.

Zuckerman, Elliott. *The First Hundred Years of Wagner's "Tristan."* New York: Columbia University Press, 1964.

Articles

Blissett, William. "Ernest Newman and English Wagnerism." *Music and Letters* 40 (October 1959):311–23.

Geduld, H. M. "Bernard Shaw and Adolf Hitler." *Shaw Review* 3/4 (January 1961): 11–20.

Groshong, James W. "George Bernard Shaw and Germany." Ph.D. disssertation, Stanford University, 1957.

Henson, Janice. "Bernard Shaw's Contribution to the Wagner Controversy in Engiand." *Shaw Review* 4, no. 1 (January 1961): 21–26.

Nickson, Richard. "G. B. S: Mosleyite?" *Shavian* 2 (September 1960): 11–14.

Painter-Downs, Mollie. "Profiles—At the Pines." *New Yorker,* 30 January 1971 pp. 31–43.

Reed, John R. "Swinburne's *Tristram of Lyonesse:* The Poet-Lover's Song of Love." *Victorian Poetry* 4, no. 2 (Spring 1966): 99–120.

Sypher, Francis Jacques, Jr. "Swinburne and Wagner." *Victorian Poetry* 9 (Spring 1971): 165–33.

Windell, George G. "Hitler, National Socialism, and Richard Wagner." *Journal of Central European Affairs* 22 (January 1963): 479–97.

INDEX

Academy, 27, 82
Albert, Prince (of England), 24
Althaus, Frederic, 18
Amateur Musical Society, 16
Androcles And the Lion (Shaw), 61
Anglo-Germans, 11, 30, 37, 38
Anti-Semitism, English view of Wagner's, 11, 20-21, 35, 46-47, 70, 75, 77-78. *See* Judaism; Racism
Antivivisectionism, 76, 171 n.18
Archer, William, 50, 59
Armbruster, Carl, 38, 40
Arnold, Matthew, 87
Athenaeum, 20, 28, 29, 34, 38
"Autumn and Winter" (Swinburne), 92

Bache, Walter, 26, 92
Back to Methusalah (Shaw), 60-61, 64, 118
Badness of Wagner's Bad Luck, The (Irvine), 79-80
Baring, Maurice, 115-17, 135
Barry, C. A., 38, 44
Baudelaine, Charles, 93-94, 97
Baughn, E. Algernon, 47
Bax, Ernest Belfort, 51, 61, 99
Bayreuth Festival, 29-33, 36-39, 41, 52, 80, 104, 108, 122, 144. *See also* English Bayreuth
Beardsley, Aubrey, 88, 99-103, 105, 115, 148
Bennett, Arnold, 113-14
Bennett, Joseph, 32-33
Benson, E. F., 114, 140
Bexfield (organist and composer), 17
Birnstingl, A. L., 38
Birth of Parsival, The (Trevelyan), 136-37
Boughton, Rutland, 143-44
"Bride-Night: Wagner's *Tristan and Isolde*—Act II, Scene 2" (Payne), 98
Brown, Ford Madox, 27, 89
Browning, Robert, 36

Buckley, Reginald, 144
Bulwer-Lytton, Sir Edward, 15
Burne-Jones, Edward, 35, 36, 89, 91, 100, 126
Burrell, Mary Banks, 143, 171 n.10
Butler, Samuel, 131

C. (Baring), 116
Cart, Henry, 46
Cashel Byron's Profession (Shaw), 58
Century of Roundels, A (Swinburne), 92
Chamberlain, Houston Stewart, 42, 44, 142, 150 n.3, 171 n.6
Chesterton, G. K., 10, 64
Chorley, Henry Fothergill, 16-17, 20, 22-23, 50
Cleather, Alice Leighton, 130-32
Conrad, Joseph, 114
Conversations in Ebury Street (Moore), 109
Conway, Moncure, 35, 134-35
Corno di Bassetto. *See* Bernard Shaw
Coward, Henry, 142
Crump, Basil, 131
Cyriax, Julius, 38, 42

Daily Chronicle, 67
Daily News, 21, 81
Daily Telegraph, 32, 38
d'Albert, Eugene, 142
Dannreuther, Edward, 26, 28-30, 34-39, 44, 50, 91-92, 144
Davidson, John, 88, 106-7, 136
Davison, James W., 16-17, 19-23, 28, 30, 37
"Death of Richard Wagner" (Swinburne), 96
Decadents, the, 99, 106, 147
De Equsquiza, R., 42
de Gasperini, August, 92
Degeneration (Nordan), 53
Dent, J. M., 100-101

187

Diarmid (Marquis of Lorne), 143
Doctor's Dilemma, The (Shaw), 61
Dowdeswell, Charles, 38, 66
Dream of Gerontius, The (Elgar), 144
du Maurier, George, 115

Edward VII (king of England), 30
Edwards, W. H., 38
Elgar, Edward, 144
Eliot, George. *See* Evans, Mary Ann
Ellerton, John Lodge, 18
Ellis, William Ashton, 20-21, 23-24, 39,
  40-44, 47, 66-67, 119, 132-34, 145-46
English Bayreuth, 51, 53, 144
Ernest II, of Saxe-Coburg-Gotha, 24
Evans, Frederick, 100
Evans, Mary Ann (pseud., George Eliot),
  35, 36
Evelyn Innes (Moore), 110-12, 119
Examiner, 28

Fane, Julian, 88, 94
Feuerbach, Ludwig, 47
Fliegende, Holländer, Der, 15, 19, 20, 26-27,
  36, 71; *L'Olandese Dannato*, 27
*Flying Dutchman, The. See Fliegende
  Holländer, Der*
Ford, Ford Madox (Hueffer), 114, 140,
  146
Forman, Alfred, 38, 40, 66, 90, 145
Frost, H. F., 38, 45
Forsyth, Peter Taylor, 120, 125-28, 147
Forthnightly Review, 27, 79, 83

Gatty, Charles, 120-21
Gissing, George, 114
Gladstone, William, 118
Glasenapp, C. F., 42
Glover, William Howard, 21, 23
Götterdämmerung, Die, 31-32, 55-56
Guardian, 92
Gurney, Alfred, 100, 120, 124-25
Gurney, Edmund, 48

Hadden, J. Cuthbert, 48
Hail and Farewell (Moore), 108-9
Haldane, R. B., 39, 65
Hardy, Thomas, 114
Harmonicum, 16
Harris, T. L., 73
Hartvigson, Fritz, 26

Haweis, Reginald, 120-23
Hawk, 63
Henley, W. E., 115
Herkomer, Herbert von, 36
Hime, H. W. L., 48
Hipkins, Alfred James, 26, 92
Hogarth, George, 18, 21, 23, 24
Holst, Gustav, 144
Hornet, 50
Hueffer, Ford Madox. *See* Ford, Ford
  Madox
Hueffer, Francis (Franz), 27-29, 35, 37,
  50-51, 66, 89, 90, 144

Illustrated London News, 21
Immaturity (Shaw), 57-58
Irvine, David: life of, 67; general
  philosophy of, 67-68; *Wagner's "Ring
  of the Nibelung and the Conditions of
  Ideal Manhood*, 68-72; *"Parsifal" and
  Wagner's Christianity*, 72-79, 85; *A
  Wagnerian's Midsummer Madness*, 71,
  79; *Wagner's Bad Luck*, 79-80; *The
  Badness of Wagner's Bad Luck*, 79-
  80, 83-84; *Metaphysical Rudiments of
  Liberalism*, 80, 85; 118, 145-47

Jacques, Edgar F. 38, 42
Judaism, 70, 73, 78. *See* Anti-Semitism
Judaism in Music (Wagner), 20, 46-47
Jullien, Louis Antoine, 16

Kant, Immanuel, 85
Kipling, Rudyard, 114
Kistler, Cyrill, 42
Klindworth, Karl, 18, 25
Kümpel, William, 26, 92

Laus Veneris (Swinburne), 88, 92-94
Lawrence, D. H., 112-13, 146
Lee, Vandaleur G. J., 50-51
Lee, Vernon. *See* Paget, Violet
Lehmann, Rudolf, 36
Lewes, G. H., 35
Lindsay, Alexander (earl of Crawford
  and Balcarres), 28
Liszt, Franz, 19, 26, 42-43, 45-46
"Lohengrin" (Swinburne), 96
Lohengrin, 18, 22, 23, 24, 25, 30, 35,
  36, 40, 42, 52, 71, 109; in Lawrence,
  112

London Germans. *See* Anglo-Germans
Lüders, Charles, 17-18, 37
Lytton, Robert, 88, 94

MacCunn, Hamish, 143
Mackenzie, Alexander, 144
Man and Superman (Shaw), 59-60
Mann, Thomas, 65
Manners, William John (earl of Dysart), 38-39, 44
Manns, August, 25, 141
Massingham, H. W., 67
Mastersinger of Nürnberg, The. See Meistersinger von Nürnberg
Maugham, Somerset, 87
Meister, 38-44, 66, 119, 146
Meistersinger von Nürnberg, Die, 25-27, 37, 41, 44, 88, 135, 144
Melbourne Argus, 67
Memoirs (Moore), 107
Mendelssohn, Felix, 16, 20-25, 46
Meredith, George, 93, 114
Meredith, Owen. *See* Lytton, Robert
Metaphysical Rudiments of Liberalism (Irvine), 80, 84
Meyerbeer, Giacomo, 18, 20, 46
Meysenbug, Malwida, 18
Modern German Music (Charley), 20
Monthly Musical Record, 29
Moore, George, 107-12, 119, 130, 146, 148
Morning Post, 21
Morris, William, 35, 88-91, 97
Moseley, J. B., 38
Mosley, Oswald, 63, 157 n.39
Murray, Alma, 38
Musical Examiner, 16, 34
Musical Review, 51
Musical Standard, 81, 141
Musical Times, 30, 32-33, 38, 141
Musical World, 16, 20-23, 25, 32, 42
Music and Morals (Haweis), 122
"Music: An Ode" (Swinburne), 96
Music-Drama of the Future (Boughton and Buckley), 144
Mystic Trumpeter, The (Holst), 144
Nature of Crime, The (Ford and Conrad), 112
Naylor, E. W., 47
Nazism, 11, 120, 124
Newman, Ernest, 23, 82-84, 141, 143, 146
New Parsifal, The (Trevelyan), 137-39

New Quarterly Magazine, 28
New York Musical Gazette, 20
Nietzsche, Friedrich, 55, 61, 75, 79, 106-7, 120, 136, 138
Nordau, Max, 53-54, 66, 95
Notes on Poems and Reviews (Swinburne), 93-94

Observer, 38
O'Connor, T. P., 51
Oliphant, Laurence, 69, 73
Osborne, G. A., 16

Paget, Violet (pseud., Vernon Lee), 115
Parker, Louis N., 38, 42
Parry, Hubert, 36, 144
"Parsifal" (Symons), 103
Parsifal, 37, 40-41, 52, 66; Irvine's discussion of, 72-79; in Symons, 103-5; discussions by Gurney, Forsyth, Cleather, Ellis, Trevelyan, 118-39, 143, 145-46
"Parsifal" and Wagner's Christianity (Irvine), 72-79, 85
"Parsifal": A Study (Gurney), 124
"Parsifal," "Lohengrin" and the Legend of the Holy Grail (Cleather), 131-32
Payne, John, 26, 66, 88-89, 97-98, 145
Perfect Wagnerite, The (Shaw), 54-57
Philharmonic Society, Old, 15-18, 21, 23, 25, 27
Picture of Dorian Gray, The (Wilde), 103
Pierson, Henry Hugh, 17
Planer, Mina, 81
Poems and Ballads (Swinburne), 91
Potter, Cipriani, 18
Powell, George, 92-93, 95
Praeger, Ferdinand, 18-21, 23, 38, 43-44, 46
Pre-Raphaelites, 27, 89, 93
Punch, 34
Puppet Show of Memory, The (Baring), 115-18
"Pyne, Evelyn", 40

Racism, 11, 75, 78, 120. *See also* Anti-Semitism
Religion in Recent Art (Forsyth), 126
Renaissance, La, 92
Revue des Deux Mondes, 92
Revue Wagnérienne, 39, 107

Rheingold, Das, 26, 32, 54, 100-102
Rheingold (Shaw), 59
Rheingold, The. See Rheingold, Das
Richard Wagner and the Music of the Future (Hueffer), 27
Richard Wagner as Poet, Musician, And Mystic (Ellis), 39, 133-34
Richard Wagner: His Tendencies and Theories (Dannreuther), 29
Richter, Hans, 34, 37, 142
Rienzi (Bulwer-Lytton), 15
Rienzi (Wagner), 16, 20, 25; Conway's view of, 135
Ring des Nibelungen, Der, 18; explanation by Hueffer of, 28; according to Dannreuther, 30, 32-33, 37, 39; according to Ward, 41; according to Hime, 48, 50; according to Shaw, 54-57, 60, 64; according to Irvine, 68-72, 81, 108, 115-16, 143, 145-46
Ring of the Nibelung, The. See Ring des Nibelungen, Der
"Ring of the Nibelung": An Interpretation Embodying Wagner's Own Explanations, The (Cleather), 131
Robert Elsmere (Ward), 118, 121
Rowbotham, J. F., 48
Royal College of Music, 26, 36
Royal Musical Association, 44, 141
Rubicon, The (Benson), 114
Rule Britannia Overture, 15
Runciman, John, 82, 120

Sacred and Profane Love (Bennett), 113-14
Saint Joan (Shaw), 61
Sainton, Prosper, 17-18, 36
Saturday Review, 38, 82
Savoy, 101-3
Scenes from Shelley's "Prometheus Unbound" (Parry), 36
Schopenhauer, Arthur, 27, 40, 42, 47, 61, 65-66, 68, 72, 75; *The World as Will and Idea,* 40, 65-66; *Schopenhauer Gesellschaft,* 67; *Neue Paralipomena,* 72, 78, 80; *Transcendent Speculations on Apparent Design in the Fate of the Individual,* 81, 85, 97, 126, 127-28, 145
Schräder, Herman Theodor, 67
Scientific Religion (Oliphant), 69
Semper, Gottfried, 18

Shakespeare, William (singer), 38
Shaw, Bernard, 10, 11, 33, 38-40, 50-64 passim, 67, 68, 118, 143, 145, 147; Corno di Bassetto (pseud.), 51; early music criticism, 50-51; first visit to Bayreuth, 52; *Sanity of Art,* 53-54; idea of Wagner Theatre in England, 51, 53; *The Perfect Wagnerite,* 54-57; *Immaturity,* 57-58; *Cashel Byron's Profession,* 58; The *Ring* as socialist allegory, 54-57, 146; *Widowers' Houses,* 59, 146; *Rhingold,* 59; *Man and Superman,* 59-60; *Back to Methusaleh,* 50-61, 64; influence of Nietzsche, 61; influence of Schopenhauar, 61; *The Doctor's Dilemma,* 61; *Androcles and the Lion,* 61; *Saint Joan,* 61
Shedlock, J. S. 45-46
Siegfried, 33, 53, 59, 112
Sister Theresa (Moore), 110, 112
Smart, Sir George, 15, 22
Smart, Henry, 22-23
Smithers, Leonard, 100
Society for the Encouragement of the Fine Arts, 133
Songs of Life and Death (Payne), 98
Sonnets (Forman), 66
Spectator, 81-82, 93
Spencer, Herbert, 36, 37, 146
Stanford, C. Villiers, 48, 141, 144
Star, 51, 52
Stevenson, R. L. 115
Studies in the Seven Arts (Symons), 104
Study of Wagner, A (Newman), 82, 84
Swedenborg, Emanuel, 73, 147
Swinburne, Algernon, 88-96, 99, 147
Sunday Times, 22, 38
Sullivan, Arthur, 144
Symons, Arthur, 99-100, 103, 105

Tannhäuser, 16, 18, 20-27, 35-36, 42, 71, 87, 115-17, 147-49; influence on poem by Fane and Lytton, 88, 94; lack of influence on Morris version, 90, 94; in Payne, 97-98; influence on Beardsley 100-102; in Wilde, 103; in Wratislaw, 106; influence on poem by Davidson, 106-7; in Benson, 114
Tannhäuser; or The Ballad of the Bards

(Temple and Trever), 88
Temple, Neville. *See* Fane, Julian
Theosophists, 128-32, 146, 148
Times, 21-22, 28, 31, 37, 51, 89, 121
Trespasser, The (Lawrence), 112-13
Trevelyan, Robert C., 120, 135-39
Trevor, Edward. *See* Bulwer-Lytton,
    Edward Robert
Trilby (du Maurier), 115
"Tristan" (Swinburne), 96
Tristan and Iseult (Symons), 103-4
Tristan and Isolde, 26, 37, 41-42, 45,
    50, 87, 92; influence on Swinburne,
    94-96; influence on Beardsley, 100;
    in Symons, 103-4; in Moore's novels,
    109-10; in Lawrence's novel, 112-13;
    in Bennett's novel, 113–114; in
    Ford and Conrad's novel, 114;
    in Baring, 116-17, 143, 145-48
"Tristan's Song" (Symons), 103
Tristram of Lyonesse (Swinburne), 92,
    94-96
Truth, 122
Tucker, Benjamin, 53
*Twilight of the Gods, The, See Götter-
    dämmerung*
"Twilight of the House of Lords, The"
    (Swinburne), 96

Under the Hill (Beardsley), 101-2
Universal Wagner Society, London
    Branch, 38-43, 53

Valkyrie, The. See Walküne, Die
Victoria (queen of England), 24, 37
Vigil and Vision (Payne), 98

Wagner, Cosima, 35-36, 67, 91, 108, 131
Wagner, Joanna, 16
Wagner, Minna Planer, 15-16, 81-82
Wagner, Richard: theory of music-
    drama, 10; first London visit, 15-16;
    second London visit, 18-24; third
    London visit, 34-37; *Judaism in Music*,
    20, 46-47; *Opera and Drama* 25, 71,
    104; *Religion and Art*, 41, 78; *Art
    and Revolution*, 40, 55, 57, 71;
role in 1848, 43; *Capitulation*, 47;
    An End In Paris, 61; Communication
    to My Friends, 71; *On State and
    Religion*, 76; *German Art and German
    Policy; What is German?*, 77; *What
    Boots this Knowledge*, 78; *Know
    Thyself; Herodom and Christianity*,
    78; *Mein Leben*, 79, 80, 83-84,
    122; World War I, 141. *See* operas:
    *Fliegende, Holländer, Der; Götter-
    dämmerung, Die; Lohengrin; Meister-
    singer von Nürnberg, Die; Parsifal;
    Rheingold, Das; Rienzi; Ring des
    Wibelungen, Der; Siegfried; Tann-
    häuser; Tristan und Isolde; Walküre,
    Die*
Wagner, Winifred, 18
Wagner and Tannhäuserin Paris (Baudel-
    aire), 93, 94
Wagner as I Knew Him (Praeger), 43
"Wagneriana" (Payne), 98
Wagnerian's Midsummer Madness, A
    (Irvine), 71, 79
Wagnerism: A Protest (Hime), 48
Wagner's Bad Luck (Irvine), 79
Wagner-Sketches: 1849, A Vindication
    (Ellis), 39
Wagner Society (1873), 28-29, 37, 38,
    66, 67, *See also* Universal Wagner
    Society, London Branch
*Wagner's "Ring of the Nibelung" and
    the Conditions of Ideal Manhood"*
    (Irvine), 68-72
Walküre, Die, 17, 26, 33, 90
Ward, Mrs. Humphrey, 113, 118, 121
Ward, William C., 41
Westminster Review, 26
Whitman, Walt, 29
Wilde, Oscar, 99, 103, 148
Women in Love (Lawrence), 113, 146
Working Men's Society, 25, 92
World, 53
World as Will and Idea (Schopenhauer),
    40, 65
Wratislaw, Theodore, 105-6

Yeats, William Butler, 111, 130
Yellow Book, 103